THE EMIGRANT'S GUIDE TO OREGON AND CALIFORNIA

Containing Scenes and Incidents of a Party of Oregon Emigrants; A Description of Oregon; Scenes and Incidents of a Party of California Emigrants; A Description of California; With a Description of the Different Routes to Those Countries; and All Necessary Information Relative to the Equipment, Supplies, and the Method of Traveling.

By Lansford W. Hastings
Leader of the Oregon and California Emigrants of 1842

THE NARRATIVE PRESS
TRUE FIRST PERSON ACCOUNTS OF HIGH ADVENTURE

Entered, according to Act of Congress, in the year 1845, by Lansford W. Hastings, in the Clerk's office of the district Court of Ohio.

The Narrative Press
P.O. Box 2487, Santa Barbara, California 93120 U.S.A.
Telephone: (805) 884-0160 Web: www.narrativepress.com

ISBN 1-58976-032-8 (Paperback)
ISBN 1-58976-033-6 (eBook)

Produced in the United States of America

TABLE OF CONTENTS

PREFACE

The importance of a work of this kind, has been frequently suggested to the author, by innumerable correspondents, in almost every portion of the Union, who have, from time to time, addressed numerous letters to him, propounding countless interrogations in reference to all the different topics, to which the following pages are devoted. Many of these correspondents the author has invariably answered; while many others, he has, from the pressure of business, found it not only extremely inconvenient, but entirely impracticable to answer, in any other manner then that which is here adopted. The above, and innumerable other manifestations, indicative of the extraordinary avidity with which all information of this nature, is every where sought, have been strong incentives to the present undertaking. But the fact, that among all the various works now extant, which treat of Oregon and California, there are none which contain that practical information, which is so much desired by the enquiring emigrant: and the fact, of the utter destitution, of all information in reference to the different routes to those countries, the equipments, supplies, and the method of traveling, have been the chief inducements to its early inception and completion. Notwithstanding the paramount importance of these subjects, nothing has heretofore, been written in relation to them, excepting the few articles, occasionally found in our western newspapers and journals, which are usually written by traveling correspondents; and which, from their necessary brevity, are found entirely inadequate to the general demand.

The design of these pages is not to treat *in extenso* of Oregon and California. but merely to give a succinct, and at the same time, practical description of those countries; embracing a brief description of their mountains, rivers, lakes, bays, harbours, islands, soil, climate, health, productions, improvements, population, government, market, trade and commerce: a description of the different routes; and all necessary information relative to the equipment, supplies, and the method of traveling. Hence it will be readily seen, that they will be found much more conducive to the interest of the emigrating portion of our community; yet, it is confidently hoped, that they may prove equally valuable and interesting to all those, who may deem it proper to give them an attentive perusal. This may, with the more propriety be hoped, as all excrescences have been cautiously lopped off, leaving scarcely any thing more then a mere collection of interesting, important and practical facts. In collecting the materials for this little work, the author has had recourse to all available and authentic sources; yet, for most of the statistical information relative to both Oregon and California, he is indebted chiefly to the gentlemen of the Hudsons' Bay Company, and the missionaries in Oregon; the gentlemen of the same company, trod other foreigners of undoubted veracity in California. All other information then that derived from the sources above alluded to, he has acquired, by his own personal observation, during an excursive journeying, of about two years duration, through those remote, yet highly interesting regions. Sincerely hoping that the following pages, may prove useful to all those, who contemplate emigrating to Oregon or California, and interesting at least, if not useful also, to the general reader, they are now submitted to the public; with the assurance that, if they shall be found either useful to the former, or interesting to the latter, the author will, in a great measure, be compensated for all the labor and expense, which he has incurred, in their preparation for the press; and thus, his most sanguine expectations will be fully realized.

Lansford W. Hastings.

Chapter 1

SCENES AND INCIDENTS OF A PARTY OF OREGON EMIGRANTS

The author long having had an anxious desire to visit those wild regions upon the great Pacific, which had now become the topic of conversation in every circle, and in reference to which, speculations both rational and irrational were everywhere in vogue, now determined to accomplish his desired object: for which purpose he repaired to Independence, Mo., which place was the known rendezvous of the Santa Fe traders, and the trappers of the Rocky mountains. Having arrived at Independence, he was so fortunate as to find, not only the Santa Fe traders, and the Rocky mountain trappers, but also a number of emigrants, consisting of families and young men, who had convened there with the view of crossing the Rocky mountains, and were waiting very patiently until their number should be so increased as to afford protection and insure the safety of all, when they contemplated setting out together, for their favorite place of destination, Oregon territory. The number of emigrants continued to increase with such rapidity, that on the 15th day of May, our company consisted of one hundred and sixty persons, giving us a force of eighty armed men, which was thought ample for our protection. Having organized, and having ascertained that all had provided themselves with the necessary quantum of provisions and ammunition, as well as such teams and wagons as the company had previously determined to be essential, and indispensable, and all things else being in readiness, on the 16th day of May, in the year 1842, all as one man, united in interest, united in feeling, we were, *en route*, for the long desired *El Dorado* of the West.

Now, all was high glee, jocular hilarity, and happy anticipation, as we thus darted forward into the wild expanse, of the untrodden regions of the "western world." The harmony of feeling, the sameness of purpose, and the identity of interest, which here existed, seemed to indicate nothing but continued order, harmony and peace, amid all the trying scenes incident to our long and toilsome journey. But we had proceeded only a few days travel, from our native land of order and security, when the "American character" was fully exhibited. All appeared to be determined to govern, but not to be governed. Here we were, without law, without order, and without restraint; in a state of nature, amid the confused, revolving fragments of elementary society! Some were sad, while others were merry; and while the brave doubted, the timid trembled! Amid this confusion, it was suggested by our captain, that we "call a halt," and pitch our tents, for the purpose of enacting a code of laws, for the future government, of the company. The suggestion was promptly complied with, when all were required to appear in their legislative capacities. When thus convened, it was urged, by the captain, as a reason why we should enact a code of laws, that an individual of the party, had proposed to capture an Indian horse, and that he had made arrangements to accomplish his sinful purpose, by procuring a rope, and setting out with that view. In view of this alarming state of facts, it was urged by the over-legal and over-righteous, that the offending party should be immediately put upon his trial, for this enormous and wanton outrage upon Indian rights. This suggestion was also readily complied with, and the offender was soon arraigned, who, without interposing a plea to the jurisdiction, declared himself ready for trial, upon the "general issue." The investigation now commenced, during which, several speeches were delivered, abounding with severe and bitter denunciations of such highly criminal conduct, as that with which the prisoner at the bar of imaginary justice, stood charged. But it was urged on the part of the accused, that in whatever light his conduct might be viewed, by the advocates of "extreme right," it amounted to no crime at all; that to talk of taking an Indian horse, was neither *malum in se,* nor *malum prohibitum.* It was not criminal in itself, for in itself it was nothing, as he had *done* nothing. It was not criminal because prohibited, for in our infant state of society, we had no prohibitory code. The jury consisted of the whole company, who now with very little hesitancy, and almost unanimously, rendered their verdict of "not guilty," when the accused was discharged, and permitted to go hence, without delay. Thus terminated the first jury trial, in our little community, whose government was extremely simple, yet purely democratic. This investigation, terminating as it did, afforded no valid reason for law-making, yet all being present with that view, and many being extremely anxious to accomplish the object for which they assembled, whether it was necessary or not, now proceeded to the discharge of the new, arduous and responsible duty of legislation. A committee was, therefore, appointed to draft a code of laws, for the future government of the company. This committee, contrary to the most sanguine expectations of the movers in this affair, reported that in its opinion, no code of laws was requisite, other then the moral code, enacted by the Creator of the universe, and which is found recorded in the breast of every man. This report was adopted by an overwhelming majority, the consequence of which was, that no code of human laws was enacted; still there appeared to be a strong determination on the part of some, to do something in the way of legislating. In accordance with this determination, a decree was passed, which required the immediate and the indiscriminate extermination of the whole canine race, old and young, male and female, wherever they might be found, within our jurisdiction. This decree was passed by a very small majority, and it gave great dissatisfaction, especially to the owners of the animals whose extermination it contemplated. Those who favored its enforcement, insisted that the subjects of "the decree of death," however athletic they might be, could not possibly be taken through; that they would die before they had traveled half the distance, and that, by their incessant barking and howling, they would notify the Indians of our locality when encamped. On the other hand, it was insisted that, if they died on the way, that would be the loss of the owners, and, consequently, their business; and that if they did notify the Indians of our position, they would also notify *us* of theirs; and hence, the conclusion was drawn, that the advantages more then counterbalanced the disadvantages. Notwithstanding this conclusion, several dogs were slain under the inconsiderate decree, when the opposition became more general and determined. The owners of the most valuable mastiffs now declared in the most positive terms, that "if any man should kill their dogs, they would kill him, regardless of all consequences." The "dog killers," however, now went out "armed and equipped," as the decree required, with a full determination to discharge their *honorable* and *dangerous* duty but they were promptly met by the owners, who were also "armed and equipped," and prepared for any emergency. At this important crisis, the captain thought proper to convene the company again, in its legislative capacity, which being done, the "dog decree," as it was called, was almost unanimously abrogated. This was our first and last effort at legislation. This legislative rebuff, however, was not the only difficulty which we here encountered.

Our misfortunes were heightened by disease and death. The wife and child of a Mr. Lancaster were taken very ill, and the child soon died. Mrs. Lancaster remained very low for several days, during which time, the company remained in camp; but as there were no prospects of her immediate recovery, and as any considerable delay in this section, might be attended with fatal consequences in the whole company, Mr. Lancaster determined to return to the States, which he could very safely do, as we were but a few days travel from the Missouri line, and as we had passed no hostile Indians. Upon arriving at this determination, we continued our journey, and Mr. Lancaster returned to the States, where he safely arrived, as I have since learned. We passed on now very agreeably, with the exception of the occasional expression of dissatisfaction with our officers, which, however well founded, grated harshly upon the ears of the order-observing, and law-abiding portion of the company. In a very few days, we met a company of traders from Fort Larimie, on their way to the States, with their returns of furs and buffalo robes, which they had accumulated during the previous year. These furs and robes were transported in wagons, drawn by oxen. Here many of our party for the first time, saw the buffalo. The only ones, however, which they saw here, were eight or ten buffalo calves, which the traders had domesticated for the St. Louis market; and so completely domesticated were they, that they followed the cows, which had been taken out for that purpose, with very little trouble to the drivers. This meeting afforded a very favorable opportunity for forwarding letters to the States, of which many of the party were happy to avail themselves. We were informed, by this party, that we would find the buffalo upon the Platte, a few days travel below the confluence of its north and south branches: upon arriving at which place, we did find them in the greatest abundance imaginable. No adequate conception can be formed of the immensity of the numerous herds, which here abound. The entire plains and prairies are densely covered, and completely blackened with them, as far as the most acute vision extends. Now the most feverish anxiety, and confused excitement prevails. Those who are accustomed to buffalo hunting, are almost instantly upon their fleet horses, and in chase, while those unaccustomed to such scenes, "green horns," as they are called, are in the greatest confusion, adjusting saddles and martingals, tightening girths and spurs, loading guns and pistols, and giving their friends, wives and children, all manner of assurances of their unparalleled success. They too, are now ready, and like the mountaineer, they dart away, as with the wings of light; but they soon observe that they are far in the rear of the mountaineer, who is now amid the buffalo, slaying them on the right and left, in the front and rear. But stimulated by the loud thundering and clattering sounds, produced by the confused rushing forth of the thousands of frightened buffalo, as well as by the extraordinary success of the mountaineer, they ply the spur with renewed energy; and giving their fiery steeds, loose rein, they are soon in the *vicinity* of the scene of action, but not in the scene of action, for to their utter surprise, and intolerable vexation, their heretofore faithful steeds, now decline the contest; and notwithstanding the renewed application of the spur, they merely hound, snort and plunge, but keep a respectful distance, until they arrive in the midst of the slain buffalo, which have been left by the mountaineer. Here their timidity is increased, and taking a new fright, they dart and leap away with great velocity, and notwithstanding the firm and steady restraint of the sturdy rider, they soon meet the moving caravan, to the infinite gratification of the mountaineer, the utter astonishment of the "green horn," and the sad disappointment of the friends, wives and children, who had anticipated so much from the first grand debut in buffalo hunting. The experienced hunter is soon seen returning to the camp, with his horse heavily laden with the choicest portions of some of the numerous buffalo which he has slain. In order that the company may now obtain a supply of the delicious fresh meat, with which the plains are strewed, it is directed to encamp, which having been done, all are soon abundantly supplied. Having been a few days among the buffalo, and their horses having become accustomed to these terrific scenes, even the "green horn," is enabled, not only to kill the buffalo with much expertness, but he is also frequently seen, driving them to the encampment, with as much indifference as he used formerly to drive his domestic cattle about his own fields, in the land of his nativity. Giving the buffalo rapid chase for a few minutes, they become so fatigued and completely exhausted, that they are driven from place to place, with as little difficulty as our common cattle. Both the grown buffalo and the calves, are very frequently driven in this manner to the encampment, where they are readily slaughtered.

By this time, the party had become greatly incensed with the officers, and had determined upon holding an election, for the purpose of electing other officers. Accordingly an election was held, which resulted in the election of myself to the first, and a Mr. Lovejoy to the second office of our infant *republic*. This election gave some dissatisfaction, to a few of the party, especially the disaffected and disappointed office-holders and office-seekers, who now, together with a few others, separated themselves from the main body, and went on a few days in advance, to Fort Larimie, where they had been but a few days, when the main body arrived. Upon arriving at Forts Larimie and John, we were received in a very kind and friendly manner by the gentlemen of those forts, who extended every attention to us, while we remained in their vicinity. While here several of our party disposed of their oxen and wagons, taking horses in exchange. This they were induced to do, under the impression that their wagons could not be taken to Oregon, of which they were assured by the gentlemen of those forts, and other mountaineers. Many others of the party, disposed of their cows and other cattle, which had become tender footed, as from this cause, it was supposed, that they would soon be unable to travel; but we found by experience, that by continued driving, their hoofs became more and more hardened, until they had entirely recovered. Before leaving these forts, the disaffected of our party proposed to unite their destinies again with ours; but the main body being so exasperated with their former course, for some time refused their consent, yet in view of the fact, that they must either travel with us, remain at these forts, or return to the States, they were permitted to join us again, when we were once more enabled to continue our toilsome, yet interesting journey.

Leaving these forts, we had traveled but a few miles, when we met a company of trappers and traders, from Fort Hall, on their way to the States, among whom was a Mr. Fitzpateric, who joined our party, as a guide, and traveled with us, as such, to Green river. From this gentleman's long residence in the great western prairies, and the Rocky mountains, he is eminently qualified as a guide, of which fact, we were fully convinced, from the many advantages which we derived from his valuable services. He was employed by Dr. White, who had received the appointment of Indian agent of Oregon, and who was under the impression, that our government would defray all such expenses; which impression, however, I think, was entirely unfounded. Perfect unanimity of feeling and purpose, now having been fully restored, we passed on very agreeably, and with little or no interruption, until we arrived at Sweet-water, near Independence rock. Here we had the misfortune to lose a young man, by the name of Bailey, who was killed by the accidental discharge of a gun. As the ball entered at the groins, and passed entirely through the body, it was readily seen that the wound must prove fatal. He survived but about two hours, which, to him, were hours of excruciating suffering, and to us, those of gloomy despondency and grief. He was an amiable young man, a native of the state of Massachusetts; latterly from the territory of Iowa. Being a blacksmith by trade, the party sustained a great loss in his death; not only, however, in reference to his services as a mechanic, but also, in reference to the important protection, which each afforded to the other, in this wild region of savage ferocity. While he survived, every possible exertion was made to afford him relief, but all to no purpose. He constantly insisted that it was utterly impossible for him to recover, that immediate death was inevitable. The physician now gave up all hopes of his recovery; his voice faltered; death was depicted upon his countenance, and every thing seemed to indicate a speedy return of his immortal spirit, "to God who gave it," yet, even now, he was to be heard, urging us all, in the most emphatic language, to be more cautious in the future, and, thereby, avoid similar accidents. He now took his "eternal leave" of all, in the most solemn and affecting manner, at the same time, most earnestly admonishing us, "to prepare for a like fate, should it be our unhappy lot, and, at all events, to make a speedy preparation for death and eternity!" This was truly a most solemn and awful scene; and these admonitions, coming from such a source, and under such circumstances, must have produced an impressive and lasting effect! He expired in the evening, and the burial took place the next morning. The grave having been prepared, at the foot of a mountain of considerable altitude, about eighty rods southwest, from the usual encampment, we now followed to the grave, the second corpse of our little company! As we thus marched along, in solemn procession, the deepest gloom and solemnity, was depicted upon every countenance, and pungent and heartfelt grief pervaded every breast! While we were silently and solemnly moving on, under arms, "to the place of the dead," the sentinels were to be seen, standing at their designated posts, alternately meditating upon the solemnity of the passing scene, and casting their eyes watchfully aroused as if to descry the numerous and hostile foe, with whom we were everywhere surrounded, and thus, to avert accumulating danger! At the same time, the young man, who was the unwilling instrument of this, our trying calamity, was also to be seen, walking to and fro, suffering the inset extreme mental agony; apparently noticing nothing that was transpiring around; seemingly unconscious of every thing, but his own unhappy existence, and the sad departure of his, and our lamented friend! The ordinary rites, after interment, having been performed at the grave, the company returned in the same solemn manner, to the encampment, where all sat down in silent mournful mood, contemplating the many trying scenes of the desolating past, and anticipating the dreaded fearful future!

Having spent several days at this place, and having, in the mean time, procured an additional supply of meat, re-elected our officers, and made all other necessary preparatory arrangements, we, once more, set out upon our dismal journey; when I thought proper to issue an order, which required all, in the future, to carry their guns uncapped or primed. The propriety and importance of this order, were clearly manifested, by the sad occurrence just related, hence it was readily and promptly obeyed. Had such an order been previously issued and enforced, our deceased friend might still have lived, and instead of sadness and dismay, hilarity and joy might have pervaded our community; but we, unfortunately, like thousands of others, were mere sophomores in the great school of experience. The fates, taking advantage of our want of experience, appeared really to have conspired against us; surrounding us everywhere, with the most inauspicious circumstances; and crowding our lonely way with innumerable and unforeseen dangers, and with death, as if determined to deluge the whole western wilds, with human misery, and to engulf us, their defenceless victims, in the deep, dark abyss of inextricable woe; and thus, to feast upon our misfortunes, and exult triumphantly over our weakness and inexperience! Sweet-water, was a bitter water to us; if it even possessed any sweetness, it had lost it all now, for it afforded us nothing but the extreme bitterness of sore affliction and deep distress.

Chapter 2

DEPARTURE FROM SWEET-WATER

The company having left our unfortunate encampment, on Sweet-water, early in the morning, soon passed Independence rock, which will be described, in the description of the routes. A Mr. Lovejoy and myself stopped at this rock, with a view of spending a few hours, in examining its peculiar structure, as well as to observe the various names, there to be seen, of individuals who have passed that way; and at the same time, to inscribe our own names, with the number of our company, the date of our passing; and whatever else might occur to us, as being serviceable to those who might subsequently pass that way. Having provided ourselves with materials for lettering, we tied our horses at the foot of this extraordinary rock, where we also left our guns, and commenced our toilsome assent up the rocky declivity. The company had, in the mean time, gone on, supposing that we would find no difficulty in overtaking them, whenever we had accomplished our purpose.

We had scarcely completed our labors, when we were surprised by the sudden appearance of seven Indians, who had descried us from some remote hill or mountain. They presented themselves to us, in the most hostile attitude, rushing towards us with the greatest vehemence; uttering the most terrific and demoniac yells; and with the most frightful gestures, seeming to design nothing but our immediate destruction. With drawn bows and guns, they thus rapidly advanced, while we were cautiously, yet hastily descending the rocky heights; winding our way with all possible haste, to the point at which we had left our guns and horses, at which place, ourselves and the Indians arrived at the same time, when we immediately seized our guns, with a view of defending ourselves. But upon seeing us take our guns, they at once lowered their bows and guns, and extended their hands in friendship. We hastily took their hands, but as hastily proceeded to mount, and to prepare for our departure. We had scarcely mounted, when they evinced a determination to prevent our leaving. One of them held Mr. Lovejoy's mule by the bit, while others laid hold of his person; and others still, stood around with drawn guns and bows. As we were now consulting in reference to the proper course to be pursued, under these peculiar and critical circumstances, their repeated demands to dismount, and their increasing determination and violence, forcibly reminded us of the eminent importance of immediate and decisive action. Finally, we determined to effect our escape, after having slain as many of our assailants as we could, which, perhaps, might have been five of the seven, as we, together, had that number of shots, upon which we might rely. Just, however, as we had arrived at the above determination, to our astonishment, we beheld the whole country, as far as we could see, completely covered with them, rapidly advancing towards us, with deafening whoops and terrific yells. They seemed to have sprung up from behind every rock, to have come down from every hill and mountain, and to have emerged from every valley and ravine. Our purpose was now, of course, changed, for resistance was out of the question; to attempt an escape by flight, was dangerous in the extreme, and to accomplish it was utterly impossible; we therefore dismounted, and determined to reconcile our minds to our fate, be that life or death. Every thing around us, appeared now, to indicate nothing but immediate torture, and ultimate death, to be inflicted by merciless savages. Their numbers had, by this time, increased to about two or three hundred; and they were still arriving in great numbers. We were treated with the utmost rudeness; our guns and pistols were taken from us; when we were compelled to sit upon the ground, surrounded by a numerous guard, who performed its *whole duty,* not permitting us to change our positions in any manner, either to avoid danger or to acquire comfort. From the time we were taken, every additional party that arrived, invariably offered some indignity to our persons, either by striking or attempting to strike us, with their bows, arrows, or the rammers of their guns. The chief, however, protected me from this insult, for which purpose, he constantly stood or sat by me; yet he appeared unable, or unwilling to protect my companion, who was repeatedly stricken with much violence. An attempt was made even to take his life, which fortunately failed. This murderous attempt, was made by an Indian who had just arrived, on horseback, and who appeared to be much more infuriated then his predecessors in barbarity. Immediately upon his arrival, he rushed most furiously upon Mr. Lovejoy, suddenly pressing his gun against his breast, and snapping it, but as it missed fire, he was foiled in his fiendlike purpose. At this critical crisis, a number of Indians gathered around Mr. Lovejoy, evidently with a view of protecting him from further insult and danger, when unparalleled consternation and confusion prevailed. While many were most vehemently insisting upon our immediate destruction, others made the very welkin ring with their boisterous and clamorous declamations in our behalf, and no doubt Mr. Lovejoy and myself, owed our preservation entirely to their persuasive barbarous eloquence. The influence of our eloquent defenders was so great, as to induce the chief to order six of his men to fire upon him, who had thus rudely assailed my companion. They promptly obeyed the command, and had the offender not been making his escape with much rapidity, he would undoubtedly have been slain. Having galloped off about two hundred yards, he commenced a most doleful lamentation, and becoming more and more enraged, he set up a tremendous howling and crying, at the same time, discharging his gun in the open air; thus indicating, in terms not to be misunderstood, his determined and settled purpose of barbarous revenge. But opposition soon become so general, that he was convinced, that returning, with hostile purpose, would be attended with imminent danger. After some solicitation on the part of his friends, he was permitted to return, upon the condition, of his abandoning his hostile purpose, and conducting himself with proper *Indian* decorum. Having returned, he kept a respectful distance from the principal scene of action, and either standing or sitting, in most sullen mood, he appeared to take no part or interest in the subsequent transactions. Some new source of discord appeared now, to have arisen, which gave rise to a most serious and animated discussion; and judging from their wild and angry tones and gestures, their boisterous and fiendish declamation; some were again insisting upon our decapitation, or destruction in some other manner, while others were again insisting upon our preservation. The discussion continued to become more and more animated; the dissatisfaction became greater; the breach became wider; some great difference evidently existed, which, to us, appeared beyond a possibility of reconciliation; the two contending parties stood forth against each other, in formidable array, assuming the most uncompromising and hostile attitude. The noisy, wild discussion now ceased to some extent, and both parties were intensely engaged in loading and putting their guns in order for action. At this critical time, for what purpose we knew not, twelve of them advanced thirty or forty yards from the main body, towards Independence rock, where they stood for a few moments, when all at once, and without any order, they discharged their pieces in the direction of a small rock, which was between them and Independence rock. We soon discovered that the victim of their wrath, was a dog which had followed us, without our knowledge, upon this, our unfortunate excursion. Upon firing at the dog, a most frightful scene ensued; one universal burst of indignation or exultation, we knew not which, resounded through the air with most terrific and fiendish roar; when all but the few who stood around us, as we sat upon the ground, rushed in quick succession, in single file towards their slain victim, each as he passed which, either thrust his spear or lance into the dead carcass, struck it with his arrow, the rammer of his gun, or kicked it; the thrust, blow or kick, being in every instance, attended with a most demoniac shriek. They continued to repeat this frightful scene, for fifteen or twenty minutes, setting out from a point near us, they formed a vast circuit around their victim, returning to the same point, when they arrived at which, they invariably uttered the most indescribable whoops and yells, which could emanate only from the wild confusion and raging madness of aboriginal barbarism.

Some degree of quietude was again restored, but, in the mean time, my horse and Mr. Lovejoy's mule had been stripped of their saddles, bridles and martingals; all the rings and straps had been cut from them; my holster had been cut and spoiled; and our arms were scattered, we knew not where, nor was it very material where, for we had very little use for *arms*, and about as little for *legs,* as we were not permitted to stand or walk. Many were again, becoming more boisterous, when, fortunate for us, a number of elderly men, who were evidently men of high distinction, just arrived for whom, it appeared that the party had been thus long waiting. It was now late in the afternoon, and we were taken early in the morning; although the time of our detention, thus far, was

short, it appeared long to us; hours were, to us, as days; the
sun seemed reluctant to go down upon the wrath of our infuriated tormentors. A very elderly man who was one of those
that had just arrived, and who appeared to be the chief, in
highest authority, after some general remarks, gave orders to
march, to obey which, all were soon busily engaged in making their arrangements. Horses were provided for us, but not
our own; and soon many of the party were on their march, but
in the opposite direction from our company. The old chief just
referred to, happened, at this time, to pass near me, when I
extended my hand to him, and accosted him in the ordinary
manner, "How do you do?" He readily accepted my hand, and
replied in the Indian language. There was a very small eccen-
tric looking man, with the chief whom I supposed to be a
Canadian half-breed. I also offered him my hand, with the
same salutation, to which he replied, in the English language,
"How do you do?" To my inquiry whether he could speak the
English language, he replied "yes" I then asked him if he
would request the chief, and all those men to stop, and tell
them that I wished to talk with them, before they went farther.
He again replied "yes," and briefly addressed the chief, who
commenced a loud harangue, to his men, and soon, those who
had commenced their march returned, when all dismounted;
and sitting upon the ground, side by side, formed a vast circle.
The chief indicated, by signs, that I and my companion,
should sit near him, which we did, when I informed them that
we were from the United States; that we were sent by our and
their "great father," the president, that we were going to the
"great waters," the Pacific, there to settle and remain; that we
were friendly with all the "red men," and that we wished to,
and would treat them kindly. It had been reported among
them, by some Canadians, at Fort Larimie, that we were
going to join their enemies, the Blackfeet, with whom they
were then at war. This I remarked, they must be satisfied, was

false, especially as we had our women and children with us, of which they were aware, as they had seen them, at Fort Larimie and elsewhere. White men, I remarked, did not take their women and children when they went to war, nor did Indians. Your party, I said, is a war party, and you have no women or children, because they can not fight. I then assured them, if they would go with us, to our party, we would convince them of our friendly designs; that we would trade with them, and make them presents; that if they went to our party, it became necessary to out very soon as it passed this place very early in the morning, and it was then late in the day. As soon as I had concluded, the interpreter to whom I have alluded, arose and addressed the chief for few minutes, when he resumed his seat, but what he said, we were, of course, unable to determine, as he spoke entirely in the Indian language, but, our opinion was, that he was repeating what I had said. This opinion was confirmed, from the fact that immediately upon his resuming his seat, the chief arose and spoke for about two minutes, apparently, with much feeling and determination. At the conclusion of his remarks, he evidently issued his order, requiring all to remount, and to change their course in the direction of our party, for all immediately mounted, and resumed their march in that direction. A much more friendly feeling was now manifested towards us; we were directed to take our position, in the ranks, at the side of the chief. We soon crossed a small creek, when I indicated to the chief, by pointing to the water, then putting my fingers to my lips, that I was thirsty; upon observing which, he directed a man to dismount, and bring me some water, which direction was readily obeyed. Upon arriving with the water, the man first offered it to the chief, who refused to take it, but directed him to give it to me; which he did, when I drank and returned him the cup, which he again offered to the chief, who again refused it, directing him to give it to Mr. Lovejoy, who having drunk, the chief then received it and drank. We now traveled on, with much rapidity, the "pipe of peace," being constantly passed around, commencing with the chief, then to myself, Mr. Lovejoy, and the principal men, who were permitted to ride side by side with us, and who, I suppose, were subordinate officers.

Having traveled in this manner, about two hours, the spies came galloping from the hills, informing the chief that they had made some discoveries, which, whatever they were, were of such importance, that the chief, at once, ordered them all to dismount, which they did; and commenced examining their guns, re-loading those which had been discharged; examining their flints and locks, and putting their bows, arrows, spears and lances in proper order. Our guns were then given to us, and we were required to re-load them; when all painted their faces and bodies, as is their practice previous to going to war; after which we were all ordered to remount, and march, which we did; but, we marched with much more confusion and disorder then before. The whole aspect of things, appeared to have undergone a material and fearful change; from harmonious, peaceable and friendly, to the most tumultuous and hostile. Although we were permitted to ride, side by side, with the chief, as before, yet, I frequently saw the Indians approach Mr. Lovejoy, from behind, with drawn spears, lances, or guns, as if with a view of terminating his existence. And Mr. Lovejoy informed me, that he observed the same conduct in reference to myself, of which, however, I had no knowledge. I here saw, for the first time, that what the spies had discovered was our company, the tents and wagons of which were then in full view. It appeared evident to us, from what we had already seen and what was then transpiring, that they contemplated an attack upon our party, and we were soon confirmed in this opinion, from what subsequently followed. When they had approached within two or three hundred rods of our camp, the young men, on each side of the chief, commenced a most furious charge, and, at the same time, uttering the most alarming and frantic yells, which left no further doubt upon our minds, but that they intended to attack our camp; unless turned from their purpose, by some fortuitous circumstance. Perceiving the inevitable tendency of this course, I suggested to the chief, by signs that he should require his men to discontinue their charge; but he was deaf to my suggestion. I then took hold of his bridle, stopped his horse, and insisted that they must stop, otherwise, our men would be compelled to repel the assault. Being, by this time, satisfied that there was, perhaps, more danger then he had anticipated, he addressed his men in a most animated manner, apparently directing them to resume their former friendly attitude, or at least, to discontinue their charge. This order was finally obeyed, though evidently, with much reluctance. Observing that our men were in the most confused state of excitement, I signified to the chief, that I would go to our camp, to which, however, he refused his assent; but being determined to attempt it, at all hazards, I disregarded his dissent, and galloped away. Two young warriors, soon came galloping up by my side, insisting that I should return; but I answered them merely by telling them, by signs, that they must go back, or our men would shoot and kill them. This had the desired effect: they returned, and I increased my velocity, in the direction of our company. Upon arriving at the camp, I found the greatest imaginable confusion prevailing; some insisting that they would fire, others opposing it: all was noisy, alarming disorder.

Mr. Lovejoy now having also arrived in camp, and order having been, to some extent, restored, I proceeded, through our Canadian interpreter, to make certain demands upon the chief. The first demand was, that he, immediately, send to our camp, my horse, and all other property which his men had

kept, which belonged either to Mr. Lovejoy or myself. This
demand he readily complied with, as far as he was able; for,
as he said, he could find but one of my pistols, which he
returned, together with every thing else which his men had
taken, with the exception of Mr. Lovejoy's bridle and martin-
gal, which he pretended were beyond his reach, and not to be
found. I then demanded, that he march his men away to a certain point of timber, and encamp during the night; to comply
with which, he at first, positively refused, insisting that an old
chief, in his own country, had a right to encamp wherever he
pleased; but he finally consented, when I informed him that
when he had encamped, as directed, he would be permitted to
return, with his chiefs and principal men; and smoke, with us,
the "pipe of peace," when we would trade with them, and
make him some presents. Of course, he, with several of his
principal men, soon returned, much more anxious, however,
to receive the promised presents, then to enter into the contemplated peace arrangements. Having formed a vast circle,
all sitting upon the ground, side by side, the "pipe of peace"
was soon called into requisition, which was most industri-
ously passed and repassed from "white chief" to "red chief"
and from "white brave" to "red brave," until we had burned
several ounces of smoking tobacco, upon the altar of peace;
the dense fumes of which, were curling thickly in the atmosphere above; appeasing the wrath of the "god of war," dis-
pelling native animosity; and restoring mutual confidence,
friendship and peace. After having concluded our "smoke"
we traded some with them and gave them some presents,
when they left us, apparently with all good feeling, which
they expressed in every possible manner, of which savage
barbarism is capable.

From this encampment we traveled a few days up Sweet-
water, where we encamped for the purpose of "making meat,"
as it is called. Here, while some were engaged in hunting the

buffalo, which were very abundant, others remained in camp, for the purpose of protecting it, and drying and preserving the meat, which was daily brought in, by the hunters. While we remained at this place, there was another accidental discharge of a gun, which produced much alarm, especially among the ladies, yet no injury resulted from it, other then a slight flesh wound in the foot of a small child, which was sitting in a wagon, through which the ball passed. At this encampment, the Indians again exhibited many indications of their hostile intentions. The small hunting parties, which were sent out for the purpose of hunting the buffalo, were not unfrequently robbed of both their meat and horses, and sent to camp on foot, happy in having made so fortunate an escape. And they not only frequently robbed the hunters, but they also came to us in great numbers; riding and parading around our camp, insisting upon being permitted to mingle with us, which, however, I absolutely refused; and at the same time, informed them, that any attempt to approach us would be met with prompt resistance. In order, however, to obviate the necessity of forcible resistance, I thought proper to terrify them from their hostile purposes, by appearances. Accordingly, I drew the men out, in front of the camp, assuming as formidable an appearance as possible, and at the same time, giving them assurances of our friendly feelings; but determined purpose, to resist any attempt to approach our encampment. This course had the desired effect; seeing our firm determination to resist them, they loitered about our camp a few hours, when they confusedly dispersed, amid the wild roar of savage clamor.

Leaving this encampment, we saw nothing more of them, for several days; but coming again, upon a tributary of Sweet-water, we met with them, in increased numbers. They numbered, at this place, not less, perhaps, then one thousand or fifteen hundred. Their numbers being now, so increased, and it being unknown whether they were hostile, I thought proper to encamp, for the purpose of receiving and disposing of them, as circumstances might require. Accordingly, we encamped, when they advanced with much rapidity, and with most furious whoops and yells, displaying, at the same time, their flags of most beautiful and variegated colors. I now, gave them the signal to stop, which they promptly obeyed, dismounted, and planted their flag-staffs; exhibiting their colors to the best possible advantage. They were now arrayed, fronting our camp, at least, fifty abreast, and ten or twelve deep; and our greatest anxiety, of course, was to ascertain whether they were peaceably inclined; for which purpose, my horse having been saddled, I mounted and galloped out to them, when I informed them, that we would "talk" with them a few minutes, "smoke" with them, and give them some presents, when we were desirous of continuing our journey. The chiefs having manifested, their approbation of this course, I invited them to our camp, to "talk" and "smoke" with us, and receive the presents, when we would all disperse. They accepted the invitation, and started with us to our camp, but as we started, the main body of the Indians also started to go with us, to have permitted which, would have been dangerous in the extreme; I, therefore, remarked to the chiefs, that the invitation, was only extended to them, and that, we would expect the residue of the Indians, to remain where they were, as much confusion, and perhaps, difficulty, might result from their intermingling with our people. They replied through their interpreter, in their brief manner, "it is good," "it is right." Then turning to their men, they gave them orders to remain, until they should return. We then proceeded to our "talk," and "smoke," which engaged our attention about two hours; when we distributed the promised presents among them, took our leave of them, and pursued our journey; while they returned to their villages, with the kindest feelings and the warmest friendship, for the "white man of the East." As we passed their villages, which were but a few hundred yards from our route, hundreds of the women and children thronged our way, gazing upon us with the utmost astonishment; and many of the men followed us, even until night, when, after having effected many profitable trades in horses and mules, they returned to their villages, rejoicing in the happy anticipation, of the extraordinary advantages, to be derived from their new acquaintances, thus favorably formed.

A few days subsequently, a rather serious difference occurred, which arose from the refusal of one of our men, to stand his guard, in conformity to the regulations of the party. His refusal being reported to the proper officers, he was subjected to a trial, and found guilty, when the ordinary sentence was passed upon him, to which he refused to submit. The officers, however, informed him, that he would be required absolutely, to comply with the sentence, or submit to expulsion from the party; after which, he would not be permitted either to travel, or encamp with the company. As he still refused to comply with the sentence, ten men were ordered to arm themselves, and remove him, and his effects, at least one mile from the encampment. They accordingly repaired to his tent, informing him of their orders, and determination to carry them into effect, unless he should, immediately, agree to comply with the sentence. He still remained obstinate refusing to comply, and at the same time, appeared to be making arrangements for his defence, against any attempt to effect his forcible removal. No one, however, apprehended the least danger from any movement on his part; for we had already, witnessed several exhibitions of his *bravery*. The men designated to remove him, now informed him, notwithstanding his threats, that it became their duty to remove him from the encampment, "dead or alive," and that they intended to discharge that duty at all hazards. This decided course soon brought him to his senses, when he, through a friend of his, or rather, a friend of order, suggested that he be allowed a re-hearing, which was accordingly granted him, by the officers. On the following day, after arriving at the encampment, a jury was summoned to investigate and determine the matter, who, after having heard the evidence, and deliberated for a few moments, acquitted the violator of orders, upon the condition that he, thereafter, punctually discharge every duty devolving upon him, in reference to standing guard, and otherwise; which he did afterwards, with unusual punctuality. He had so profited by this lesson, that day or night, rain or shine, he was always to be found at his post; or from it, as the various orders happened to suggest.

Nothing further, worthy of remark, occurred until we reached the Colorado of the west, or Green river, where we encamped for several days. During our stay at this place, it was suggested that we leave our wagons, in order to facilitate our progress. This proposition was made, and insisted upon, by those who had an anxiety to reach Fort Hall, at an early day, for reasons unknown to us; and for the promotion of interests foreign from ours; yet, so urgently was it insisted upon, and so cogent were many of the reasons, which were urged, that several of the party determined to leave their wag-ons, and to prosecute the residue of their journey on horse-back; while I, together with a majority of the party, was of the opinion, that it was not necessary to leave the wagons, conse-quently, we determined to take them to Fort Hall, at least, that being the extent to which they had been previously taken. We accordingly, proceeded to make our arrangements to go on with our wagons, leaving those behind, who had determined to leave theirs, as they were under the necessity of convening them into packsaddles, which, by the by, was attended with much labor and inconvenience. Our guide, Mr. Fitzpateric, concurring in opinion, with those who had determined to leave their wagons, remained with them, the consequence of which was, that we were under the necessity of prosecuting the residue of our journey without a guide; unless we should accidentally fall in with one, elsewhere. Many of those who designed to leave their wagons, urged us to leave ours also, insisting that if we took them on, we would arrive at Fort Hall, so late in the season, that we would be under the necessity of remaining there during the winter; or that we would perish in our attempt to cross the Blue mountains. Others insisted that as we had no guide, it would be utterly impossible for us to find our way to Fort Hall, and that, consequently, we would inevitably perish by the way. We, however, confident in our own ability to do what others had done; and believing that "some things could be done as well as others," determined to pursue our journey at all events, and at all hazards, with or without a guide, as circumstances might determine. Seeing our determination, a Mr. Meek, who had formerly passed through that region, as far as Fort Hall, offered his services as our guide. Believing that he might be found serviceable to us, to some extent, at least, we employed him, when we were soon in readiness for our departure. The order being given to march, our friends now crowded around us, for the purpose of taking their leave of us, and, at the same time, lamenting the necessity which impelled our separation. Some still insisted upon our remaining, while others, in their terrified imaginations, already saw us winding our fearful way over mountains of perpetual snow, falling victim to raging famine, and the piercing cold, of eternal winter; and others still, by a more enlarged view of futurity, saw us very distinctly, deviating far from the proper route, falling victim to the savage ferocity of the more than barbarous Blackfeet. There were others still, who not having as clear a view, as their friends, of the hidden mysteries of futurity, examined its dark pages, in vain, for conclusive evidences of our destiny;

hence they determined, that separating now, we were separated forever; that no traces of us would ever afterwards be found. Amid this disparity of prophetic opinion, as well as the urgent solicitations of our friends to remain, which were insisted upon with much anxiety and sincerity, even to the shedding of tears, we now took a most solemn and affectionate leave of each other; some expecting to be so fortunate as to meet again at Fort Hall; others never expecting to meet again in this world; while others still, lost all hope of uniting again, either in this world, or the world to come. Leaving our obstinate friends, as we thought them, we now moved onward, while they resumed their extraordinary business of converting wagons into packsaddles. We had passed on but a few days, when contrary to our own expectations, and contrary to all the lights of prophecy before us, we all arrived, about the same time, at Fort Hall; we with, and they without their wagons.

Upon arriving at this fort, we were received in the kindest manner, by Mr. Grant, who was in charge; and we received every aid and attention from the gentlemen of that fort, during our stay in their vicinity. We were here informed, by Mr. Grant, and other gentlemen of the company, that it would be impossible for us to take our wagons down to the Pacific, consequently, a meeting of the party was called, for the purpose of determining whether we should take them further, or leave them at this fort, from which place it appeared, that we could take them, about half way to the Pacific without serious interruption. Some insisted that the great convenience of having wagons with us, would amply warrant taking them as far as we could; while others thought as we would eventually be under the necessity of leaving them, it would be preferable to leave them at the fort, especially as we could there obtain tools, and all other means of manufacturing our packing equipage, which we could not do elsewhere. Another reason which was urged in favor of leaving them was, that we could, perhaps, sell them for something at this place, which we could do, at no other point upon the route. The vote having been taken, it was found that a large majority was opposed to taking them any further, the consequence of which was, that there was no alternative for the minority, as our little government was purely democratic. Mr. Grant purchased a few of our wagons, for a mere trifle, which he paid in such provisions as he could dispose of, without injury to himself, He could not of course, afford to give much for them, as he did not need them, but bought them merely as an accommodation. Those who did not sell to Mr. Grant, got nothing for theirs; but left them there, to be destroyed by the Indians, as soon as we had commenced our march. This was a serious loss, as most of the wagons and harness were very valuable. Eight or ten days were occupied, in consummating our arrangements for the residue of our cheerless journey. In the interim, those of our company who left us at Green river, had accomplished their preliminary arrangements, and had gone on, several days in advance. We were enabled, at this fort, to exchange our poor and way-worn horses, for those which had not been injured by use; having done which, to considerable extent; having purchased many; having procured such additional provisions as could be obtained; and having convinced ourselves that we were invincible, we, once more, resumed our dangerous journey, over the burning sands, and through the trackless deserts of Oregon.

Upon this portion of our journey, we had anticipated many difficulties and hardships, especially, as we were entirely unacquainted with our new method of traveling, and as we were unable to procure a guide; yet, we proceeded with much less difficulty then we had anticipated. Arriving at Fort Boisia, we were very kindly received and entertained by the gentleman in charge, who kindly proffered to let us have such provisions as we needed, and to render us any additional service in his power. Here we learned that a young man, of the advance of our party, was drowned, in crossing Lewis' river. It appeared that the portion of the party to which he belonged, crossed this river at the usual ford, which is considered entirely safe, by those who are acquainted with it, but this young man deviating from the usual crossing, and disregarding the directions of his friends, was swept away in an instant. He soon became detached from his horse, and appeared to be standing permanently upon the bottom, when several called to him, requesting him to stand until they could come to his relief. He, however, not heeding, or perhaps, not hearing what was said to him, leaped fearfully from his position, as if with a view of swimming to the shore, but he was swept away by the current, with the rapidity of lightning; and neither himself, nor his horse, was ever seen, or heard of after. He was a German, the same unfortunate young man, who caused the death of Mr. Bailey, of which I have before spoken. The portion of the party to which I belonged, did not cross the river, but kept directly down it, upon the south side. Leaving Fort Boisia, the next place of note, at which we arrived, was a presbyterian mission, in charge of which, is a Dr. Whitman, who is a very kind and hospitable gentleman. He received us with the utmost kindness and attention, and insisted upon our remaining a few days with him, in order to obtain some relaxation of both body and mind, to which proposition, we finally acceded. Our stay with the doctor included the Sabbath, during which day, we attended divine service, at his residence. In the forenoon, he delivered a discourse to the Indians, in their own language, to which they appeared to be very attentive, evidently comprehending the truths and doctrines inculcated. Having had a few hours intermission, we again convened, when the doctor delivered a very able discourse to our company, the other members of the mission, and his family. This scene was the more interesting to us, as we had then, for the last four months, heard nothing but the terrific howl of wild beasts of prey, and the furious midnight yell, of a hostile and barbarous foe. The doctor is not only a very kind and hospitable gentleman, but he is no doubt, a very good man, and a devoted christian. He appears to be rendering great service, in christianizing and civilizing the natives. We spent a few days at this place, during which time, we were enabled to exchange many horses with the Indians, as well as, to purchase many, and also, to obtain our additional supply of provisions, which, having been done to the extent that we desired, we again proceeded upon our dismal journey.

The first day after leaving this mission we passed Fort Wallawalla, at which place we stopped but a few minutes, when we passed on, and in a few days, arrived at the methodist mission at the dalles. Mr. Perkins is in charge of this mission. He bestowed every attention upon us, and rendered us every aid in his power. We, however, remained but a few days here, when we, once more, re-commenced our pilgrimage; and without any thing further worthy of remark, we arrived, on the fifth day of October, in the lower settlements of Oregon. The mind was now naturally thrown back upon the past, brought to contemplate upon the present, and led to anticipate the future. Having left the land of our nativity, having torn ourselves from our relatives and friends, having passed through innumerable dangers, both seen and unseen; having been for the last four long months surrounded only by hordes of barbarous Indians, herds of wild beasts of prey, and danger and death in all their various and varied forms, we had now, arrived at our place of destination; and were about to locate in the wild forests of Oregon. Here we were, cut off almost entirely, from all communication with our connections and friends; in a wild uncultivated region; more then two thousand miles from the land that gave us birth; with no promise of support or protection from our government; exposed to the inclemencies of a dreary rainy season, of about five months, of almost incessant rain, hail, sleet and snow; without houses, without a sufficiency of clothing, or provision; entirely destitute of the means of agriculture; and surrounded with innumerable savages, with whose disposition as to peace or war, we were entirely unacquainted. Under these circumstances, we were very naturally led to inquire, how long this state of things was destined to exist. If this country is such as it has been represented, if it is so fertile and productive; if it is so eminently calculated to promote the prosperity and happiness of man, will not our government, soon extend her jurisdiction and laws over it, so as to insure our future protection; to encourage emigration and to promote enterprise? An affirmative answer to this question, was all our hope, all our consolation, for otherwise, as circumstances and things were, we could see nothing to warrant this tremendous leap into these dark and wild regions, of the "western world." The country did not appear to us, to be in reality, that delightful region which we had thus long and laboriously sought. Dismay and dissatisfaction appeared to be visibly impressed upon every countenance, and deep discontent pervaded every breast. All, however, soon obtained temporary residences, Doctor McLoughlin kindly proffered to render them any assistance in his power. He proposed to sell goods on a credit, to all those who were unable to make immediate payment. He also commenced building extensively, at the falls of the Wallammette, and thereby gave immediate employment, at the highest wages, to all those who wished to labor. Many engaged in labor for the doctor, others for the mission, while others selected and settled upon their "claims," in the various portions of the country, improving them as they best could, under these very unfavorable circumstances. In the spring, it was found that the dissatisfaction had, in a great measure, subsided, yet, many were still, much dissatisfied, and determined to leave the country, as soon as an opportunity should present. Some desired to return to the States, while others determined to avail themselves of the first opportunity of going to California, to which latter country, many of them, have subsequently gone, where they are entirely satisfied.

Chapter 3

A DESCRIPTION OF OREGON

The reader having now arrived in Oregon, he is, no doubt, anxious to enter upon an exploration of that much admired region. I will therefore, proceed with him, to take that brief view of the country, which the title-page contemplates. The extreme brevity of this description will, however, undoubtedly, render it more or less unsatisfactory; yet I shall endeavor to crowd together, as much useful and practical matter as possible upon the few pages, which, from the very narrow limits of this little work, I am allowed to devote to this branch of my subject.

Oregon territory is bounded on the east by the Rocky mountains; on the south by Upper California; on the west by the Pacific ocean; and on the north by the British possessions. The southern boundary was determined in the year 1819, by a treaty between the United States and Spain, which is commonly called the Florida treaty. It stipulates that the boundary between the possessions of the two nations, west of the Mississippi river, shall be as follows: "following the course of the southern bank of the Arkansas to its source, in latitude 42 degrees north, and thence, by that parallel of latitude, to the South sea." This boundary was confirmed by Mexico, as the successor of Spain, in the year 1828, consequently, there is no dispute or difference as to the southern boundary. The northern boundary was settled in 1823, by treaty between the United States and Russia, at 54 degrees and 40 minutes north

latitude. These treaties then, fix and determine the boundaries, as between the United States, Spain, Russia and Mexico, which are, in truth, the only powers that ever had any just
claim, to any portion of that territory.

Great Britain, however, latterly asserts a pretended claim,
adverse to that of the United States, to a portion of that country. But so far from having any valid claim to any portion of
it, she has no right even to occupy it; other then that right
guarantied to her, by the convention of 1818, the third article
of which provides, that any country that may be claimed by
either party, on the northwest coast of America, westward of
the Stony mountains, shall, together with its harbors, bays and
creeks, and the navigation of all rivers within the same, be
free and open for the term of ten years, from the date of the
signature of the present convention, to the vessels, citizens
and subjects of the two powers. It being well understood, that
this agreement is not to be construed to the prejudice of any
claim, which either of the two high, contracting parties, may
have to any part of said country." The same provisions were
indefinitely extended by the convention of 1827; with the further agreement, however, "that it should be competent for
either party, at any time after the 20th day of October, 1828,
on giving due notice, of twelve months, to the other contracting party, to annul and abrogate said convention." It is my
purpose here, however, merely to state the boundaries of Oregon, to give the authority by which they are established; and
to give the authority by which, the subjects of Great Britain
occupy that country, conjointly with citizens of the United
States. Having done which, to an extent sufficient for ordinary purposes, I will now, enter upon a more detailed description of Oregon territory. This territory is naturally divided
into three distinct divisions or sections, which, for convenience, I shall call the Eastern, Middle and Western sections.
The Eastern section includes all that country between the

Rocky and the Blue Mountains; the Middle section that between the Blue and the Cascade mountains; and the Western section, that between the Cascade mountains and the Pacific ocean. These ranges, which thus divide this country into distinct sections, together with their spurs, will now receive a more particular notice; commencing with the Rocky mountains. The course of this range is, generally, from the southeast to the northwest; and its distance from the sea is, generally, from 500 to 1000 miles: it is of great altitude and is usually covered with perpetual snow. The greatest elevations in all Oregon are found in this range, many of which are more then 25,000 feet above the level of the sea. From the foregoing remarks, and from the well known fact, of the entire sterility of all this range, it will be readily seen, that it is in no wise adapted to the support of man or beast. Instead of vegetation and timber, in the more elevated regions of this range, nothing but mountains of eternal snow are any where seen. From the extraordinary altitude and sterility of this range, it would be utterly impassable, were it not for certain gaps, or passes. Of these, there are five, which are known, and through which emigrants, traders, trappers and Indians annually pass, in greater or less numbers, depending upon the inducements, and the practicability of the pass. The principal of these, is the well known great southern pass, at latitude 42 deg. north, through which companies of emigrants and others, are annually passing, from the United States to Oregon and California. That through which the fur-traders of the Hudsons' Bay Company annually pass, is situated between Brown's and Hooker's peaks; a third between the sources of Maria's and Clarke's rivers; and a fourth is near the southern head waters of the Missouri; and the fifth is between Henry's fork of Lewis' river, and Big-horn, a branch of Yellowstone. The first of these passes is much the most important, and hence, it will receive a further notice upon a subsequent page. This range, like all the ranges of this country, has numerous spurs, many of which, are also of extraordinary altitude, The principal of them, I will now briefly describe. The first, which I shall notice, is that lying north of Frasier's river, and in which that river takes its rise. It has many high peaks, several of which are covered with snow the greater part of the year. It is a vast concatenation of peaks and heights, which are covered here and there, with a small growth of firs and pines. From this spur, another puts out for a considerable extent, down the Columbia river; and another branch of the same spur, extends down Frasier's river, about the same distance. The altitude of both branches of this spur, is less then that at the source of Frasier's river, yet it has several high peaks, near the Columbia. It is generally rather sparsely timbered; but in many places, it is covered with dense forests of low pines. A spur of lofty elevations, and of extraordinary sterility, lies south of mount Hooker, in the great bend of the Columbia; it is slightly covered with vegetation and shrubs, but, generally, it produces no kind of vegetation whatever. Between the Flat-bend and the Flat-bow rivers, there is another spur, which is quite similar to that just described, or, if possible more sterile and worthless. Between the Flat-head and the Spokan, there is also another spur, which has several very elevated peaks. The greatest part of this spur is thickly covered with trees, shrubs and the grasses. The only remaining spur, worthy of notice, in connection with this range, is that ranging near the Koosk-ooske river. It consists of high, rugged cliffs and peaks, many of which are entirely destitute of timber, or vegetation, yet the less elevated portions of them, are thickly covered with firs, pines, and a thick undergrowth of shrubs and bushes. This spur appears to be connected with the Blue mountains and to form a portion of that range.

The Blue mountains commence between the forty-fifth, and the forty-sixth degrees of north latitude, and run south, to the southern boundary of Oregon, where they intersect the Klamet range. They constitute a very irregular range, and are thought by many not to be a distinct range, but to consist entirely of spurs of the Rocky mountains; but the better opinion is, that they are, of themselves, a distinct range; for they are entirely separated from the Rocky mountains, by several large valleys. The general direction of this range is about north and south, and its distance from the coast is usually from three to five hundred miles. Its altitude is much less then that of either of the other ranges mentioned, yet it has several peaks, which are about ten or eleven thousand feet above the level of the sea, and which are covered with perpetual snow. This range is much less sterile then the Rocky mountain range; it has numerous depressions, elevated plains, and valleys of limited extent, which produce an abundance of grass, and most excellent timber; consisting principally of fir, pine and cedar of the best quality. This range, like that before described, has numerous spurs, some of which are immediately connected with the range, and others appear to have little or no connection with it; but upon examination, are found to be spurs of that range.

The Cascade mountains constitute that range which lies nearest the coast, and which is tailed the Cascade, or President's range. The course of this range is nearly parallel with the coast; its average distance from which, is from one to two hundred miles; and it is surpassed in altitude only by the Rocky mountains. It has twelve lofty peaks, several of which are from twelve to eighteen thousand feet above the level of the sea, rising in perfect cones, and covered perpetually with snow. Five of these have received the names of the former deceased presidents of the United States. These names were given them, by a Mr. Kelley, a traveler from the United States, several years ago, and they have ever since retained them; hence it is that this range is now called the Presidents' range. The other seven of these extraordinary conical peaks have received their names from various English travelers and navigators. But five of this seven, have latterly received the names of five other presidents of the United States. These names, I will also adopt, as I much prefer our own names, for our own property. The remaining two of these singular elevations, are called mount Fareweather, and mount St. Elias, both of which, are situated north of the northern boundary of Oregon. Now having our own names for each of these, which are within our own territory, I will proceed to give a brief description of them, in their proper order. Mount Washington is situated near latitude 44° north, about seven leagues south of the cascades; it is conical in form, rising about eighteen thousand feet above the level of the sea, and covered with perpetual snow, at least 12 thousand feet from its top downwards. Mount Adams is near the parallel of 45° north latitude, about eight leagues north from the cascades. About five hundred feet of its surface from its top, are covered with snow perpetually. Mount Jefferson is a vast and lofty peak, situated near latitude 42° north; it is also covered perpetually with snow several thousand feet downward from its top, and is seen from almost any part of the southern country. Mount Madison is near latitude 46° north; it is a vast massive peak, covered with snow to a very great depth. Mount Monroe is also a vastly elevated peak, extending far into the snowy region; it lies near latitude 43° and 30' north, and is seen at a great distance. Mount John Q. Adams, situated at latitude 42° and 10' north, is also a vast peak, towering high above the snow line. Mount Jackson is among the most elevated peaks, and is surpassed only by mount Washington; it is situated near the forty second degree of north latitude. Mount Van Buren is a very high peak, situated on the isthmus, between the Pacific and Pugets' sound. Mount Harrison is also a very lofty peak, terminating in regions of perpetual snow; it lies about forty miles west from Pugets' sound. Mount Tyler, being vastly elevated and covered with snow, is seen at a very great distance; it lies about eighty miles north from mount Harrison. All these are most extraordinary conical formations; some of which are seen from every part of the country. Here, wherever you are, you behold these ancient pyramids of eternal ice and snow, fearlessly rearing their majestic heads, high in the ethereal regions, amid the howling tempest, the flashing lightnings, and the roaring thunders above; presenting their eternal battlements, in bold defiance of the foaming billows, the raging floods, and the quaking and volcanic earth below. Enduring monuments of time! All this range of mountains is much less sterile then those before described. It has numerous elevated plains and valleys, and extensive depressions, all of which, abound with vegetation of various kinds; lofty trees of fir, pine, cedar and oak, of most extraordinary growth.

Besides the main ranges of mountains here described, there are several other smaller ranges worthy of notice, which appear to have very little connection with the main ranges, yet in some instances, may be traced as spurs of those ranges. Among them is the Claset range, which lies on the north side of the Columbia, running in a north westerly direction, along the straits of Juan de Fucas, to the waters of Pugets' sound. This range has many high peaks, a number of which rise very considerably above the snow line, but from their proximity to the sea, they are covered with snow, only about nine months of the year. It is generally covered with dense forests of fir, pine and cedar of immense growth. A small range also extends from the cascades, on the north side of the Columbia, to cape Disappointment on the coast. This range has many depressions and elevated plains, and is, generally, covered with dense fir and pine forests. There is a similar range to that just described, also on the south side of the Columbia, which commences at the cascades, and running nearly parallel with that river, terminates near its mouth. It is a continuous succession of low mountains and hills, having no elevations of more then about three thousand feet above the level of the sea, the greatest of which, are near the cascades. This range is also covered with stately pines and firs, of centuries growth, and of unparalleled dimensions. There is still another range, which extends along the coast, from the straits de Fucas, to Upper California. Its greatest elevations are immediately upon the coast, where they present high, dark cliffs of basaltic rock, which are seen at a very great distance from the ocean. This range descends gradually from the coast to the east, terminating in undulating plains. That portion of it nearest the coast, is generally entirely destitute of timber or vegetation, and presents a very irregular, broken and stony surface; but the east side presents those dense forests, undulating plains and prairies, peculiar to this section of Oregon. The last range which I shall notice, is that called the Klamet range, which is perhaps, properly a spur of the Rocky mountains. It extends from the Rocky mountain range, in latitude 42° north, in a direction west by north, to the Pacific ocean, and has many high peaks covered with snow. In its course from the Rocky mountains to the Pacific, it is intersected by the Blue mountains and the Cascade or Presidents range. It is usually destitute of timber, and in many places, entirely devoid of all kinds of vegetation.

The rivers next deserve our attention. The principal of these, is the Columbia, which is a grand and majestic stream. It is about fifteen hundred miles in length, including its meanders, entering the Pacific ocean, at latitude 46 degrees north. The general course of this river, from the confluence of its two great branches, is about west by south. Its northern branch takes its rise in the Rocky mountains, at latitude 50° north, and longitude 116° west. The course of this branch, from its source to McGillivarys' pass, at the base of the Rocky mountains, is generally, about northwest. This pass is at latitude 53° north, where those traveling from Oregon to Canada, make a very extensive portage, which is attended with much difficulty and danger. The river, at the base of the Rocky mountains, is 3,600 feet above the level of the sea, and its waters are urged down with great rapidity. Here, bearing to the south, it runs but a few miles, when it passes through a very narrow rocky channel, which is called the Upper dalles, through which, the waters are thrown with such tremendous force, that they whirl and dash with such violence as to produce a most frightful appearance. About thirty miles below the Upper dalles, are the Lower dalles, which like the Upper dalles, is a narrow channel, walled in by immense ledges of rocks, through which also the waters pour with great force. These dalles, seriously interrupt the navigation of the river, and detract very much from the importance of the surrounding country. From the Lower dalles, the river continues the same course, to Fort Coleville, in its course to which place, it receives several tributaries, among which are Kootanie, or Flat-bow, and the Clarke rivers from the east, and that of Coleville from the west. In its course to this place, it also forms a line of lakes, two of which I will now briefly describe. They are called the Upper and Lower lakes, the former of which, is about twenty miles in length, and about five in width. It is situated in an extremely rough and mountainous country, surrounded by high towering cliffs, and dense forests of pines. Between this and the Lower lakes are the "straits," as they are called. Here, for an extent of about five miles, the waters are compressed into a very narrow channel, through which they are thrown with great impetuosity. The Lower lake is about twenty five miles in length, and six in width. It has, in its vicinity, forests of beautiful timber, and limited prairies and plains, of fertile land. Clarkes' or

Flat-head river, enters the Columbia but a few miles above Fort Coleville. It takes its rise near the head waters of the Missouri river. It is a large stream, and has as much the appearance of being the main river, as does that portion which is called the Columbia. The lake Kullerspelm is formed by this river, in its course, about one hundred miles above its junction with the Columbia. This lake is about thirty-five miles in length, and eight in width. The immediate country through which this river passes, is extremely mountainous and sterile, with the exception of that in the vicinity of the lake, much of which is fertile and delightful. Hootanie or Flat-bow river, also has its source in the Rocky mountains, and running in a westerly direction to the Columbia, it passes through a high broken region, yet it passes through some tolerably extensive and fertile valleys. Its length, following its meanders, is about three hundred and fifty miles, a very small portion of which, is navigable, for any other craft, than canoes and barges.

From Coleville, the Columbia continues a westerly course, receiving a tributary from the east, called the Spokan, which takes its rise in the Lake Couer d'Alene, among the spurs of the Rocky mountains. This river has worn its way through a vastly mountainous and sterile region. Its banks are generally high basaltic cliffs, covered in some places, with sturdy pines and lofty cedars. In the surrounding country, are found some limited valleys and plains, many of which produce abundance of vegetation and are surrounded by dense forests of good timber. This river, can not be said to be navigable, for any kind of craft, except such as barges and canoes. The lake in which it takes its rise, is about thirty miles in length, and ten in breadth. There are some very fertile plains and valleys in the vicinity of this lake, which produce an abundance of grass and timber, as well as a great variety of wild fruits. The Columbia still tends westward: about sixty miles below its junction, with the Spokan, to its conflux with the Okanagan, above which point, it receives several small tributaries. The Okanagan takes its rise in a line of lakes of the same name, which are situated in the mountains, about one hundred and twenty miles from its mouth. These lakes are all navigable to considerable extent, for canoes, barges and boats. The country through which this river passes, is usually extremely sterile: with the exception of a very few small plains which are covered with vegetation, and a few hills, which are thinly timbered. From the mouth of the Okanagan, to Fort Wallawalla, the course of the Columbia, is about south southwest. In this distance it receives the Y'Akama, the Piscous, and the Entyatecoom, from the west; all of which take their sources in the Cascade range. Within the above distance also, it receives the great Saptin, or Lewis' river from the east, which flows into Columbia at latitude 46° and 8' north. This great tributary of the Columbia has its source in the Rocky mountains, near latitude 42° north. Its general course is about north west, and its length is about five hundred miles, following its meanders. It lies between the Rocky and the Blue mountains, dividing the one from the other, by its extensive valleys. It is navigable only for canoes and barges, and for them only between its various rapids and falls, which are very numerous. It winds its tortuous way alternately, through high perpendicular cliffs, sterile mountains, limited, yet fertile valleys, barren hills and plains. In its course it receives the Kooskooske river from the east, and the Salmon river from the west. The Kooskooske rises in the Rocky mountains, near latitude 46° north, and is navigable only for canoes and boats, for a very short distance. The Salmon river takes its rise in the Blue mountains; it is not navigable even for canoes, but is a very beautiful little stream. At Fort Wallawalla, the Columbia is about 1280 feet above the level of the sea, and about 200 rods wide. Near this place, it receives the Wallawalla river, from the south; a small stream, which is not navigable, nor is it of any particular importance for any purpose other, then to water the country through which it passes; it is, however, a very beautiful stream. The course of the Columbia from Fort Wallawalla, is very nearly due west. Between Wallawalla and the dalles, it receives the Umatilla, Quisnels', John Day's, and de Chutes rivers, from the south, and Cathlatates from the north. Neither of the last mentioned streams is navigable, yet they all water some very rich and productive, but small valleys. About eighty miles below Fort Wallawalla, the Columbia is much interrupted in its course, by rapids, falls and cascades. The first fall of importance, is that about ten miles above the dalles, where the water falls about fifty feet perpendicular, over vast ledges of rocks, down which it leaps and whirls with thunder's roar; then rushing, thundering and foaming through a deep narrow channel, formed by high ledges of massive rocks, it winds its noisy, tortuous way onward to the dalles; pouring its mighty volumes over cliffs, into cavern, after cavern, and trench, after trench, with such tremendous force, as to cause the very earth to groan and quake.

The dalles, is a name applied to an elevated section of country, of about ten miles in extent, of solid dark rock, rising in irregular, high cliffs, hills and mountains, which have braved the fury of this great river for ages past; but have finally given way to its repeated assaults. Stratum, after stratum, has given way, until it has worn a deep, frightful, cavernous channel, the walls of which are solid rock, from fifty to four hundred feet in height. Into this deep, narrow channel, are all the waters of the great Columbia compressed; but averse to confinement, they force their way through these narrow defiles, with the velocity of lightning, and the roar of thunder. The course of the river is not materially varied by these repeated interruptions, nor is its navigation entirely destroyed. Provisions and merchandise are annually transported, in great quantities, by the Hudsons' Bay Company, from Fort Vancouver to all the interior forts, which is effected by repeated portages. The last and most formidable obstruction to its navigation, are the cascades, at the base of the Cascade mountains, about one hundred and twenty miles from the ocean. From the dalles to the cascades, the Columbia pursues its onward, noisy course and forcing its way through the vast, massive, solid rocks of the elevated cascade range, it pours its immense volumes down the rocky declivity, four hundred feet perpendicular. The roar of this unparalleled cataract, is heard at a great distance, and to those who are near it is almost deafening. The volume of water and its fall are so great, that its whole bed, dashes and thunders down, with such fury, as to make the very earth quake and tremble, with such violence, as to cause you very much to doubt the permanency of that upon which you stand. From the cascades to Fort Vancouver, a distance of about thirty miles, the river assumes a much milder character, and spreads, and extends its water, to a much greater extent. At Fort Vancouver, which is ninety miles from the coast, it is three hundred and sixty rods wide, and of great depth. Between the fort and its mouth it receives the Wallammette from the south, and the Cawlity from the north, both of which, aid much in increasing the volume of its waters. From its mouth to the cascades, it is a beautiful, and grand stream, and is navigable to that extent, at the lowest stage of water, for ships drawing two fathoms. It enters the ocean between mount Adams and cape Disappointment, where several sand bars are formed, which are a great and dangerous obstruction to its navigation, and which render it extremely difficult and hazardous of entrance.

The Wallammette rises in the Cascade mountains, near latitude 41° north; its course is generally north, northwest, to its mouth, where it enters the Columbia river at two distinct points, and thus forms a large triangular island, called the

Wappato island. The upper mouth of the Wallammette, is about five miles below Fort Vancouver, and the lower mouth is about twenty miles below that place; which shows the extent of the Wappato island, to be fifteen miles on the Columbia. The Wallammette receives the Klackamus and the Putin rivers from the east, and the Fualitine and the Yamhill rivers from the west. Besides these rivers, it also receives numerous less important tributaries, both from the east and the west. The Wallammette is navigable for vessels of a light draught, to the mouth of the Klackamus, which is about twenty miles from its conflux with the Columbia. Here, its navigation is seriously obstructed by rapids and sand bars, the latter of which, are formed by the waters of the Klackamus, which annually wash down immense quantities of sand, and which are deposited at the junction of the two rivers. The falls, which are a few miles above the mouth of the Klacka-mus, are a further, and more serious obstruction to its naviga-tion. Here, its vast volume of water, is poured precipitately down a ledge of rocks, of about thirty feet perpendicular; and although this fearful cataract, forms a great obstruction to its safe navigation, yet it is highly important, as it affords an almost inexhaustible water power. Above the falls, the Wal-lammette is again navigable, for vessels and steam-boats of light draught, for one hundred miles, or perhaps more, with little or no obstruction. This river and its tributaries, water one of the most fertile and delightful regions in all Oregon. From its source to its mouth, a distance of about three hun-dred miles, it passes alternately through high mountains and hills, undulating, rich plains, and fertile and beautiful valleys. The Klackamus takes its rise in the Cascade mountains, near latitude 43 degrees north. It is a very rapid stream, and is nav-igable only for boats and barges of light draught, and for those only during high water. The Fualitine river enters the Wallammette about a mile above the falls: it takes its rise, in the elevated and mountainous regions near the coast, and is about one hundred miles in length, a greater part of which distance, it is navigable for boats, barges, and steam-boats of light draught, a greater part of the year. The Yamhill empties into the Wallammette about twenty miles above the falls; it also has its source in the mountainous region near the ocean, and is about one hundred and twenty miles long. About one half of its length, is navigable, perhaps, two thirds of the year, for boats, pirogues and the like crafts. The Putin river empties into the Wallammette about twelve miles above the falls, after having wound its tortuous course, about one hundred miles from its source, which is in the Cascade range, near latitude 44 degrees north. This stream is navigable only a small portion of the year, and then only for small crafts of very light draught. The Cawlitz is a beautiful little stream, which enters the Columbia below the Wappato island; it can not be said to be navigable, for any kind of crafts, only during high water, and even then, only for those of the lightest draught; though it is highly important, as it waters a large extent of country, which is well adapted to grazing purposes. I will give no further description of the tributaries of the Columbia, as most of them have already been partially described, in the description of that river; but I shall proceed to give a brief description, of those which lie north, and south, of that great river.

The largest and most important river north of the Columbia, is Frasier's river, which rises in the Rocky mountains, near latitude 55 degrees north. Its general course is about north by west, a distance of seventy or eighty miles, when it changes to south southwest, which course it continues, to the parallel of 49 degrees of north latitude, at the Cascade mountains. In its course to this place, it receives Stewart's river, which takes its rise in a chain of lakes, near latitude 55 degrees north, then passing through a sterile mountainous region, it receives the Chilcotin and Pinkslitsa from the west, and the Thompson's and Quesnells' rivers from the east. The last mentioned rivers water an extremely broken and mountainous country, yet they are said to be navigable to some extent, though with repeated interruptions, which arise from their numerous falls, rapids and cascades. Frasier's river cuts its way through the Cascade range, and thundering down cataracts, and over falls and rapids, it pursues a westerly course, to the gulf of Georgia, near latitude 49 degrees and 7 min. north, where it finally empties its vast floods of water into that great gulf. The whole length of this river is about three hundred and sixty miles, but a small portion of which is navigable. That portion of it, above the Cascade range, is navigable only for canoes, boats and the like, and for those only during high water, and even then, with numerous obstructions; but that portion below the Cascade range, a distance of about eighty miles, is navigable without interruption, for vessels of two fathoms draught. No obstruction whatever, is found any where in this portion, except a bar which is found at its mouth, and which is a serious obstruction to those unacquainted with its entrance. The country through which this stream lies is, with some exceptions, rough, mountainous and sterile; studded occasionally with those lofty pines of ages, and towering, icy monuments of time! I shall notice but one other river lying, north of the Columbia, which is the Chilkeelis, and which heads in the mountainous region north of the Columbia, by three distinct heads. Receiving several other streams, which have their sources in the mountainous region, near the head of Pugets' sound, it runs westward, pursuing a winding and circuitous course, through elevated plains and high mountains, forming numerous falls, and rapids, and finally, empties into Gray's harbor. This river waters one of the most barren and broken regions in all Oregon; it is navigable only for boats of light draught, between its numerous cataracts and rapids.

There are several other rivers on the north side of the Columbia, which however, are unimportant. I shall, therefore, proceed to the description of those on the south side of that river. Besides the tributaries of the Columbia, there are but three rivers on the south side of that river, which deserve particular attention. The first which I shall notice, is the Umpqua, which rises in the Cascade mountains: near latitude 43 deg. north, pursuing a westerly course, it enters the ocean at latitude 43 deg. 30 min. north. It is generally about a half of a mile wide, and is confined, in many places, within high banks of basaltic rock. Having a very large bar at its month, the entrance is very difficult, and the harbor very unsafe. The water upon this bar is about two fathoms deep, yet the channel is subject to such sudden changes, that at times, it is with the greatest difficulty it can be found. The tide flows up this stream, about forty miles from its mouth, which would aid in its navigation, very much to that extent, were it not for the vast bar at its entrance. The country through which this stream passes, is, generally, broken and hilly, but in many places, there are valleys and undulating plains, which are very rich, and of very considerable extent, with the exception of the valleys and plains, it is usually covered with thick forests of lofty pines, firs and oaks. This stream is perhaps navigable for steam-boats, about forty miles from its mouth, beyond which, its navigation is repeatedly interrupted, by falls and rapids, yet it is navigable still above, for boats and barges to considerable extent. The river lying next south of the Umpqua, is the Rogue's river, which has its source in the Klamet and Cascade ranges, near latitude 42 deg. north. It pursues a course about west by north, winding its way through alternate sterile mountains, high hills, rich, fertile valleys, and beautiful plains, and finally, empties into the ocean, at the parallel of 43 deg. north latitude. The entrance of this river, is also much obstructed by a vast sand bar, at its mouth, which is entirely impassable, the greater part of the year. This river is about the same width of the Umpqua; its current is very rapid, and it has numerous falls and rapids, which much obstruct its navigation: even for boats and canoes. Its bed is generally about fifteen or twenty feet below the surface of the earth, hence its waters are very difficult of access. It is navigable, perhaps, about eighty miles, for boats and canoes. The country through which it passes, is usually, very well timbered, well watered, and much of it is very rich and productive.

The only river which remains to be noticed, is the Klamet, which rises in the Klamet range, near latitude 41 deg. north, whence it runs a northwest course, about ninety miles, where it changes its course to west, and pursues a very serpentine course for many miles, when, finally: it runs about west by north, to the ocean, where it empties, near latitude 41 deg. 40 min. north, in California. This river waters the most barren and mountainous portion of country, in the southern part of Oregon. With the exception of a few small valleys and plains, it is everywhere walled in, with high mountains and cliffs of solid rock, most of which, are entirely destitute of timber. But a very small portion of this stream, is navigable for any crafts larger then canoes and boats; but that portion of it near its mouth, is, perhaps, navigable for steam-boats, a distance of thirty or forty miles, without serious obstruction. As is the case, with all those streams, emptying into the Pacific, it has an extensive bar at its mouth, which entirely prevents the safe entry of vessels, although there is a sufficient depth of water. All those rivers putting into the Pacific, south of the Columbia, have from two to eight fathoms of water upon their bars; but it is hazardous in the extreme, for a vessel to attempt an entrance, at many seasons of the year, because of the tremendous surf, that sets in from the ocean; and the extreme narrowness, and variableness of their channels. All the various

rivers of Oregon, are subject to extraordinary rises and over-
flows, which take place, in those heading in the different
ranges of mountains, at different seasons of the year. In those
which rise in the Cascade range, the rise takes place in
November and February, annually. These rises are produced
by the great quantities of ruin, which fall in those regions, of
which, more will be said, upon a subsequent page. The rise of
those rivers having their sources in the Blue and Rocky
mountains, is, generally, in the months of May and June, of
each year; it is occasioned by the melting of the snows of
those mountains. The rise in all these streams is very great,
especially in those having their sources in the Cascade range.
The Columbia usually rises from ten to fifteen feet, and of
course, inundates much of the surrounding low country. The
Wallammette frequently rises from twenty to twenty-five feet
perpendicular, and thus submerges large sections of the adjacent country, and occasions very great damage. Such is also
the case with the Cawlitz, Umpqua and Rogue's rivers; and in
fact, all those rivers which are in the vicinity of the low lands.
There is also a rise in the Wallammette and the Cawlitz,
which is occasioned by the backing of their waters, during the
rise in the Columbia. The rise in the rivers heading in the Cascade range, is, generally, very sudden, but that in the Columbia, and other rivers which have their sources in the Rocky
mountains, is usually, gradual, unless there happens to be
very heavy rains in the interior, about the time of their annual
rise, which is not generally the case, though it sometimes happens, and when it does occur, the country is submerged to a
great extent, both man and beast are driven to the hills and
mountains for their safety, and irreparable losses are frequently sustained.

Chapter 4

A DESCRIPTION OF THE ISLANDS

There are several islands adjacent to the main land, which now deserve our attention. The most important of these, is Vancouver's island which is two hundred and sixty miles in length, and fifty in width, and like the main land in its vicinity, its surface is broken and mountainous, yet it has some plains and valleys, of considerable extent and fertility. An abundance of good fresh water is produced by its numerous springs and streams, which rise in its interior; and it is generally well timbered, and in all respects well adapted to grazing and agricultural purposes. Washington, or Queen Charlotte's island, is about one hundred and fifty miles in length, and thirty in width. It is quite similar to Vancouver's island, in its adaptation to grazing and agricultural purposes, and it has also an abundance of good fresh water, which is produced from its numerous springs and rivulets rising in its interior. Its surface is also broken and hilly, having however, many small valleys and plains, which are very rich, and which abound with good timber; it, like Vancouver's island, is well adapted to the support of a small community. Besides these, there is also an archipelago of islands, near the southern extremity of Vancouver's island. The surface of these islands, is, generally, much broken, and they are much less fertile, then those just described. They generally, have a sufficiency of timber, but an insufficiency of fresh water, which is, no doubt, the cause of their being uninhabited. There are a few other islands also, near the main land, which are called the Prince Royal islands, and which are uninhabited, and in all other respects, quite similar to those last described. The first two above described, are as thickly inhabited as the main land, by various tribes of Indians, who resort to them, in large numbers, for the purpose of hunting and fishing.

Very few safe harbors are found in all Oregon. As has been elsewhere remarked, all the various rivers, which empty into the ocean, have extensive sand bars at their mouths, which render them extremely difficult, and dangerous of entrance. These bars are formed by the immense quantities of sand, which are brought down by the water, during the annual over-flows, and which, are thrown back into the mouths by the lashing surf. Thus, the waters of the rivers, pressing upon the one side, and the surf upon the other, the sands are formed into bars, which so much interrupt the navigation of all those otherwise navigable, and important streams. Permanent bars, are not however, thus formed; the constant action of the water, having a tendency to confine the sand within indefinite limits, but not to render it permanent. Hence it is, that the bars are constantly changing their positions, from side to side, which renders the entrance into all those rivers, the more difficult and dangerous. The pilot who well understands the channel this year, knows nothing of it the next. Entrance or departure, through many of these channels, is entirely impracticable, the greater part of the year. These bars are not only changing their positions, but they are constantly increasing; yet the fact that the depth of the water upon them, has never been known to diminish, induces the belief, that notwithstanding the changes, and increase of the sands, they will never afford any greater obstruction to the navigation, than they do at present. Gray's harbour is considered very safe, when entered, but vessels only of a small class can enter it, there being but about ten feet of water at the entrance, and the anchorage which it affords, although safe, is very limited. The northern part of Oregon affords many extensive and safe harbours, the principal of which, are those of the straits Juan de Fucas. Many of these harbours are very extensive, and entirely secure, and are capable of receiving any class of vessels. They are, no doubt, ample for all the commercial purposes of northern Oregon, but that portion is the least fertile, and the least valuable part of all that country, consequently, commercial advantages, in that section of the country, are of much less importance. Much of that part of the coast north of latitude 49° north, is cut and intersected, in almost every direction, by innumerable deep inlets, which have high perpendicular walls, of solid rock, but which afford no anchorage or harbors. But the sterility and roughness of that portion of the country are such, that harbors there, would be of little or no importance. Some of the islands of which I have spoken, have a few very good harbors, but they are very limited in extent of anchorage. Vancouver's island affords the best, but Queen Charlotte's island affords some very good ones, so also do several others of the larger islands. South of the Columbia, there are but two harbors of any importance, which are found at the mouth of the Umpqua and Rogues rivers, and which have vast sand bars at their entrances, that render ingress and egress, not only very difficult, but extremely hazardous. A further and more serious objection, to all those harbors formed by the rivers, is, that after an entrance is effected, the anchorage is entirely insecure, owing to the exposure of vessels, to the winds, and surf of the ocean, to which they are dangerously exposed, everywhere in the vicinity of the mouths of all these rivers. There is not, in fact, a good, convenient, or safe harbor, on all the coast of Oregon, south of the straits of Juan de Fucas, and the gulf of Georgia.

A more particular description of the face of the country will now be given. In giving this description, I commence with the Eastern section, or that section which lies between the Rocky, and Blue mountains. It is much diversified in surface, as it is intersected in almost every direction by innumerable spurs of the Rocky and Blue mountains. Very little level land is to be found, in any portion of this section, but many extensive, broken and hilly prairies, are found, which are entirely sterile, producing neither grass nor timber; the only vegetation seen being the prickly-pear and the wild wormwood, or artemisia. The only vegetation which is found in any part of this section, is in the vicinity of the streams, with occasional patches of "bunch grass" off the streams. Persons in traveling through this section, are under the necessity of traveling a certain number of hours each day, and at a certain rate of speed, in order to reach those places, where water and grass may be found, for the sustenance of themselves and their horses. Notwithstanding the general sterility, of this section, it has some tolerably, and some very rich valleys and plains, all of which, however, are extremely limited in their extent. The first of them, which I shall notice, is the valley of the great Bear river. The river upon which this valley lies, is of considerable importance; rising east of the Rocky mountains, it runs through the great southern pass, at latitude 42° north, and empties into the great Salt lake, or lake Timpanagos, in Upper California. The valley of this river, lies principally in California also, but my present purpose is to describe that portion only of it, which lies in Oregon. Much of this valley is very rich, producing vegetation in great abundance, but its principal importance, consists in its peculiar local situation. It is through this valley, that the route from the United States to Oregon and California, is destined forever to pass. Being the most eligible, and in fact, the only practical wagon route, that has, as yet, been discovered, by which the emigrant may travel with ease and comfort; it is destined, beyond any doubt, to become the great thoroughfare to all the western country. When we reflect that even now, hundreds and thousands of our citizens are annually passing by that route down this valley, we can not fail to arrive at the conclusion, that this must soon become a vastly important region. At some point in this valley, will be found the most favorable point, on the whole route from the Atlantic to the Pacific, for the emigrant to encamp for a few days, in order to acquire that relaxation and repose, which he so much needs, after his long and fatiguing journey, as well as to obtain supplies, and to refit, for the residue of his toilsome expedition. But this is not the only importance attached to this peculiar section of country. In this valley, are found the soda springs, the "steam-boat springs," and numerous other wonderous objects, which are well calculated to attract the attention of the curious, and the admirer of nature.

The soda springs are situated about one hundred miles west of the dividing ridge, of the Rocky mountains, and about fifty miles east of Fort Hall, within twenty rods of Bear river, on its north side, and near latitude 42° north. They are in the midst of a beautiful grove of small cedars, and surrounded by rich valleys and plains, high, rolling hills, and volcanic vales and mountains. Upon approaching within their vicinity, you are struck at once, with the extraordinary appearance which they present, as well as the hissing noises which they produce, occasioned by the perpetual effervescence of their bubbling, noisy waters. There are six of these, which are from five to ten feet in diameter; the waters of which, are from two to three feet below the surface of the earth. Their waters are perfectly clear, and very delicious to the taste, and in all respects, like the water obtained at our common soda fountains in civilized life. When dipping the water from the springs, the effervescence is still going on in your cup, until you place it to your lips, when, if you can withstand its suffocating fumes, you have a most delicious draught. In the vicinity of these springs, there are also, several other soda springs, which, however, are much less important, then those just described. Near them also, are several very singular conical elevations, about five or six feet in height, in the apex of each of which, is an aperture, of about six inches in diameter, from which the water gushes out, and running down the sides of these cones, it leaves upon them a sediment, which is thrown up by the water, and which has, no doubt, in the process of time, produced these extraordinary conical formations, which now much more resemble the work of art, then that of nature. These singular evomitions of water and sediment, are produced by the escape of great quantities of gas, generated by the evolving waters in the subterraneous caverns below. The ceaseless commotion of the waters, in those vast reservoirs, produce a constant rumbling and gurgling sound, which is distinctly heard a distance of several rods from the springs, and the emition of gas, produces a kind of puffing, and blowing sound, which is also heard several rods. About one hundred rods below these springs, is the "steam boat spring," as it is called, which discharges water and gas in the same manner, as those just described, but in much greater quantities, and with a report quite similar to that produced by the emition of steam from the escape pipe of a steam-boat, hence the name "steam-boat spring." These evomitions of water and gas, are from the face of a vast rock, and are frequently heard at a hundred rods. In the immediate vicinity of the soda springs are innumerable other springs, the waters of which, are highly impregnated with soda and sulphur; and north, and in fact, in every direction from them, the whole country wears a striking and volcanic appearance, especially, at the north, where the entire earth, seems to have been burnt out, leaving scarcely any thing, but masses of burnt rock and lava. Numerous hot springs are also found, in the immediate vicinity of these springs, which produce water from blood heat, to the boiling point, in many of which, meat is cooked perfectly done, in less then four minutes. The whole surrounding country here, affords ample evidences of former, vast, and numerous volcanic eruptions. This valley, and especially that portion of it, in the immediate vicinity of these springs, is really a very extraordinary section of country, and is destined, beyond any kind of doubt, to become immensely important and valuable; because of its peculiarly favorable locality; its extraordinary, wonderful, and delightful scenery; and perhaps, the medicinal properties of its inexhaustible mineral waters.

There are several very extensive valleys in the vicinity of Fort Hall, upon the river, as well as extensive plains, which produce a great sufficiency of vegetation and timber, but the surrounding country, more remote from the fort, is extremely hilly, mountainous, and sterile, generally producing neither timber, nor vegetation. There are also several very extensive plains and valleys, in the immediate vicinity of Fort Boisia, which are quite fertile, and capable of producing grain and vegetables, in great abundance; yet, the surrounding country is generally barren and mountainous. About seventy miles below Fort Boisia, in a direction northwest by north, is a valley of very considerable extent, which abounds with various kinds of vegetation, of most luxurious growth. This valley is situated upon a tributary of Lewis' river, which appears to afford great sufficiency of durable water. In the midst of this valley, is a single pine tree, which is called *l'arbour seuel*, the lone tree, from which circumstance, the valley is called the "Lone Tree valley." There is not a sufficiency of timber in the immediate vicinity of this valley, but in the surrounding mountainous region, there is perhaps, ample timber, and that of a very good quality. Forty or fifty miles south southeast from this valley, the country has a very romantic, and volcanic appearance. Large extents of country appear to have been visited by earthquakes, which have torn the stupendous mountains of rock asunder, and strewed the plains below, with their confused fragments; while other sections, having been the seat of desolating volcanoes, are thickly covered with vast, massive heaps of burned rock and lava. Here innumerable hot and boiling springs are also found, the waters of which, are so hot, as to cook any kind of flesh, sufficiently for the table, in a very few minutes. These springs are not unfrequently, found within a few feet of running streams of pure cold water, into which, they pour their boiling waters, which are so hot, even when commingled with this cold water, as to kill the fish in an instant, which happens to be swimming within its caloric influence. About forty miles northwest, from the "lone tree," in the midst of the Blue mountains, is a very extensive valley, which is rich and productive, and which is well timbered, and well watered. It is about fifty miles in extent, in either direction, and is surrounded in every direction, by hills and mountains, which, in many places, are covered with luxuriant growths of pine and cedar. The form of this valley is nearly circular, hence its name, "la Grande rounde," the Grand round. This is one of the most fertile valleys, found any where in this section, and is perhaps, as well adapted to agricultural and grazing purposes, as any portion of Oregon. It has some timber upon its streams, but not sufficient for all purposes, yet the surrounding hills and mountains abound with the best of timber. This valley is destined soon, to be occupied, and to become a very valuable, and important section of country. All the northern part of this section, is one vast concatenation of hills and mountains, which are generally, spurs of the Rocky and Blue mountains, and which, in many places, are thickly clad with timber and vegetation, but they are generally, entirely destitute of either. Many of these hills and mountains are densely covered with forests of huge firs, pines and cedars; so also are many of the valleys which are found upon the rivers and smaller streams. Besides the few limited valleys, which are found in this part of the Eastern section, there are also, many undulating prairies, elevated plains, and depressions of some extent, which are tolerably rich, and which have a most beautiful and picturesque appearance.

The face of the country, in the Middle sections, presents a continued series of rolling hills, high cliffs, and undulating plains, which are almost everywhere, intersected by innumerable, stupendous mountain spurs, which are offsets of the Blue, and Cascade mountains, and which are generally, covered with a kind of short fine grass, called "bunch grass," wormwood, and prickly-pear. Some of these, in the northern part, are also thickly covered with forests of lofty firs, pines and cedars. In this section too, there are numerous small valleys, worthy of notice, several of which, however, have received partial notice, upon another page. There is a very beautiful valley on the Wallawalla river, in the vicinity of Dr. Whitman's mission. This valley is sufficiently large for forty or fifty farms, and is very well adapted to farming purposes. There are also other valleys in this vicinity, of considerable extent, and of more then ordinary fertility, which are situated upon John Day's, Umatilla, Quisnell's and de Chute rivers, and which, together, afford a large extent of very excellent country. These valleys are well watered, not only by the rivers just referred to, but also, by numerous other smaller streams and rivulets, running through them in every direction. There are also several small valleys in this vicinity, on the Columbia, which are very rich and productive, though of much less importance, because of their very limited extent. The principal valleys of this section, south of the Columbia river, are those in the extreme southern portion, between latitude 43 deg. north, and the southern boundary, where several very productive and extensive valleys are found, which are admirably adapted to farming purposes, much the greater portions of which, are better adapted to the purposes of pasturage. The scarcity of timber, in all this portion of the section, will however, in all probability, forever remain, an insuperable barrier, to its extensive and successful cultivation or occupation; though some of these valleys may, perhaps, be supplied with timber, from the surrounding mountains, many of which afford timber in considerable abundance, especially, the spurs of the Cascade mountains. Timber is also occasionally found, on some of the streams, which water these valleys, though generally, in very small quantities, and of inferior quality. That part of this section, which lies north of the Columbia river, much more broken and mountainous then the southern part, but unlike that portion, it is, in many places, thickly covered with compact forests of lofty firs and pines. In this portion also, are many small, though productive valleys, of several of which, I have spoken in the description of the rivers. Besides these, there are several others, of much greater extent, but of less fertility, as well as several high, rolling prairies, many of which are tolerably well adapted to the purposes of pasturage, though but illy adapted to farming purposes, because of the extreme variableness of the climate.

The surface of the Western section only, now remains to be described. That portion of this section, which lies north of the Columbia river, has innumerable mountain spurs, high cliffs, and rolling hills, interspersed throughout almost every portion. These are generally thickly clad with compact forests, of high and enormous trees, of centuries growth, the like of which, is seldom, if ever seen. In many places also, the undergrowth of shrubs, bushes, vines and briers, is so dense, that it is actually impenetrable; in such places, however, the soil is extremely productive. Many small, though rich valleys, tolerably fertile plains, and prairies, are also found, throughout this northern portion, which are very well adapted both to the purposes of pasturage and farming. Several prairies and plains are also found, on the Columbia and the Cawlitz, some of which, are quite extensive and productive. There is a very rich section of country, in the immediate vicinity of Fort Vancouver which, by trial, is found to produce the various kinds of northern grains and fruits, with much luxuriance. Below this fort, are several valleys and prairies, of considerable importance, especially on the Cawlitz, where some rather extensive valleys and prairies are found, though they are not generally very productive. Above, and in the vicinity of this fort, a number of plains and valleys are also found, which are very fertile, though much less extensive, then that just described. In the various portions of the timbered country, many plains are found, which are surrounded with almost impenetrable forests, of majestic firs and pines, of unequalled growth. Adjacent to Pugets' sound, large tracts of Prairie country are also found, which are sufficiently rich, for all agricultural purposes, and which yield a great abundance of vegetation. At and in the vicinity of the straits de Fucas, are some extensive plains and prairies, which, although not sufficiently rich, for farming purposes, afford every advantage for grazing. All the plains and valleys of the northern portion of this section, are much better suited to the rearing of herds, then the growing of grain, though there are several of them which are adaptable to the latter purpose, as well as the former, yet not with the same prospects of success. The portion of this section, which is found south of the Columbia river, contains much the most extensive and productive plains and valleys of all Oregon, which are in all respects, by far, the most valuable portions of that country. The most extensive valley here found, is the Wallammette valley, which lies upon the Wallammette river, and is about one hundred and fifty miles in length, and thirty or forty in width, on each side of the river. It is a very beautiful and productive valley, and as it is well timbered, well watered, and as it yields a superabundance of all the grasses, and the various other kinds of vegetation, it is admirably suited to agricultural, and grazing purposes. In the vicinity, and northwest from this valley, are the Fualitine plains, which are about fifty miles in length, and fifteen in width. These are equal in beauty and productiveness, if not superior to the Wallammette valley. They produce the various kinds of vegetation, with much profusion, and they are very well timbered, and well watered; hence their adaptation to the purposes of grazing and farming, are readily seen. Further south, numerous other beautiful, and rich valleys, are also found, the first of which, I shall notice, are those lying upon the Umpqua river, in the immediate vicinity of Fort Umpqua, a valley of about thirty miles in length, and ten in width, is found, which is everywhere surrounded by an extensive, broken and mountainous country, but which is a very beautiful and rich valley, abounding with all the various grasses, and good timber. There is also another valley upon this river, of much greater extent, which commences about ten miles above the eastern extremity, of that just described, and extends up, and south of the river, about seventy miles. This is among the most beautiful, and productive valleys of all Oregon; abounding with the various grasses, and good timber of most luxuriant growth, and having an unusually deep, rich soil, it is peculiarly fitted both to the purposes of grazing and farm land. South of this, upon Rogue's river, are several other very extensive and unusually rich valleys. The principal of them is found upon that river, about sixty miles from the ocean. It is about eighty miles long, and averages from ten to forty miles in width, on each side of the river. For beauty of scenery, richness of soil, abundance of timber and vegetation, and for its peculiar adaptation to both grazing and agricultural purposes, this valley much surpasses all others, in any part of Oregon. Besides this, there are also several others, which are found upon, and in the vicinity of this river, and which, are much less extensive, but equally productive of both timber and the various grasses. All these valleys, however are surrounded by stupendous mountains, high hills, and elevated plains, which are generally, entirely destitute of timber, and, in many places, devoid of all vegetable productions. The only valleys which remain to be noticed, are those found upon the Klamet river, where numerous valleys are to be found, which, although very limited in extent, possess a very rich soil, and yield a superabundance of good timber, and most luxuriant vegetation. Throughout all this section, besides the various valleys before enumerated, and more particularly described, there are numbers of others, which are equally productive, and valuable, though of much less extent. Upon, and in the neighborhood of the Umpqua, Rogue's and Klamet rivers, there are not only the valleys referred to, but there are also several others, as well as numerous sections of high lands, undulating, elevated plains, and rolling prairies, which are also very productive, and which are admirably suited to the purpose of grazing, as well as that of farming. This southern portion of the Western section, is by far, the most valuable and delightful portion of Oregon, and in point of richness and productions, it very much resembles the unequalled plains and valleys of California.

The soil of all the Eastern section is, for the most part, extremely poor; that of the plains is generally, a light, sandy loam; that of the valleys, especially in the immediate vicinity of the rivers, and smaller streams, is rich and aluvial, while the hills and mountains generally present a most barren and desolate surface, which, for many miles together, presents nothing but burning sands, and hills and mountains of unsurpassed sterility. Here, however, every variety of soil is found, from the extreme sterility of the burning sands of the Arabian deserts, to the deep rich alluvial soil of the most fertile Egyptian valleys. The prevailing rock of this section is generally basalt, granite, pudding stone and talcon slate, which in many places, extend entirely to the surface, for several miles together. It may be estimated, with a close approximation to exactness, that not more then one twentieth part of all this section, is, in any wise, suited to agricultural purposes, while one tenth part of it, may perhaps, be found to be tolerably well adapted to pasturage. The soil of the Middle section is, as a general thing, a light yellow sand, clay or loam; that of the valleys, is usually, a black, alluvial, vegetable loam. South of the Columbia, the hills and mountains present a surface of extraordinary sterility; but those north of that river, have a soil of a light, brown loam, or a thin, brown, vegetable earth. The rock of this section is, generally, confined to the hills and mountains, and in the northern part, it consists principally, of granite, pudding stone and basalt: that of the southern part, consists chiefly, of granite, basalt, talcon slate and bornblend. Although this variety of rock will be found highly serviceable, in the ultimate improvement of the country, yet as it rises entirely to the surface, for miles together, it adds very much to the sterility, and impenetrability, of many portions of this, otherwise, sufficiently sterile, and forbidding region. Of all this section not more, perhaps, then one tenth part, is at all susceptible of successful cultivation, nor is more then one fifth part of it, well suited to grazing purposes. The soil of the Western section, varies very much, in the different portions. North of the Columbia river, that of the hills and mountains, is generally a light, brown, loam or vegetable earth, upon a stratum of gravel or sand; that of the plains and prairies, is usually, a deep, brown, vegetable mould, having a subsoil of sand and clay; and that of the valleys and lower sections, is a deep black loam, upon a substratum of clay or trap rock. The principal rock of this part of the section, appears to be granite and pudding stone, especially in the extreme north, but in many parts of the more southern portion, are found basalt and hornblend. South of the Columbia river, the soil of the valleys is very fertile, being generally, decomposed basalt or a deep, black, vegetable loam, upon a stratum of gravel, sand or unctuous clay; that of the plains, is usually, a deep, brown, vegetable loam, the substrata being stiff clay, gravel and sand: and that of the hills and mountains, is a light, brown, and thin vegetable earth, upon a stratum of gravel or sand. Many of the hills and mountains, however, are entirely sterile, and are principally composed of basalt, stone and slate, yet in the extreme southern part, the rocks are usually primitive, and consist principally of talcon slate, hornblend and granite. Of this section, about one fifth part, is arable land, and one third is, perhaps, seldom surpassed in its adaptation to grazing purposes. I am well aware that the fertility and productiveness of Oregon, are viewed, by many who have visited that region, in a much more favorable light, than the above and foregoing, would seem to indicate; but however that may be, I design merely to give facts, as they occur to me, leaving their corroboration to the concurring testimony of others, and the developments of time.

Chapter 5

A DESCRIPTION OF EASTERN OREGON

The climate of Oregon is, perhaps, as varied and variable, as that of any part of the known world, which fact is attributable to the great diversity of local positions, which the various portions of the country occupy, in reference to those regions of perpetual snow, and the Pacific ocean, as well as the altitude of each portion, in reference to the other. The same diversity of climate, as of soil, prevails in the different sections, and the climate, like the soil, is much more diversified in the Eastern section, then in either of the others. In many portions of this section you experience perpetual winter, while in others you have continued spring, depending upon the position which you occupy; and even in the same portion of the country, one day, you have the extreme heat of a southern summer, and the next, the excessive cold of a northern winter. There are other portions of this section where, in the short space of 24 hours, you experience four distinct changes, corresponding in temperature, with a northern spring, summer, autumn and winter. The mercury in Fahrenheit's scale, rising to 50° in the morning, to 120° at noon, and falling again to 50° in the evening, and to 12° below zero at night. These remarks, however, are designed to apply only to a portion of this section. In many other portions, it is both much warmer, and much colder, the mercury frequently rising to 160° and falling to 18° below zero. The mean temperature, of course, differs very much in the various sections, but it is said to be about 50° of Fahrenheit, in the vicinity of Fort Hall. Those portions which have a climate of this variable character, are generally in the immediate vicinity of the regions of perpetual snow. Rain very seldom falls in any part of this section, during the spring or summer, nor do great quantities fall during the autumn or winter. In the winter, snow falls very frequently, though not to a great depth; it lies but a short time in the valleys, but eternally on the mountains. Hence then it appears, that you may enjoy every possible variety of climate, from perpetual winter, to perennial spring. The climate of the Middle section, is not as variable as that of the Eastern section, but much more so then that of the Western section; it is subject however, to very great extremes of heat and cold. In the summer, the mercury in Fahrenheit's scale, frequently rises to 180°, in the shade, and as frequently, falls as low as minus 28° of Fahrenheit. As in the Eastern section, the temperature of the various portions, differs very much, depending upon the altitude of each portion, and its proximity to the snowy mountains, yet the mean temperature is said to be about 52° of Fahrenheit at Fort Wallawalla, and the daily difference of temperature, is said to be, about 40° of Fahrenheit, at and in the vicinity of that place. It very seldom rains in this section, during the spring, summer or autumn, consequently, there are about nine months of continued drought, during which time, here, as in the Eastern sections, dews seldom fall, hence a dryness and aridity of atmosphere prevails throughout both these sections, which are seldom elsewhere known.

The climate of all the Western section is very mild, and notwithstanding its northern latitude, it has no excess of cold, nor has it any excess of heat. The mean temperature of this section, at Fort Vancouver, is 57 deg. of Fahrenheit. Snow very seldom falls more then four or five inches in depth, and generally disappears in three or four days. Running water never freezes south of the Columbia river, and that river has been closed, opposite Vancouver, but three times within the last forty years, and even then, it remained closed but a very few days. It is so mild in latitude 45 deg. north, and even in 50 deg. north, that it does not become necessary either to house, or feed any kind of stock during the winter. The valleys are generally thickly covered with the grasses, and various other kinds of vegetation, during the entire winter. Farther south, the vegetation puts forth very soon after the rains commence to fall, and continues to grow all winter, so that the pasturage for stock, is equally, as good at that season, as at any other, and perhaps, better than it is in the summer. Here during the winter, not only the valleys, but the hills and mountains also, are everywhere covered with green, fresh grass; but in the latter part of the summer, and fore part of the fall, from the continued drought, all vegetation is generally, completely dried and divested of its principal nutriment. The rainy season commences in November, and continues until March inclusive, and during all the residue of the year, scarcely a drop of rain falls. In the rainy season, rains fall almost incessantly, but not in great quantities; though they usually fall in such quantities, and so continually, as to prevent the advantageous transaction of most kinds of business. The cold, or winter weather, is chiefly confined to the months of December, January and February. From what has already been said, in reference to the climate of this section, it will be readily perceived, that there is a very great difference of temperature, in the same latitude, on the Atlantic and Pacific coasts. There are more then ten degrees difference between the temperature on the east and west side of the Rocky mountains, in the same latitude, especially, on the coasts. It is milder in latitude 50 deg. north, on the Pacific coast, then it is in latitude 40 deg. north, on the Atlantic coast. The chief cause of this extraordinary difference of temperature, in the same latitude, is perhaps, the prevailing winds, on the Pacific coast, from the north during the summer, and from the south during the winter. The climate of the extreme southern part of this section, is much milder, and more delightful, then that just described. Here snow seldom falls, and there is much less rain during the winter, or rainy season; the climate here, in fact, very much resembles that of Upper California. From the foregoing facts, in reference to the climate, very correct conclusions may, perhaps, be formed in reference to the health of Oregon. Febrile diseases are seldom if ever known, in any portion of the Eastern or Middle sections; and as no local febrific causes are found in any part of these sections, the presumption is, that they will always possess superior advantages, in point of healthfulness. The Western section is also very healthy, yet intermittent fevers prevail to a limited extent, in some portions. These fevers, however, are found to be of a much less obstinate character, then those which prevail on the east side of the mountains, as they yield very readily to any of the ordinary curatives. Cases of remittent fevers, have scarcely ever been known, in any portion of this country. It has been remarked, that although this country appears to be entirely exempt from all local causes of disease, yet it has, at some former period, been very unhealthy. As a proof of this view, you are referred to the numerous, and extensive burying-grounds of the natives; but the devastation which disease has evidently made among them, has been much more attributable to the rude treatment, which they adopt, then to the obstinacy of the disease.

The productions of the Eastern section are much more limited, both in variety and quantity, then those of the Western section, yet they are in all respects, very similar to those of the Middle section. The same diversity obtains, throughout all those sections, in reference to productions, as well as to soil and climate, which will be fully seen, from what will now follow. As before remarked, timber is found in some portions of the Eastern section, in sufficient quantities for all valuable purposes, but as a general thing, there is a very great deficiency of timber. Wherever it is found, however, it usually grows with great luxuriance. It consists chiefly of white and yellow pine, white and red cedar, fir, spruce, hemlock, arbour vitae, cherry and willow. Many portions of this section are well suited to the producing of wheat, rye, oats, barley, buckwheat, hemp, flax, potatoes, turnips, and in fact, all kinds of vegetables, common to a northern climate, as well as such fruits as apples, pears, peaches, plums, grapes and cherries. In addition to these fruits many wild fruits are also found, in the greatest abundance. Indian corn will not mature in any part of this section which is attributed to the very cold nights, and early frosts, to which every portion of this section is subject. The productions of the Middle section, very much resemble those of the Eastern, yet there is perhaps, a slight shade of difference, in some of the different portions. The timber of this section, consists for the most part, of fir, pine, cedar, spruce, hemlock, oak of several kinds, ash, arbutus, arbour vitae, maple, willow and cherry, in the north; and fir, pine, cedar, oak, ash, arbutus and willow in the south. This section is also capable, in many places, of producing wheat, rye, oats, barley, beans, peas, hemp, flax, tobacco and most kinds of vegetables, in considerable abundance. Several kinds of fruits may also be produced here, in quantities sufficient for all ordinary purposes. Such fruits as apples, pears, peaches, plums, cherries, grapes, and several kinds of wild fruits, grow most luxuriantly, in various portions of this section. But very few agricultural experiments have, as yet, been made in either the Eastern or Middle sections, but sufficient has been determined: in this respect, to warrant the foregoing statements. In the Middle, as in the Eastern section, it has also been determined that our common Indian corn, will not mature, which is owing to the same cause as that before mentioned.

In the Western section, we find a much greater variety, and abundance of productions. The timber of this section consists chiefly of pine, fir, cedar, red and white oak, ash, arbour vitae, arbutus, maple, poplar, willow and cherry. The undergrowth consists, generally, of hazel, rose, grape vines, and a great variety of shrubs and bushes, all of which together, form an undergrowth so dense, that in many places, it is actually impenetrable. Timber of the most extraordinary growth is found in many portions of this section. Both in the north and south, it is not uncommon to see fir and pine trees three hundred feet in height, and from twenty to sixty feet in circumference. Their usual height, however, is from fifty to two hundred feet; and their circumference from ten to thirty feet. There are very few portions of the world, perhaps, which afford a greater variety, and quantity, or a better quality of timber, then this section of Oregon. The timber south of the Columbia, although it is, in many places, equally as large and thrifty, yet it is not as valuable for lumber, as that north of that river. In the south, it is much more spungy and porous, then in the north, consequently, it is much more subject to contraction and expansion, when manufactured into lumber. The south side of the trees, in the south, also possess much more porosity then the north side, consequently, lumber made of this timber would be much less valuable, as one part of it would be much more subject, then the other, to excessive contractions and expansions. Both the climate and the soil in many portions of this section are well suited to the growing of wheat, rye, oats, barley, flax, hemp, beans, peas and tobacco, as well as the various kinds of garden vegetables. Indian corn does not mature in any part of this section, as far as it has been tried, but there is no doubt but that it, as well as cane, cotton and rice, may be grown with much success, in the extreme southern part of this section. Several kinds of the northern fruits succeed here, extremely well, especially apples, pears, peaches, plums, grapes and cherries. For the growing of all the northern fruits, there are very few countries better adapted then this section, the extreme southern part of which, is also admirably suited to the growing of many of the tropical fruits. Wheat is the principal grain grown in this section as yet, the greatest quantities of which are produced at the Wallammette valley, the Fualitine plains, and the farms of the Hudsons' Bay Company, at Vancouver, Nisqually and the Cawlitz. The average crop, is about fifteen bushels to the acre, yet, I have no doubt, but that portion of this section, which lies south of the Columbia river, and which is susceptible of cultivation, may, with proper agricultural skill, be made to produce twenty-five or thirty bushels to the acre. The northern portion will never produce so abundantly, as the southern part, for, as has been before remarked, its soil is generally, much less fertile, and its climate much less adapted to the luxuriant production of any kind of grain or vegetables. Wherever wheat has been grown as yet, the first crop is found to be of very little value; so valueless in fact, that in many instances it is not harvested. I was informed by several respectable farmers, that from the first sowing, they could not, as a general, thing, rely upon receiving more then the seed sown, and that, in many instances, even the seed sown, was not received. But a fact was also stated to me, by several respectable gentlemen, which clearly shows the peculiar adaptation of this country, to the growing of this species of grain, especially, after it is reduced to a proper state of cultivation. The fact alluded to is, that after having subdued the land properly, having sowed your wheat, and having harvested it, a spontaneous growth will spring up the succeeding year, and you will receive a very good crop without a second sowing.

As has been stated upon a former page, all the different sections of Oregon, are much better suited to the rearing of herds, then to farming purposes. Some experiments in this respect have been made, in all the different sections. In the Eastern section, at Forts Hall and Boisia, both horses and cattle are reared in large numbers, where they thrive most admirably. The Indians of this section also, rear horses in vast numbers, and of a very superior quality. In the Middle section, horses and cattle are also reared in great numbers, by the missionaries, at their different stations, and by the gentlemen of the Hudsons' Bay Company, at the different forts. The Indians here also rear horses, in the various parts of this section, in very large numbers. Both the horses and cattle of these sections thrive exceedingly well, and that too, without the ordinary attention of feeding and housing. The Western section is seldom surpassed, as a grazing country, and it is to this purpose that it is most eminently adapted, especially, the southern portion, where cattle, horses and sheep, may be reared in any numbers, with no other expense then that of employing herdsmen and shepherds. The necessity of feeding and housing any kind of herds, is here obviated, by the mildness of the climate, and the putting forth of the vegetation, during the winter season. Vast herds of horses, cattle and sheep, are latterly driven to this section, from Upper California, by which means, the entire country is destined, in a very short time, to become extensively stocked. Each farmer has, even now, from twenty to a thousand head of cattle, about as many horses, and from twenty to one hundred head of sheep. Notwithstanding the ease and facility with which herds are here reared, they are equally as valuable, if not more so, here then they are in the States. Horses are worth from twenty to fifty dollars per head; oxen from forty to eighty dollars per yoke; cows from ten to thirty dollars per head; other grown cattle, from eight to fifteen dollars per head; and sheep, from one to four dollars per head. Cattle and horses however, which are driven from the States, are considered much more valuable, then those which are driven from California, as they are thought to be better blooded; which view, I think, is entirely unfounded. But the preference of our people, for every thing that is American, every thing that is reared in their own country, as well as the great difficulty of driving cattle and horses to that country, will always cause them to command a much higher price. Oxen driven from the States are worth from fifty to one hundred dollars per yoke; cows from twenty to fifty dollars per head; and other grown cattle, from fifteen to forty dollars per head. Horses driven from the States, are generally, worth from fifty to one hundred and fifty dollars per head. I have frequently heard the belief expressed, that neither horses nor cattle, driven from the States, would thrive in that country, because of the incessant rains of the winters there, and their not being housed during that inclement season; but experience proves, that they thrive most admirably, and even better then they do in the States.

All the various rivers of Oregon abound with a great variety of fish, of the very best kinds. They are very abundant in all the different sections; but the streams of the Western section afford the greatest abundance. They are found, however, in each of the other sections, in quantities sufficient to supply a very dense population. There are innumerable and inexhaustible fisheries on the coast, and in all the different rivers, throughout all the different sections, both in the north and south. These abound with fish in the greatest abundance, and of almost every variety, consisting, chiefly, however, of salmon, salmon trout, cod, carp, sturgeons, flounder, ray, perch, lamprey and herring. Most of these are taken throughout the year, but in much greater quantities, during the months of May and October; at which seasons, all the different tribes of Indians, are congregated at the different fisheries for the purpose of obtaining their supplies for the residue of the year. Most of the Indians of all Oregon subsist almost entirely upon them, either in their fresh or dried state. In drying them, no salt is used; they are either exposed to the rays of the sun, or hung or spread in houses provided for that purpose, and dried in the shade. The atmosphere is so pure and arid, that they are perfectly cured in a very few days, even in the shade, without salt, and without any danger whatever, of putrefaction. The Indians not only take them in such quantities as to supply their own wants, but also in sufficient quantities, to supply all the different settlers, during the entire year. They usually take them with seines, which they make for that purpose, and which, in fact, are nearly as well constructed as those used by our own people. Spears and peculiarly constructed traps, are also used in taking them, in some portions of the country; and in others, the Indians take them very readily, even with their hands. In small streams, for the purpose of taking them more readily, with their spears or hands, they drive small stakes, thickly in the bottom of the streams, side by side, entirely across their beds, which prevent the fish from passing up or down, but do not materially interrupt the flow of the water. The fish, being thus interrupted in their course, congregate in great numbers, at the stakes, passing from space to space, endeavoring to get through, when the Indians, taking advantage of their confusion, wade among them, and take them with all ease, either with their spears, hands or otherwise. Upon the coast, several kinds of shell fish are found, such as crabs, clams, muscles and oysters, all of which, are used by the natives, in that vicinity, as a principal article of food. The oysters of Oregon are very small, but they are of a very excellent kind, and are perhaps, not inferior, to those taken any where on the Atlantic coast. Along the coast, the entire extent of the country, whales are found in great numbers, and they are frequently taken by the Indians, especially at the straits of Juan de Fucas. The American and English whale ships, very seldom visit that region, although they might find it very profitable to do so, as whales are as abundant there as in any other portion of the north Pacific.

The game of the Eastern and Middle sections is not very abundant. It consists chiefly of bear, wolves, elk, antelope, muskrats, foxes, beavers and martens. Buffalo are also found in the Eastern section; but in much less numbers, than in the country east of the Rocky mountains. No game can be said to be very plentiful, in either of these sections. Persons may travel through many parts, of both these sections, for weeks together, and not see a wild animal of any kind, during the whole time. The fur-bearing animals are the most numerous, but they are much less numerous latterly, and they are constantly diminishing in numbers. Other than the fur-bearing animals, the game of the Middle section is of very little or no importance, that of the Eastern section is important only for the fur-bearing animals and the buffalo. Water-fowls are very seldom met with, in either of these sections, which, may perhaps be attributed to the temperature of their waters, the sterility of their soil, and the variableness of their climate. The game of the Western section is much more abundant; yet, it can not be said to be very plentiful, even in this section. It consists principally of elk, antelope, deer, wolves, bear, foxes, martens, muskrats, beavers, otters and seals. In the southern part of this section, several kinds of game, are very plentiful, especially, the deer, elk, antelope and the bear. In many parts of this section also, the fur-bearing animals are very numerous, but, they are by no means as numerous now, as they formerly were; and it is said, that they are annually decreasing, because of their being taken, without regard to the proper season. The decrease has been so great, in fact, that several of the trading posts, of the Hudsons' Bay Company, have been abandoned, as they did not defray expenses. Whenever that company, however, has had the entire control of the trade, the decrease has been much less perceptible; as the trappers of that company, are required to trap, with strict regard to the proper season; and to observe every particular circumstance, which may tend to prevent a diminution of the fur-bearing animals. In that part of this section, where the settlements are now being made, by our citizens, deer and wolves are the most numerous game, of the quadruped kind. The latter of these animals, are very numerous, and troublesome to the surrounding settlers, among whom they make frequent incursions, destroying their sheep, hogs, and even young calves, in great numbers. In addition to the game before referred to, all the various rivers of this section abound with innumerable flocks, of geese, ducks, brants, cranes, pelicans, swans, gulls, and a great variety of other water-fowls. Besides these, there are numerous other feathered animals, such as hawks, eagles, ravens, thrushes, pheasants, woodpeckers, partridges, grouses, snowbirds and robins. Robins are very seldom found in the northern part of this section, but, are numerous in the southern part, as are also bluebirds, and several other birds common in the States. The water-fowls, above enumerated, are very numerous, in the spring and autumn, when they appear to have congregated, from all the surrounding country, and from their incessant croaking, squeaking and flapping of wings, you would be inclined to think, that they were convened, in sporting convention, from all parts of the world. So numerous are they, in fact, that their tumultuous croaking, and plunging and dashing in the water is, in many places, noisome in the extreme. It is scarcely necessary here to remark that it is entirely unnecessary, for emigrants to take either beds or feathers, from the states to that country. Feathers of the best quality can be obtained from the Indians, in any desired quantities, for any trivial compensation.

The settlements and improvements in Oregon, are principally confined to the forts of the Hudsons' Bay Company, and

the missionary stations, in the different sections. But besides
these, there are several other settlements, as well as towns,
and other improvements, latterly commenced, in various sections of the country, which are disconnected, with the forts
and missions; all of which, will now be noticed in successive
order. These small settlements, called forts, are mere trading
posts, established for the purpose of carrying on trade, with
the various tribes of Indians, and are now, all possessed and
occupied by the Hudsons' Bay Company, for that purpose. In
all, there are eighteen of these, two of which are situated in
the Eastern section; eight in the Middle section; and eight in
the Western section. Instead of describing each of them particularly, I shall merely give a description, of one of the principal of them, in each section; and give the locality of each of
the others, which, it is believed, will be found sufficient, for
all the ordinary purposes, of the emigrant. The most important of these posts, found in the Eastern section, is Fort Hall,
which is situated on the Lewis' or Saptin river, about sixty
miles, west by north, from the soda springs, and near latitude
42° 30' north. It was constructed by captain Wythe, of Boston, in the year 1832, for the purpose of prosecuting trade,
with the various tribes of Indians, found in that region. It is
now owned by the Hudsons' Bay Company, who purchased it
of captain Wythe, and who is now carrying on a very extensive business at that place, in the fur trade. This fort consists
of a small extent of ground, inclosed by a wall of about sixteen feet in height, and three in thickness, which is constructed of "adobies," or large dried brick, with bastions at the
corners, which command each side. Within this inclosure, are
the residences of the different officers, and mechanics, as
well as the various offices, shops and store-houses. Mr.
Grant, who is in charge, at this place, and of whom I have
before spoken, has at his command, and under his control,
about sixty Canadians and half-breeds, who serve the com-

pany as trappers, herdsmen and domestic servants. Large numbers of horses and cattle are reared at this fort, which are protected from the incursions of the Indians, by an inclosure of high walls, constructed in a manner similar to those of the fort. This inclosure, is called a "caral," and is designed not only for the protection of the horses at night, at which time they are regularly driven in, but also upon the approach of hostile and thievish Indians.

In addition to these securities, herdsmen are constantly kept out who repel all inferior forces, and give timely notice of that which is superior. With this kind of expensive precaution, the company is enabled to rear any requisite number of either horses or cattle, and that too, without the expense of feeding or housing. Several kinds of grain and vegetables, are produced here, with ordinary success, though the company has not, so far, been able to grow sufficient grain and vegetables for the consumption of the post, yet this may be attributable to defective cultivation. The remaining fort, in this section, which belongs to the Hudsons' Bay Company, is Kutanie, which is situated on Flat-bow river, about one hundred and fifty miles from its mouth. It is constructed much like Fort Hall, and is kept up, and conducted, in a similar manner, and for similar purposes. Fort Boisia, is also situated in this section, and although abandoned by the company, it is still kept up, and occupied by a Mr. Payette, who occupies it for the purpose of trade with the Indians. This Fort is situated in the midst of this section, on the north side of Lewis' river, about forty rods from its northern bank. It is constructed much like those just mentioned, but is the seat of a much more limited business, than either of those above, described.

Fort Wallawalla is the principal establishment of this kind, in the Middle section. It is situated on the south side of the Columbia river, within a few rods of its bank, at latitude 45 deg. north. From the central position of this fort, in reference to those on the coast, and in the interior, it is made the great depot, for all those in the more remote and mountainous regions. An extensive trade is here carried on, with the surrounding tribes of Indians, and herds of horses and cattle are also here reared, in such numbers as to afford ample supplies of both, to many of the interior posts. Grain and vegetables are also grown at this fort, in sufficient quantities for the consumption of the post. This fort is constructed in a manner, quite similar, to Fort Hall, though it is much less extensive. Fort Okanagan is situated on the Columbia river, about two hundred miles above Wallawalla, and near latitude 48 deg. north. Fort Coleville is also on the Columbia, about one hundred miles above Okanagan. It is situated, in the midst of a beautiful and fertile plain, where an abundance of grain and vegetables are grown, and herds of cattle and horses are reared. The remaining five forts of this section, are Alexandria, Barbine, St. James, Kamloops, and Chilcothin, all of which, are situated upon Frasier's river, and its tributaries. These are all constructed upon a plan, similar to that of those before described, but upon a scale more or less extensive, as the business in the portion of the country in which they are situated, seems to demand.

Of the forts of the Western section, Vancouver is, by far, the most important, as it is the great depot of the Hudsons' Bay Company; for all that region of country west of the Rocky mountains. It is located on the north side of the Columbia river, about eighty rods from its north bank, and ninety miles from the ocean, at latitude 45 deg. 30. min. north, and longitude 122 deg. 30 min. west. It was established in the year 1824, by Governor Simpson, and was designed as the great commercial depot of that herculean company. This fort is about fifty rods in length, and thirty in width, and is inclosed by a palisade, which is about eighteen feet high, with bastions at the corners. Within this inclosure, are about forty cheaply constructed buildings, which are occupied as dwelling houses, offices, store-houses, shops and lodging apartments. Within this fort, you see nothing but stirring activity, and the most persevering industry; officers, clerks, mechanics and servants, are always to be seen constantly passing and repassing, each intent upon the prompt and efficient discharge, of his individual duty; which, together with the diligent and incessant plying of the hammers, sledges and axes, and the confused tolling and ringing of bells, present all the impetuous commotion, rustling, tumultuous din and rumbling of a city life, in the oriental world.

Dr. McLoughlin, who is chief factor of the Hudsons' Bay Company, west of the Rocky mountains, is in charge. He is courteous, intelligent and companionable, and a more kind, hospitable and liberal gentleman, the world never saw. Every possible attention, kindness and hospitality are extended to all those who visit him, either upon business or otherwise; some of whom he invites to his own table, where they are treated with all the courtesy and etiquette of English refinement. For all others, a rapacious apartment is provided, which is called the "bachelor's hall," and which contains a convenient sitting room, a dining room, and several comfortable lodging apartments, all of which, are provided expressly for those who are not invited to his private table. Those who occupy the "bachelor's hall," are also furnished with all the luxuries of the fort; servants are in readiness to give them any attention, and, although they remain for weeks, or even months together, as many have, the kindness, attention and hospitality of the doctor, are still, unremittingly bestowed. But the kindness and hospitality of this gentleman, do not end here, for when his guests wish to return to their homes, a cart with servants, is sent, to convey their baggage or goods to the river; and all this too, without promise or hope of reward. A Mr. James Douglass, who is occasionally in charge of this fort, in the absence of the doctor, is also an intelligent gentleman, and is alike courteous, kind and hospitable as the doctor. This gentleman is now in charge of a fort, which the company was building, when I left that country. About one hundred rods below Fort Vancouver, and near the river, is the village, which is connected with the fort, and which consists of about fifty small and cheaply constructed buildings, which are occupied by the servants of the company. In connection with this fort, there is also a very large farm, consisting of about three thousand acres of land under fence; the cultivating of which, gives constant employment to about one hundred hands, who are generally, half-breeds and Indians. Near the fort also, are a saw and flouring mill, both of which run day and night, during the entire year, and hence, do a most extensive business. This site has been well selected, in reference to the future improvements of the country; and I am of the opinion, that it is much the best site for a town or city, to be found upon the Columbia; and I am of the further opinion too, that the time is not distant, when the present site of Vancouver, will be occupied by a great commercial city.

Fort George is situated, on the south side of the Columbia, upon the hill side, near the river, but a few miles from the mouth, and near latitude 46 deg. north. The buildings of this fort consist of three small log-houses, which are occupied by persons in the service of the company, for the purpose of trade with the Indians, and also for the purpose of keeping the officers of Fort Vancouver, duly advised of the arrival of ships, and such other occurrences as may be deemed important. The only importance which is now attached to this fort, is derived from the fact, of its being the former site of Astoria; the establishment of John Jacob Astor, of New York, which was made in the year 1811; taken possession of by the British, as an act of war, during the war of 1812; and restored to the United States in 1818, in accordance with the treaty of Ghent.

Nothing now remains of Astoria, but a few remnants of the old palisade, scarcely sufficient to identify the seat of that great enterprise; the classic narrative in reference to which, has spread the name and fame, of both John Jacob Astor, and Washington Irving, wherever the English language is read. The importance of the remaining forts, of this section, will not warrant a minute description of each; I shall therefore, merely give their respective locality. Fort Simpson is situated on Dundas island, at latitude 54 deg. 20 min. north. Fort McLoughlin is on Millbank sound, near latitude 52 deg. north. Fort Langley is at the outlet of Frasier's river, near latitude 49 deg. 25 min. north. Fort Nisqually is situated at latitude 47 deg. north, near Pugets' sound. Fort Cawlitz is on the Cawlitz river, about thirty miles from the Columbia, and near latitude 46 deg. 40 min. north. The only remaining fort of this section is Fort Umpqua, which is situated at the mouth of the Umpqua river, at latitude 43 deg. 30 min. north, and longitude 124 deg. west. These are all constructed much like Fort Vancouver, but they are much less extensive, yet, they are generally, seats of extensive and lucrative trade. Besides the improvements in connection with Fort Vancouver, the company also has very extensive farms at the Cawlitz, Nisqually, Langley and the Fualitine plains. At each of these considerable grain is grown, and many horses and cattle are reared. That at Nisqually, is more particularly designed as a grazing farm, to which purpose, it is eminently adapted. Upon this farm, the company keeps about eighty milk cows; has an extensive dairy, and makes both butter and cheese, not only in quantities sufficient for home consumption, but it also makes much for exportation. The farm at the Cawlitz, is a most beautiful place, containing about six hundred acres, under a high state of cultivation, which yield both vegetables and various kinds of grain, in great abundance. At the Fualitine plains also, grain and vegetables grow most luxuriantly, and produce abundantly. The foregoing is but a faint exhibit of the power, and the agricultural and commercial resources, of this great heremitical company. Since it is true, as above seen, that this gigantic company, of British subjects, holds the almost entire control, not only of the trade, but also of the agricultural and commercial resources, of all Oregon, a brief description of that company, may not be deemed inappropriate. This great company, was created in the year 1670, during the reign of Charles II, by a charter which was granted to certain British subjects, under the name and style of the Hudsons' Bay Company. This Company was created, with the view of carrying on the fur trade in Oregon, where it soon established, and held the uninterrupted control of the entire trade, of all that country, until the year 1787, when the North American Fur Company was chartered. This Company also established in Oregon, and commenced a very extensive trade, throughout the different portions of that country; but it soon came in competition and coalition with the Hudsons' Bay Company, which gave rise to many serious difficulties. The attention of the British government was soon directed to these companies, and as there was no probability of reconciliation, an act of parliament was passed, uniting the two companies, under the name and style of the Hudsons' Bay Company, under which name it has continued its operations, up to the present time, wielding an almost unbounded trade, with unparalleled success. The officers of this company, as now organized, consists of a governor general, chief factors and chief traders. The governor general has charge of all the different trading posts or forts, in North America, and for that purpose resides at York Factory, on Hudsons' Bay. The chief factors have the control of a certain number of forts or trading posts, within a certain district, or section of country, subject however, to the general superintendence of the governor general. The chief traders also have control of a certain number of trading posts, within a particular district, being subject to the superintendence of the chief factors. Thus, we have briefly noticed, the origin, and the present organization, of that powerful company, which has, so entirely, wielded the destinies of Oregon, for more then half of a century.

Chapter 6

SETTLEMENTS AND IMPROVEMENTS

The various missionary stations, together with the improvements in connection with them, next deserve our attention, in describing which, I shall for the sake of brevity, confine my remarks chiefly, to the more important stations. In all there are eight stations in Oregon, four of which are in the Middle section, and four in the Western section. There was, also a station, formerly, in the Eastern section, but it is now abandoned. This station was called Kaima, and was situated on Koosekooseke river, in the vicinity of Fort Boisia. The principal station found in the Middle section, is a presbyterian station, which is situated on the Wallawalla river, about twenty-five miles easterly from Fort Wallawalla. This is the station, to which I have alluded upon another page, as being under the superintendence of Dr. Whitman, and which is called Dr. Whitman's mission. At this station, there is a very large farm, under a good state of cultivation, which produces a great abundance of both grain and vegetables. The buildings are very convenient, consisting of two large dwelling-houses, one of which, was not entirely completed, when I was at that place. The walls of these buildings are constructed of "adobies" or large dried brick. In connection with these, there is also a flouring-mill, which answers all the purposes of the missionaries, and the dependent natives. Near this mill, there is also, a large "caral," or inclosure, into which, the cattle and horses are daily driven, as at Fort Hall, and elsewhere, throughout this region. Large numbers of American cattle, and Skiuse, and Wallawalla horses, are reared at this place, and they all thrive most admirably, notwithstanding the inclement winters, of this excessively cold region. There are two other stations, at the east, and north of this, called the Lapwai and the Chimekaine stations; but the only remaining station of this section, which I shall more particularly notice, is that at the dalles, which is situated about a mile from the Columbia river, on the south side, upon the adjacent high lands, just below the dalles. Between this station and the river, is a most beautiful and fertile valley, on which, herds of fine cattle and horses, belonging to the missionaries, are always to be seen grazing, in great numbers. The buildings of this station consist of a dwelling-house, a school-house, workshops and several outhouses. This is a beautiful station, and the missionaries here appear to be in very comfortable circumstances. There is not a very extensive tract of land, under cultivation, in connection with this station, but both grain and vegetables, are grown in sufficient quantities, for the consumption of the missionaries, and the natives in their service. The missionaries of all this section, and especially, those at the presbyterian stations, are laboring with much success, both in christianizing, and civilizing the natives. Agricultural pursuits, have already been introduced among them, to a very considerable extent; and many of them, even now, grow considerable grain, rear large herds, build houses; and in fact, exhibit an extraordinary advancement in civilization, considering the brief duration of missionary labors in that region.

The missionary stations of the Western section, are located at the Wallammette valley, the Wallammette falls, Clatsop and Nisqually. That station situated in the Wallammette valley, is the principal and most important station of this section. It is situated about fifty miles above the falls, a few miles east of the Wallammette river, where the buildings in connection with the station, consist of dwelling-houses, barns, shops, store-houses, churches, school-houses and mills. In all, there are about fourteen buildings, belonging to this station, which are located at different points in this valley, varying from one to eight miles in distance, from each other. At the Indian school, thirty or forty Indian children, are now being taught the rudiments of the English language, with a view of facilitating the promulgation of the doctrines of the christian religion. There are also two large farms, in connection with this station, which are very extensive, and which produce ample grain and vegetables, for the consumption of all the different stations of this section, as well as much grain for exportation. Here too, cattle, horses, sheep and hogs, are reared in much greater numbers, than at any of the other stations. There is also a store, connected with this station, where goods are annually sold, both to the settlers, and the Indians, to the amount of several thousand dollars. The Rev. Jason Lee is in charge at this station, and is the general superintendent, of all the Methodist missionary stations in Oregon. He is gentlemanly, kind and hospitable, and with all, a very energetic and enterprising man. He extends great kindness and hospitality, to the numerous emigrants who are constantly arriving in that country. The station at the falls, is situated but a few rods below the cataract; the buildings consist of two dwelling-houses, a store-house and a ware-house. At this place also, as at the valley, there is a store, at which large quantities of goods are daily sold, by the missionaries, to both whites and Indians, from which extensive profits are annually derived. The Indians in the vicinity of this station, are occasionally convened, either at the falls, or the Klackamus, for the purpose of religious instruction; but it appears to be with the greatest reluctance, that they assemble, upon such occasions. The stations at Nisqually and Clatsop, are much less important than those just described, as there are but a very few missionaries stationed at each, merely for the purpose of imparting religious instruction to the few Indians, who are connected with each station. Nor is there any additional settlements of whites, in connection with either of these stations, which will enable the missionaries, to extend their labors among them, as religious teachers. At both of these stations, grain and vegetables are grown, to some extent, and cattle and horses are reared in numbers sufficient for the purposes of the stations. Although the station at the falls, may have been and may at this time be, of some importance, as a means of imparting religious instruction, to the natives, yet the time is not far distant, when it can be of no further importance, in that respect; for it is evident, from the importance of that point, for manufacturing and commercial purposes, that the Indians will not be permitted long to remain either there, or in the immediate vicinity. And my impression is, that none of those missionary establishments, can long exist, as such, in that part of the Western section; for there are but very few Indians, in the immediate neighborhood, of any of these stations, to require the attention of missionaries. And, as that is far the most fertile, and delightful portion of Oregon, which is as yet occupied, it is very evident, that the natives will, in a very few years, at farthest, be required to change their locations.

The settlements and improvements, which are disconnected with the forts and missions, are chiefly at the Wallammette valley, the Fualitine plains, and the Wallammette falls. The settlement at the Wallammette valley, is at present, the most extensive settlement in the country. It contains about one hundred families, who have extensive farms, and who are otherwise comfortably situated. Each of the farmers in this valley, generally have, from one hundred to five hundred acres of land under fence, and in a good state of cultivation, upon which, they grow annually, from five hundred to a thousand bushels of wheat for exportation, besides beans, peas and potatoes, turnips and various other vegetables, which they grow in great abundance. They also usually rear cattle, horses, sheep and hogs, in large numbers; each farmer generally having from fifty to five hundred head of cattle, from ten to one hundred head of horses, and as many sheep and hogs; for all of which, the continued, annual emigration, affords an ample market. In the Fualitine plains, there are about fifty families, all of whom have selected, and are now improving their farms. They generally have from fifty, to a hundred acres of land, under fence, with cattle, horses, hogs and sheep, in large numbers. The settlers here, however, like those of the Wallammette valley, devote their principal attention, to the growing of wheat, of which, they sell annually, from one hundred to a thousand bushels, besides beans, peas, turnips, potatoes and the like, for all of which, a ready market is found in the country, as will be seen upon another page. The settlement at the falls, is less extensive then those just described, but from its very favorable situation, it is, perhaps, more important then either of those. In the winter of 1843, a town was laid off near the falls, which has since improved, with unparalleled rapidity. It was surveyed under my direction, but at the expense of Dr. McLoughlin, who claimed, and then occupied the site, and who, after having surveyed it, for a mile in extent, up and down the Wallammette river, permitted all persons who wished to do so, to take as many lots, as they would build upon and improve, requiring them merely to pay for the drawing of the writings, in reference to them. During the winter, there were numerous lots taken, upon these terms, and in the following spring, there were thirty buildings, in Oregon City, which was the name given it, at the time of its surveyal. In the autumn of 1843, there were fifty-three buildings in this town, among which, were four stores, four mills, two of which were flouring mills, one public-house, one black smith's shop and various other mechanic's shops; a church was also in contemplation, and in fact, commenced. Many of the lots, which were obtained gratuitously, only the spring previous, were then worth at least one thousand dollars each, and their value was daily increasing, with the improvements of the town. Such were the improvements of Oregon City, in the autumn of 1843, but about eight months, after its emergent appearance. Oregon City is situated upon a very favorable site for a town, and it is, beyond a doubt, destined to become a place of very considerable manufacturing and commercial importance. This opinion is strengthened, when we take into consideration, the fact, of its being near the head of slack-water navigation, and the fact, of its possessing a water power, scarcely ever surpassed. For the present, and until other towns spring up, emigrants will, in a great measure, concentrate at this place, especially merchants, mechanics and those of the learned professions. But other towns are already springing into existence, as additional evidences of the unbounded energy and enterprise of American citizens. A town has been recently laid off, upon the west side of the Wallammette river, about five miles from its mouth, near the head of sloop navigation, and about ten miles below Vancouver; called Linnton, in honor of the lamented Dr. Linn of Missouri. This is also a very favorable site for a town, and is improving, with extraordinary rapidity.

The improvements of the settlements, both in the valley and plains, are quite similar to those in our western states. The buildings being usually constructed of logs, some of which are hewn, and others round, are intended only for temporary residences; but many of them are very comfortable, and convenient. There are some exceptions to the above remarks, for there are several very commodious, and well-finished framed buildings, both in the valley and the plains. The buildings in Oregon City, are, with a few exceptions, framed and well-finished. Including saw and flouring mills, there are now fourteen in Oregon, many of which are doing a very extensive and profitable business; and there are innumerable sites for mills and other machinery, which are destined, soon to he occupied. There are perhaps, very few countries which afford more numerous, or more advantageous sites for the most extensive water power then Oregon. The people of this territory, in their anxiety to provide for their individual necessities, and to promote their individual interests, have paid but very little attention to the making of roads, and other public improvements. Traveling and transportation, are, as yet, chiefly on horseback, and by water, but from the nature of the soil however, there can be no difficulty, in making good roads, and thereby, rendering intercommunication easy, and transportation cheap, throughout all portions of the country. The foregoing facts, in reference to the improvements of Oregon, afford a few evidences of the very enterprising character of the Oregon emigrants; but a further evidence is found in the fact of their having recently sent to New York for a printing-press and a steam-engine, which will be received sometime during the next summer or autumn; when the same energy and enterprise that procured them, will soon put them into extensive and successful operation.

The entire population of Oregon, may now be estimated at about twenty-four thousand, including both whites and Indians, and the white population, including Canadians and half-breeds, now amounts to about four thousand. The emigrants, up to the autumn of 1844, and the former American settlers inclusive, increase the American population to about three thousand. The officers of the Hudsons' Bay Company, the Canadians and half-breeds, number about one thousand; and hence, it is seen, that the Indian population is about twenty thousand. The American population, and the Canadians and half-breeds, who are disconnected with the company, are, as

before remarked, chiefly settled at the falls of the Wallammette, the Fualitine plain, and the Wallammette valley. They
are industrious, orderly, and good citizens; devoting their
entire time and attention to the improvement of their farms,
the growing of grain, and rearing of herds; they all appear to
be intent, only upon the advancement of the general good. In
every thing that tends to the advancement of the interests of
the country, there appears to be a hearty co-operation,
between the gentlemen of the Hudson Bay Company, and the
American citizens. As one instance of extraordinary, and
entire devotion to the best interests of the country, the whole
community, with one unanimous voice, determined to abandon the use of all alcoholic or inebriating liquors; and to prevent their introduction or sale, under any state of
circumstances. In this measure, the gentlemen of the company perform a very efficient part, and although their own
store-houses are full of intoxicating liquors, they sell none to
any person. Upon the arrival of a vessel freighted with ardent
spirits, the doctor, McLoughlin, has been known to purchase
the whole cargo, in order to prevent its sale among the settlers, when at the same time, he had hundreds of barrels in his
own store houses. A course equally prompt and energetic, is
also pursued by the settlers themselves, as is seen in this
instance. A Mr. Young, commenced the erection of a distillery, in the vicinity of the principal settlements, of which the
settlers, were all soon advised, when a public meeting was
called, for the purpose of adopting such measures, as might
immediately arrest this work of death. Upon due deliberation,
and full consideration of the subject, the meeting unanimously resolved, that Mr. Young should be paid for his building, already commenced; but that he should also abandon the
further prosecution of his most nefarious purpose, which if he
did not do, his buildings and whatever else connected with
them, however often erected, should as often, be demolished.

This resolution, accompanied by an appropriate preamble, was presented to Mr. Young, who, after a few moments reflection, saw the full force of these mandatory admonitions, and finally, consented to abandon his unrighteous enterprise. This certainly speaks volumes, for the morality and intelligence of the citizens of Oregon, and it is, no doubt, the chief cause of all that order and quiet, which so universally prevail, throughout all the different settlements.

A kindness and hospitality exist, among those pioneers of the west, which is almost unparalleled. Upon the arrival of emigrants, in the country, immediate arrangements are made by the former settlers, to provide them with houses and provisions, and every aid is rendered them in making their selections of lands, and procuring houses for themselves. The doctor McLoughlin, also, affords them every aid in his power; furnishing them with goods and teams, upon a credit, if they are unable to make immediate payment, providing them with wheat for their bread and seed, and receiving wheat the next year in payment; and letting them have cows and other cattle, to be returned in such time as shall be agreed upon, with a portion of the increase. This kindness and generosity of the doctor, are not confined to emigrants upon their arrival merely, but they are extended to every settler, and respectable inhabitant, in all the various portions of the country. Schools and churches are already established throughout the country, and unlike all other new countries, a very great anxiety prevails, for the speedy promotion, of the moral and intellectual improvement, of the rising generation, as a consideration, of high and paramount importance. Divine service is regularly attended, in every inhabited portion of the country, at least, once or twice each week, upon which occasions, sermons are delivered by the clergymen, of the various christian denominations. In point of morality, and virtue, this little community, loses nothing, by a comparison with any community, on the east side of the Rocky mountains. Mechanics of all kinds, and men of all the learned professions, are even now, to be found in Oregon, and for so limited a population, there is a very fair proportion of talent and learning. And I may add, that the Oregon emigrants are, as a general thing, of a superior order to those of our people, who usually emigrate to our frontier countries. They are not the indolent, dissolute, ignorant and vicious, but they are generally, the enterprising, orderly, intelligent and virtuous.

There are several powerful and warlike tribes of Indians, occupying each of the different sections. The principal tribes inhabiting the Eastern section, are the Shoshonies, or Snakes, the Blackfeet, and the Bonarks. The Nezpercies also frequent this section, but their country is properly in the Middle section, where they are principally found. The Indians of this section are much less advanced in civilization, than those of the other sections. They are all said to be friendly, excepting the Blackfeet, who have always been hostile. Emigrants, however, very seldom meet with them, in traveling to Oregon, by the way of Fort Hall, as their country lies far to the north of that route. They are not to be dreaded, however, when met by a large party of whites; even forty or fifty armed men, are ample to deter them from any hostile movements. They should always be considered, and treated as enemies, whatever may be their pretensions of friendship. The Shoshonies or Snakes, the "Root-diggers," (a lower order of the same tribe,) and the Bonarks, although said to be friendly, are, in fact, not strictly so, in the sense in which that term is used in civilized life. The word "friendly," as used by mountaineers, in reference to the Indians, only implies that they are not arrayed, in armed and hostile opposition to the whites; that they are not actually seeking their indiscriminate destruction. This is a Rocky mountain definition, of the word "friendly." However "friendly" these Indians may be, they seek every

possible opportunity, to steal your horses, and every thing
else upon which they can lay their hands, and they avail themselves of every favorable occasion, for forcibly taking from
you, every thing that you possess, which they chance to desire
or admire. There is no exception to this, only in the immediate neighborhood of the various forts, where they are held in
awe by superior force. At these places, they appear to be
inclined to accomplish their thievish purposes, with much
more caution, and upon a much more limited system. Petit
larceny is the most common offence committed at these
places, while grand larceny, and robbery are constantly being
committed by them elsewhere; but as they are "friendly",
murder is an offence which they seldom commit.

The principal tribes of the Middle section, are the Nezpercies, Skyuses, Wallawallas and Chenukes. The first of these
tribes, here mentioned, rear large numbers of horses, and
some cattle, and they are notorious, not only for horse-trad-
ing: but for horse-stealing. The Nezpercies rear a much the
greater number of horses, then any other tribe in Oregon; I
was informed, that one Nezpercie chief, had eleven thousand
of fine horses; this number, however, I suppose was perhaps,
rather exaggerated. The best horses that I have ever seen, I
saw among the Nezpercie, the Skyuse and Wallawalla tribes.
The horses of these tribes, differ very much from those of the
various other tribes; they are large, well proportioned, and
extremely fleet and hardy. The Chenukes also, have some
horses, but very few, in comparison to those of the tribes just
mentioned. Many of these Indians, grow a small kind of corn,
and potatoes and melons, in considerable quantities, which
are grown by some for food, and by others for the purpose of
barter with the Indians of the Eastern section, for which they
receive buffalo robes and meat in exchange. The women have
been taught, by the missionaries, to spin, weave and knit, in
which manner, many of them employ much of their time,

when their services are not required in the fields. They are also entirely "friendly," that is, they are not inclined to take your life, if they can accomplish all of their thievish purposes without. But a more villainous and treacherous race of thieves, can scarcely be found. Notwithstanding all the religious instruction, which they are daily receiving, and the moral influence, which is hourly exerted among them, they will unhesitatingly, steal your knives, forks, plates, cups, horses, or any thing else, whenever an opportunity is afforded; and almost any kind of an opportunity, answers their purpose. Like those in the Eastern section, they will also rob you, whenever they are satisfied, that they have the preponderance of power, and that there is no probability of chastisement, from any other source.

The most numerous and important tribes, of the Western section, are the Shatshet, Squamish, Toando, Chalams, Classet, Chenook, Clatsop, Klacksinus, Klackatats, Kallapuyas, Umpquas, Killamucks, Rogues, Klamets, Shasty and Celkilis tribes, which like all other tribes of the country, have, by many, been thought to be migratory, and wandering tribes, but this appears not to be the case. They are always to be found within their own proper territories, sometimes passing and re-passing, however, from fishing to fishing, or from hunting ground to hunting ground; yet, their usual haunts are very seldom, if ever, entirely abandoned. They all subsist almost entirely upon fish, which they are enabled to take in any abundance, and at any, and every season of the year. Some of them also hunt, but hunting appears to require too much active exertion, to comport with their inherent and hereditary indolence, therefore, as a means of livelihood, it is not very generally adopted. They generally live in small huts, constructed in the most simple and artless manner imaginable. Uprights of about eight feet in length are obtained, which are inserted about one foot into the ground, side by side, forming either a square or circular inclosure, of about ten feet in diameter. At the side of these uprights, about two feet from the ground, and also about five feet from the ground, poles are placed horizontally, and attached by means of barks or withes to the uprights, when the walls are completed. The roof or cover, is of bark or branches and twigs of trees, which, thrown on in the roughest manner, completes these primitive, rude dwellings, of the Oregon aborigines. These Indians are of much service to the settlers, as they can be employed for a mere nominal compensation, to perform various kinds of labor, at many kinds of which, they are very expert, especially paddling canoes, rowing boats, hunting and driving horses, and bearing dispatches. With the exception of those in the extreme northern and southern portions of the country, they are entirely friendly and inoffensive. Such is the character, particularly of those, in the immediate neighborhood of the different settlements, yet, it is true, that the settlers here, are not entirely free from the little pilferings, and low treachery, to which all Indians are, more or less addicted. They very seldom steal any thing but food and clothing, though they frequently drive the horses of the settlers off, in order that they may be employed to find them, and this they do, in order to obtain food and clothing, as a reward for their services. The word friendly, is here used, in the sense in which it is used upon a former page, signifying merely, that they will make no unprovoked attack upon your person, or that they will not kill you; but not that they will not steal, for stealing appears to be an inborn vice, to which all barbarous Indians, are habitually addicted. The statement, which I have seen in several of our western papers, in reference to the burning of Dr. Whitman's mill, by the Indians, as an act of war or hostility, is entirely unfounded. The burning of this mill, occurred while I was in that country, and it was wholly accidental; no fault or design whatever, was attributed to the Indians. It is also reported, that all the various tribes in the neighborhood of the settlements, are combining, for the purpose of making a simultaneous attack, upon the settlers. This report is also, without foundation, for that unanimity of feeling does not exist among them, which would be indispensable to such a combination. But if they were hostile, and should combine, for warlike purposes, still, no danger whatever, would be apprehended from them, for they have neither the means, nor courage, to enable them to prosecute an efficient warfare.

A civil organization has recently taken place in Oregon, and an infant republic is now in full operation. Several attempts had been made to effect an organization, prior to the spring of 1843, but they had all proved ineffectual. The present organization took place, in the spring of 1843, in accordance with the expressed wishes, of a great majority of all the settlers. An election was held, during the same spring, when the various officers, such as members of the legislature, a supreme judge, justices of the peace, sheriffs, constables, a treasurer, a secretary, and the different prothonotaries, were elected. No executive was elected, consequently, the government must, of course, prove very inefficacious; though it was designed merely, as a substitute for a government, until the United States shall afford them a government, more enlarged, and more effective; to which event, the people of Oregon look forward, with a deep, and abiding interest. The legislature convened in the month of May 1843, at which time, it adopted the statute laws of Iowa, with such alterations and amendments, as local circumstances seemed to require. Neither the officers of the Hudsons' Bay Company, nor any persons in the service of that company, took any part in this governmental organization, nor did many of the Canadians or half-breeds: who had formerly been engaged in the service of that company. The reason assigned by the gentlemen of that company, for the neutral course which they pursued, was that they were British subjects, and hence, amenable to the laws of that government, which were already extended to that country, and in full force; therefore, whatever necessity might exist, on the part of American citizens, to enact a temporary code of laws, no such necessity existed on the part of British subjects. Those gentlemen, no doubt, pursued the proper course, in reference to their duty, as British subjects, for it is strictly true, that by an act of parliament, the jurisdiction and laws of Upper Canada, are extended over all that country, occupied by the British fur traders, whether such country is owned, or claimed by the British government. In accordance with this law, several gentlemen of the Hudsons' Bay Company were appointed, and now officiate, as justices of peace; having jurisdiction of all civil matters of controversy, where the amount claimed, does not exceed two hundred pounds sterling. The jurisdiction of these justices, in criminal cases, only extend to the examination of those who stand charged with the commission of criminal offences; against whom, if sufficient evidence is found, they are sent to Upper Canada, for final trial. This jurisdiction does not extend, as some have supposed, to the citizens of the United States; but, as is thus seen, there are two distinct forms of government, now established in Oregon, which will most likely, conflict, and thereby, produce serious consequences, if they are long continued.

Great Britain, then, has already done, by actual legislation, what our government seems willing to concede, that we have no right to do, under the existing circumstances. Although Great Britain, has already extended the jurisdiction and laws of Canada, over that country, when it is proposed to extend the jurisdiction and laws of Iowa, over the same country; or in any other manner to establish a government there; it is insisted that the government of the United States, has not the right. It is claimed by the United States; that Oregon territory belongs to her alone, and that Great Britain has no right whatever, to any part of it, upon any recognized principle, of the laws of nations. Now if this is true, may not our government, extend its jurisdiction over that country, and that too, in any manner which she may deem proper? But, it is remarked, that by the treaty of London, the stipulations of the treaty of Ghent, are indefinitely extended, which gives British subjects, the same right to settle, and trade in Oregon, as citizens of the United States have; that is true, but how does this permission, destroy the right of this government, to extend its jurisdiction and laws over its own territory? Admitting however, that it is doubtful whether the country, in fact, all belongs to the United States, as the question of title is yet unsettled, still, have not the United States, the same authority, the same right, to extend their jurisdiction and laws over that territory, that Great Britain has, to extend her jurisdiction and laws over the same country? In any view of this subject, it is not only clear, that this government has the right to extend its jurisdiction over that country, in any manner that it may think expedient, but also, that it is its duty to do so; a duty which it owes to its own interests; its own security; and above all, to its own, thus far, neglected citizens, in that wild and perilous land, of doubtful and heterogeneous jurisdictions.

The market, trade and commerce, of this infant country, are even now, much more extensive than the most prophetic, could possibly have foreseen. An ample market is now afforded, in the country, and at the very doors of the farmers, for all their surplus produce. The Hudsons' Bay Company has certain arrangements, by which, it is enabled to take the products of the country, at the highest prices, even at the doors of the farmers, which is a very great convenience to the farmer, as well as a great saving of time and expense. The American merchants, also afford an additional market, for the wheat and the various other productions of the country; all of which, as well as labor of all kinds, bear a very good price. Wheat is worth from sixty cents to one dollar per bushel, flour from four to five dollars per barrel; potatoes from twenty five to fifty cents per bushel; beans from seventy-five cents, to one dollar; oats from twenty five to fifty cents; beef from four to eight cents per pound; pork from five to ten cents; fresh salmon from one to four cents; salted salmon from four to six cents, or from eight to twelve dollars per barrel; butter from twenty to thirty cents per pound; and all things else, in the same proportion. Labor of ordinary hands is worth from one to two dollars per day; that of mechanics, from two to four dollars; and that of Indians, from twenty five, to fifty cents per day. All kinds of dry goods and groceries, are generally, afforded here, as cheap as they are in any of our western states; especially, by the Hudsons' Bay Company, the merchants of which, very much undersell those of the United States. This may be attributed to the fact, that this company ships its annual supplies of goods, directly from England, free of duty, which enables it to sell at prices much lower, than those of the American merchants; hence it is, that almost the entire trade of Oregon, is as yet, confined to that vastly wealthy company. No unfairness, however, can be attributed to the company in this respect, for its course of dealing is the most honorable and commendable; but this result is the natural consequence, of such an unequal competition. We see that English merchants, sustain themselves, with much success, in competition with our merchants in the States, notwithstanding the high duties imposed upon many of their imports; to remove these duties that, as in Oregon, must necessarily, give the English merchant, for many years to come, a decided preponderance in trade.

The chief trade of Oregon, as yet, is the fur trade, which is almost entirely, monopolized by that company. This trade, however profitable it may formerly have been, and although it is still very lucrative, yet, it is rapidly decreasing, owing to the great decrease of the fur-bearing animals, which was alluded to upon a former page. The peltries annually collected in Oregon, by this company are, at this time, estimated at about one hundred and fifty thousand dollars, which, however, is far less, then the returns of former years. The trade in grain and lumber is also chiefly confined to this company, which ships the former, in large quantities to Sitka under a contract with the Russians; and the latter, in very great quantities, to the Sandwich Islands, where it is sold for about forty dollars per thousand. The staples of this country, will eventually be grain, pork, beef, hides, tallow, fish, wool, lumber and coal, all of which, may be produced, in abundance, for exportation; and the Russian settlements, China and the various islands of the Pacific, will undoubtedly, forever afford, an ample market, for all its surplus productions. For many years to come, however, the continued, and increasing emigration will afford a home market, at least, for most of the grain, vegetables, pork, beef and lumber, which the country will produce. Such is now, the case; the emigrants annually purchase most of the provisions, as well as cattle, horses, hogs, sheep and lumber, of which the former settlers wish to dispose. This country possesses a very decided advantage, over all the other newly settled countries, of the United States, from its proximity to the Sandwich Islands, which afford an extensive market, at which all its surplus productions, are readily, exchanged, for the various tropical productions. This country also possesses many commercial advantages, much superior, to those possessed generally, by other newly settled countries of the States. Its commercial advantages, as before remarked, are tolerably extensive in the northern part, although they are rather inconsiderable, in the immediate vicinity of the settlements, and in the southern portion; yet its commerce is, at this time, tolerably extensive. There are frequent annual arrivals, at all the different accessible ports, from the Russian settlements, the Sandwich Islands, California, the United States and England. In all, there are eight or ten vessels, engaged in the Oregon trade, of which, the company has five, measuring from two to seven hundred tons. They are all engaged, the greater part of the year, in importing goods from England, and exporting wheat, furs, fish and timber in return. One of these ships arrives every spring, with a stock of goods, designed to supply the different trading posts, which having been disposed of in that manner, a cargo of lumber is taken to the Sandwich Islands, or a cargo of goods and flour to Sitka or Kamschatka. Having disposed of their freight, at the places last mentioned, these vessels return to Vancouver, in the latter part of the summer, where the furs, collected during the previous year, are shipped for England. These vessels, although designed merely, to carry on trade between the places above mentioned, are all well armed with cutlasses, muskets and cannons. Besides these, the company also has a steam-vessel, which is well armed, and which plies along the coast, and in the inlets and bays, northward from the Columbia. There are also four or five American vessels, which touch annually, at the different ports of Oregon, by the way of the Sandwich Islands. They usually arrive in the spring and autumn, bringing goods, and receiving hides, tallow, furs, wheat and fish in return. Besides the merchant vessels, which trade in the Pacific, there are numerous whale-ships, and ships of war, which cruise in the north Pacific, but which, however, very seldom touch at any of the ports in this country. It is believed, that the foregoing will give a view sufficiently enlarged, for the purposes, for which this little work was designed, of the present, and at least, a faint prelude, of the future, agricultural and commercial advantages of Oregon.

Chapter 7

SCENES AND INCIDENTS OF A PARTY OF CALIFORNIA EMIGRANTS

Having remained in Oregon, as long as I had originally designed, I now proceeded to make preliminary arrangements, for an over land tour to California, to visit which country, was also among my original proposes. But traveling from Oregon to California, like traveling from the States to Oregon, is attended with imminent danger, from innumerable hostile Indians; hence it became necessary to obtain a party of armed men, sufficient in numbers, to secure our protection. I, therefore, visited the different neighborhoods, with that view, when I soon found, that there would be no difficulty in obtaining a party, ample in numbers, to insure our entire safety. Upon designating a place of rendezvous, on the Wallammette river, about twenty miles above the falls, we soon had fifty-three emigrants, of whom, twenty-five were armed men, when myself having been again honored with command, on the 30th day of May, 1843, we were outward-bound for the second and last paradise of the west, California. As the presumption is, that many of the Oregon emigrants will, eventually, emigrate to California, and that too, by the same route which I traveled; I have deemed it proper, to give some of the principal scenes and incidents, of this party of California emigrants. This I do, in order to put the future emigrants upon their guard, and thereby, to enable them, to avoid the innumerable dangers and difficulties, which we encountered, and of which, we were wholly unadvised.

Leaving our place of rendezvous, as above stated, nothing of importance occurred, until we arrived at Rogue's river, which we were under the necessity of crossing, by the aid of the Indians, who soon appeared with their canoes, and proffered their aid, which we were under the necessity of accepting; but we proceeded with the utmost caution, for as we were well advised, several parties had been robbed at this place, under quite similar circumstances. In view of the peculiarity of our perilous situation, I directed twelve men to cross the river, in advance, in order to receive and guard the baggage, as it should be sent across. The residue of the men, remained, in order to protect the women and children, and to guard the horses and baggage, previous to their being sent across. During all the time, which was occupied in crossing the river, great numbers of Indians thronged around us, on each side of the river, frequently rushing upon us, in such a manner, that it became necessary for us to draw our forces out, in battle array, against them, when we were under the necessity, of discharging a gun or two occasionally, in the open air, in order to deter them from any further hostile movements. Upon discharging a gun, they would, invariably, fall back, and flee in every direction, with the greatest confusion; but after the lapse of a very few minutes, they would again, crowd and huddle around us, in increased numbers, when we would again dispel them as before. Their object in crowding upon us, in this manner, was to intermingle with our people, to such an extent, as to produce general confusion and disorder, when they designed to steal and plunder and if they could produce disorder and tumult, to the extent that they desired, they, no doubt, intended to make a direct attack upon us, not only with the view of stealing and robbing, but also, with a determination to effect our indiscriminate extermination. By the above system of caution, however, we finally, succeeded in crossing the river, in perfect safety, and were enabled to leave them, to enjoy the wild howlings of their timid confusion, without the loss to ourselves, of either life or property. Upon emerging from the boisterous confusion, of these more than barbarous beings, we continued our journey, for several days, without anything worthy of remark, until we met a company of cattle drovers and emigrants, who were on their way from California to Oregon, the former, with cattle for the Oregon market, and the latter, designing to locate in Oregon, where they hoped to find refuge, from the oppression, which they had suffered, in California, of which I shall speak more fully hereafter.

Upon meeting this party, both parties immediately encamped, where we remained together, all that day and night, as well as a part of the ensuing day, which time was spent, in discussing the comparative advantages, and disadvantages, of our respective places of destination. We, of course, had nothing very favorable to say of Oregon, for we were then in search of a desirable place of abode, which in our view, could not be found in Oregon; nor had they much to say in favor of California. They all concurred in the opinion, that California was, beyond any doubt, one of the most delightful countries in the known world, both in point of mildness of climate and fertility of soil; but they remarked, that they had been seriously oppressed there and that they would seek refuge, *for the time being*, in Oregon. This discussion terminated in very disastrous consequences to us; for about one third of our party, was prevailed upon to return to Oregon. This reduced our number of armed men to sixteen, and that too, in a region where our full forces, were more than any where else required; in a country where we were everywhere surrounded by a numerous and hostile foe; where our "sixteen" were, at anytime, liable to be attacked by thousands of unrestrained, and barbarous Indians. But the most distressing circumstance, at this particular juncture, was, that our guide also left us, with a view of returning to Oregon, contrary to our wishes, and repeated solicitations to remain. This left us, not only without a force sufficient for our future protection, but also, without any knowledge of the route, or any means of obtaining that knowledge; and also, without any knowledge of the haunts and prowess of the countless savages, with whom we were now everywhere surrounded. The time of our separation had now arrived, when we proceeded to take our leave, of these our friends of long standing, with whom we had traversed the great western prairies, immersed in doubt, and surrounded with fearful dangers innumerable; and with whom we had penetrated the deep, wild recesses of Oregon, amid the howls of beasts of prey, the yells of frantic savages, and desolation and death, in all their various and varied forms. We were sad, sad indeed, and grieved too, even to the shedding of tears. Much did we regret the necessity, which impelled our separation, and as much, did we dread the danger, attendant upon that separation; but to accomplish our purpose, we were determined, regardless of all consequences. So leaving our friends, we traveled on, silently and solemnly, contemplating the cheerless past and the fearful future.

As I moved on, in this mood of mind, a half or three quarters of a mile, in advance of the party, my meditations were interrupted by the sudden appearance of two Indians, who were in close pursuit of a fine fat cow, which had strayed from the party to which I have just alluded. I immediately gave chase to these intruders upon my solitude, without being observed by them, until I had approached within about thirty yards of them, when I fired upon them, but whether I wounded either of them, I could not ascertain; but at all events, I so alarmed one of them, that he yelled most furiously, and with tremendous leaps, soon reached a deep ravine, which afforded him a secure retreat, as its banks were thickly studded, with willows. Turning to the other, I found him still in hot pursuit of his intended prey; but as he saw that I had turned my attention to him, he also fled with unusual rapidity, and took refuge with his comrade, among the same willows, near to which, I had no inclination to approach, as willows are thought by mountaineers to be "dangerous things." The party soon came up, and the cow very soon fell a victim to our returning appetites; but we saw no more of our noble competitors. Perhaps the one was engaged, in some secluded place, extracting buckshot from the lower limbs of his fellow. As we continued our journey, we frequently saw the Indians, far upon the mountain's height, viewing us as we wound our serpentine way, through low, deep valleys, up high, towering hills, or over beautiful, expansive plains. Thus, remaining upon the extreme height of the surrounding mountains, they always kept their eyes fixed upon us, until we had encamped at night, when they would approach us, with a view of stealing or killing our horses. We, however, met with no serious difficulty with the Indians, until we arrived at a small tributary of Rogue's river, called the Chasty river, where we encamped, for the night. About midnight, we were attacked by them, the first indication that we had of which, was the cry, by one of the guards, of "Indians," "Indians," which soon brought the men "to arms," when a brisk, random fire commenced, in all directions from the camp, which soon dispelled our midnight assailants, not, however, until they had severely wounded one man and two horses. The man who was wounded, was a Mr. Bellamy, who happened to be posted as guard, at the most vulnerable part of the camp, and near the river. He was the guard who gave notice of the attack, which however, he did not do, until several arrows had been thrown. The first knowledge which he had, of the presence of the Indians, was the reception of an arrow in his back, which, I suppose, he thought to be "striking proof," "pointed evidence," of their presence, if not of their omnipresence. The arrow was immediately extracted, but from the intensity of the pain, which it appeared to produce, it was feared, by some, that it would be attended with fatal consequences. In the morning, it was thought, from the increased pain, that in all probability, the spinal marrow was affected, and hence, that it would be unsafe to move that day; but we determined to make the attempt, which we accordingly did, and were happy to find, that it was not attended with serious consequences.

From this encampment, we now moved on, without any thing worthy of remark, until we arrived at the Sacramento river, in California, about one hundred and fifty miles above the bay of St. Francisco. Here, we were just on the point of encamping, when we were surprised by the sudden appearance, of several hundred Indians, who appeared to have been advised of our approach, and to have remained there, in ambush, with a view of attacking us, upon our arrival. Upon observing our peculiarly unfavorable position, I immediately altered my purpose, and directed four of the men, to take the women and children, as well as the horses, into the plains, and there remain. Myself, and the residue of the party, dismounted, and at the same time, turned our horses loose, which were also driven into the plains, while we held our position, for the purpose of receiving the enemy, whose numbers, during this time, had increased to about four hundred. They continued to advance, with most terrific and frantic yells, which together with their fiendish gestures, and demoniac grins, too clearly indicated their hostile designs. They now rapidly advanced, with increased yelling, gesticulating, and grinning, as though mere frantic gesticulations, wild noises, and demoniac grins, constituted irresistible weapons of warfare. They were now, within about thirty yards of us, and every moment seemed to indicate, nothing but an immediate attack, yet, as it was possible, that I might mistake their design, I paused for a few moments; but every moment only confirmed our suspicions; every moment showed most conclusively, that they were preparing for a desperate and deathlike attack. Still, hoping to deter them from their hostile purpose, I discharged a gun, in the open air, upon which, they all fell to the ground, while, at the same time, the chief was heard, haranguing them, at the top of his voice, while the men were everywhere seen, stringing their bows, and preparing for the charge. They were now rising, to make their deadly onset; the arrows from their rear, were already falling thickly among, and around us; there could be no further doubt, as to their designs, nor could there be any further delay; we fired, and fourteen of them fell, victims to their own ignorance and insolence. The residue now fled, in every direction, taking refuge behind trees, shrubs, and in ravines; but they continued to throw their arrows in increased numbers, and with increased violence, for about two hours, when finally, from some cause, their fury and violence were abated. Our men had, in the mean time, cut them off occasionally, as they would venture to emerge, from their temporary hiding places. Their loss was about twenty killed, besides many, who were mortally wounded, and whom we saw, either crawling away, upon the ground, or being dragged away by their friends.

Now finding, that they were inclined to abandon the contest, we proceeded to make our arrangements, to join that portion of our party, which remained in the plains; but, as we commenced our march, they renewed their charge, which they continued, until they arrived at the point, where the attack was made, and where the ground was still strewed with the dead. Upon arriving at this place, and perceiving for the first time, that their companions in arms, were actually dead; they commenced a most tremendous howling and yelling, which plainly indicated that this was the first knowledge, which they had, of the desolating ravages, that death had made in their ranks. This was further evinced, from their throwing down their bows and arrows, and falling upon the dead bodies, of their companions, and their most piteous howling and lamentation, with which they now rent the air. They paid no further attention to us, but continued to howl and yell most furiously, falling upon their dead, and pulling and hauling them about, in every direction, evidently, so utterly confused, that they knew not what they did; entirely insensible, of all surrounding circumstances. Perceiving their indisposition to molest us further, we now left them, when their howlings and lamentations increased, to such an extent, that they were distinctly heard, at the distance of three miles.

We traveled that evening, but about five or six miles, from the "field of battle," where we encamped with the strictest regard, to our successful defence, in case of an attack, which we had some grounds to anticipate. As fortune would have it, however, we were not attacked; but upon examining the country, in the vicinity of our camp, we found that they had, during the night, approached within a few hundred rods of us, in increased numbers, and clearly, with the view of attacking us; but upon perceiving our peculiarly favorable position, and profiting by the sore and deadly chastening, which they had so recently received, they no doubt, thought it the part of prudence, if not of bravery, to abandon their dangerous enterprise. So concluding, they left us, and in the morning, we left them, to enjoy their degraded solitude, sincerely hoping, never to be so unfortunate, as to meet again, any where this side of eternity; and no doubt, they had as little anxiety, to renew our acquaintance.

We, afterwards, neither met with them, nor any other hostile Indians, but continued our journey, without any serious difficulty or interruption, other than the loss, for the time being, of two of our men, who were lost, and absent from the party, for several days, without ammunition, and hence, without food; but after having suffered extremely, both from hunger and thirst, they both arrived, on the fourth or fifth day, in the settlements of California. One of them arrived at Capt. Sutter's fort, on the Sacramento, and the other, at a farm about forty miles above that place, about the same time, that the main body of the party, arrived at the Sacramento, opposite New Helvetia. The whole company, received every possible attention, from all the foreigners in California, and especially, from Capt. Sutter, who rendered every one of the party, every assistance in his power; and it really appeared, to afford him the greatest delight, to be thus enabled, to render important aid, to citizens of his former, adopted country. All those who went with me to California, as well as all other foreigners, who are residing there, are extremely delighted with the country; and determined to remain there, and make California the future home, not only of themselves, but also, of all their friends, and relatives, upon whom, they can possibly prevail, to exchange the sterile hills, bleak mountains, chilling winds, and piercing cold, of their native lands, for the deep, rich and productive soil, and uniform, mild and delightful climate, of this unparalleled region. This delightful country, will form the subject of several successive chapters, which it is believed, will fully show, that the casual allusions, heretofore made to this country, are, by no means, mere gratuitous exaggerations.

Chapter 8

A DESCRIPTION OF UPPER CALIFORNIA

Having conducted the reader to California, I will now proceed to give a brief description, of that highly important country, which is latterly, so justly attracting the attention, of the various civilized powers of the world. From the extremely narrow limits of this small work, I am compelled, to confine my remarks, entirely to Upper California, notwithstanding, both Upper, and Lower California, are properly, and naturally united, and have always been, so considered, for governmental, and other purposes; but to treat of both those countries, would extend this description, far beyond, either of my original or present purpose; I shall, therefore, content myself, with giving a description of the former alone. The former, is selected in preference to the latter, because of its greater extent, both of territory and of population; and because of its being that portion of the Californias, to which, the attention, not only of the enterprising emigrants, but also, that of the avaricious and jealous powers, of the civilized world, are now being turned, with high hopes, either of its present, or ultimate acquisition.

Upper California is a Mexican province or state, situated on the Pacific Ocean, between the forty-second, and thirty-second parallels of north latitude. It is bounded on the east, by the Cordilleras mountains, which are a continuation, of the Rocky mountain range; on the south, by Sonora, the gulf of California, and Lower California; on the west, by the Pacific ocean; and on the north, by Oregon, or the forty second parallel, of north latitude. It is six hundred miles in extent, from north to south, and about eight hundred miles, from east to west; having a superficies of about 480,000 square miles; more then four times as large as Great Britain; twice as large as France; and equal to twelve states, as large as that of Ohio.

It is naturally divided, into two great sections or divisions, by the California mountains, which together with the Cordilleras, and the Klamet mountains, constitute the only mountain ranges, of this country. The Cordilleras mountains run very nearly north and south, the whole extent of the country, ranging generally, from six hundred, to a thousand miles from the coast. Like the Rocky mountains, in Oregon, they are generally covered perpetually with snow. This range is, also, of extraordinary altitude, and has many, very elevated peaks, which are from ten to twenty thousand feet, above the level of the sea. Several eligible passes, or gaps, are also found, in this range, the most important of which, is that in the vicinity of Santa Fe, near the latitude 34° north. There is already very considerable passing and re-passing through this gap, which is no doubt, destined to increase, very much as the emigration increases to that country. The chief emigration will, however, undoubtedly, always be through the great southern pass, near latitude 42° north, which was alluded to, in the description of Oregon. All this range is, for the most part, entirely sterile and unproductive, producing nothing but low shrubs of pine and cedar, the prickly-pear and wormwood; amidst, and in the immediate vicinity, of the mountains, however, there are numerous small, but extremely, fertile valleys, as well as many elevated plains and prairies, which abound with vegetation. Upon, and in the vicinity, of the various streams, heading in this range, very good timber is also found, in sufficient quantities, for all ordinary purposes.

The California mountains are a continuation of the Cascade, or Presidents' range, of Oregon; their general course is also nearly north and south, ranging, usually, from two, to four hundred miles from the coast, and terminating near the head of the gulf of California, at latitude 32 deg. north. This range is much less elevated, than the Cordilleras or Rocky mountains, yet, it has several very elevated peaks, many of which are from ten to fourteen thousand feet, above the level of the sea. There are several very easy, natural passes, through this range also, the principal of which, and that through which the chief emigration will eventually pass, is near latitude 40 deg. north, through which, it is said, load-wagons may now be driven, without serious interruption. There is also another, near latitude 38 deg. north, through which, the chief trade in the northern part of the country, has been carried on, as the more northern pass has not, until quite recently, been known. This pass at latitude 38 deg. north, affords a very eligible route for wagons, but it will never become as extensive a thoroughfare, as that at latitude 40 deg. north, as that is in a direct route, from the great southern pass, in the Rocky mountains. But the pass near latitude 38 deg. north, is of the utmost importance, as it affords the means of intercommunication, between the two great sections, lying east and west of the California mountains. Besides these two passes, this range has another also, near latitude 34 deg. north, through which, the Santa Fe traders and others, annually pass, and which, not only connects the two great valleys, which lie on the east and west sides of the California mountains, but it also affords a great thoroughfare, by which the southern emigrants will eventually, travel by hundreds and thousands. The California mountains are much more fertile, then the Cordilleras or Rocky mountains, which is evidenced, by their being generally covered with a great variety of vegetation, as well as by their affording, in many places, a great abundance of good timber. This range is also interspersed with innumerable limited valleys, elevated plains and prairies, which abound with both vegetation and timber, of most luxuriant growth. The Klamet range was described, in a former page, in the description of Oregon, as commencing at the Rocky mountains, at latitude 42 deg. north, and running in a direction, west southwest to the coast, at latitude 41 deg. north. This range has numerous spurs, of small extent, which are usually covered with the grasses, and various other kinds of vegetation, as well as a growth of small timber, while the principal range is, generally, entirely sterile. It is also thickly interspersed with small, though extremely productive valleys, all of which, are well timbered, and well watered; and like the Cascade range, it also has several very high peaks, some of which are covered with perpetual snow. There is but one eligible pass in this range, which is found near latitude 41 deg. 30 min. north, and longitude 117 deg. west from Greenwich, through which wagons can be driven, with very little inconvenience. This pass is destined to become of great importance, both to Oregon and California, in facilitating intercommunication and commerce, between the two countries.

Besides these distinct ranges of mountains, there are several others, which, in many places, intersect the country in various directions, all of which, however, may be traced as spurs of the ranges before described. Some of them, and especially, those found between the California, and the Cordilleras or Rocky mountains, have been thought, by some, to constitute a distinct range: but, upon a more particular examination, they will be found to be mere spurs, of the ranges last mentioned. These, like the main ranges to which they belong, also have high peaks, or elevations, many of which, rise considerably above the snow line, which is here found to be about seven thousand feet above the level of the sea. Here, as in Oregon, wherever you are, you are always in view of some of those extraordinary conical elevations, which are always covered with snow, several thousand feet deep; but there are much fewer of them here, than in Oregon. Besides these snow-capped, conical elevations, there are several others, which are alike conical in form, but which do not rise above the snow line. The highest and principal of these, are the three butes, as they are called, which are situated near latitude 39 deg. north, and about one hundred and fifty miles east, from the coast. They are cones in form, rising about five thousand feet above the level of the sea; and being entirely isolated, they serve as great land marks for the mountaineer, and emigrant. In a clear day, they are frequently seen, at a distance of fifty or sixty miles, by persons in the valley; but by persons, upon the adjacent mountains, they are not unfrequently seen, even at eighty or ninety miles.

Here we cannot avoid observing some of the peculiarities, of this very extraordinary country. We find it almost entirely walled in, by stupendous natural walls, which are perfectly impregnable and impassable, everywhere, except at those natural gateways or gaps. These gaps appear to have been designed, by nature, to enhance the importance of this, otherwise important and valuable country, by affording easy intercommunication, and facilitating trade and commerce with all the surrounding country. The great southern pass in the Rocky mountains, near latitude 42 deg. north, connects this country with the United States; that near latitude 34 deg. north, connects it with Texas; that near latitude 41 deg. 30 min. north, connects it with Oregon: and the three gaps in the California mountains, connect the two great sections or valleys, at the most important points; and thus, not only gives this country, ready and easy access to, and commerce with, the family of republics; but also, renders intercommunication easy, and transportation cheap, from one portion of the country to another. But these are not all the advantages, to be derived from the peculiarities of this country. These natural walls, which almost entirely inclose the whole country, afford it perfect security against an invading foe, from those quarters. Nature, as if designing to ensure more perfect security to that country has, in erecting the great walls, which inclose it, heaped mountains, upon mountains, whose heads, now mingle, with the clouds above; but lest these even might not afford sufficient security, they are thickly, deeply covered, with perpetual snow, or eternal sand, either of which, is equally forbidding, to the approach of man or beast.

Having given this brief description of the mountains, I will next notice the various rivers, the most important of which, is the Colorado of the west, or Green river. This great river is to California, what the Columbia is to Oregon, the Mississippi to the United States, or the Amazon, to South America. It rises near latitude 43 deg. north, its head waters interlocking with those of the Platte; its general course is about south, southwest: to its emboguing, at the Gulf of California, near latitude 32 deg. north. Following its meanders, its length is about twelve hundred miles, about two thirds of which distance; its course is very serpentine, and much interrupted, by innumerable rapids, cascades and deep chasms or channels. Its vast torrents of water, rushing and lashing over the former, foaming and dashing through the latter, make the very welkin ring, sending their misty spray in volumes to the clouds. As might be expected these repeated interruptions almost entirely destroy its navigation, for about eight hundred miles. The remainder of its distance is much less interrupted, but its navigation is also here seriously interrupted, with the exception of about one hundred miles, from its mouth, which are without interruption, and which are navigable for vessels of two hundred tons burthen. The greater portion of this river from its source, lies through a very broken, mountainous country, breaking, through lofty mountains, pouring over high cliffs, down vast perpendicular cataracts, and into deep chasms, with perpendicular basaltic walls, five hundred feet in height. The latter part of its distance, for four or five hundred miles, is through alternate rolling hills, undulating plains, and beautiful valleys and prairies. All the different tributaries, of the northern portion of this river, water an extremely mountainous, sterile, and entirely worthless region, with the exception of the limited, though numerous valleys, which are interspersed among the mountains. But the various tributaries of the southern portion of this river, water many extensive plains, beautiful prairies, and fertile valleys. Its tributaries from the north, in the southern part, interlock with those of the Sacramento, and they water much the most extensive and fertile regions. The Colorado and its tributaries, water much of the northern portion, most of the southern, and all the eastern portion of Upper California. The tide sets up this river about one hundred miles, the extent to which it is navigable, and very much aids its navigation to that extent. Many portions of this river, its entire extent, will be found to be navigable for short distances, and although it will require repeated, and in many places, extensive portages, yet it will be found serviceable, for purposes of navigation, in all the different portions of the country, through which it passes.

The Sacramento is the next river in importance, and although, it is a less stream than the Colorado, yet in many respects, it is even more important than the Colorado, especially as it waters all of the most fertile, and extensive valleys of that country, and as it empties its vast torrents of water, into the great bay of St. Francisco. It rises in the California mountains, by two distinct heads, the one of which, is near latitude 41° north, and the other is near latitude 38° north. The course of the former of these, to their confluence, is south southwest, and that of the latter, is west by north. Their junction, is near latitude 40° north, and near longitude 117° west, above which, in their course, they receive innumerable small tributaries, both from the north and south, which swell their waters to immense volumes. From the junction of these branches, the general course of the river to its mouth, is south west, receiving in its course, a river, which I shall call Dry river, from the north, and Feather river, the American fork, and the Tulare from the south. Its length is about eight hundred miles, following its meanders, about three hundred miles of which, are navigable without interruption, for vessels and steamboats; and it may be rendered navigable, to a much greater extent, with very little expense. By actual survey, it has been determined to be navigable for vessels of two hundred tons, about one hundred and fifty miles from its mouth. From the confluence of its two branches, to its mouth, it waters a vastly extensive, and fertile valley, while above that point, each of the branches pour their waters, alternately over rapids, down cascades, through mountains; and winding their way amid undulating plains, rolling prairies, and fertile, though small valleys, they finally contribute largely, in forming the great Sacramento. The tide flows up this river, about one hundred and fifty miles, which adds much to its safe and convenient navigation. Dry river rises in the Klamet range, near latitude 41° north, whence it runs southeast, about thirty miles, then forming a semi circle, it runs nearly parallel with the Sacramento, but in the opposite direction, when finally, it empties into that river, near latitude 40° north. Its length is about one hundred and forty miles, including its meanders; it waters a large portion, of the great valley of the Sacramento, as well as several limited valleys, in the mountains, in which it has its source. Some portions of the country, immediately upon this river, are entirely sterile, being mere beds of sand and gravel; but they are comparatively, very small in extent. It is from the fact of its watering these sandy and dry sections, that I have deemed the name, Dry river appropriate. There are several other small streams, putting into the Sacramento, from the north, which also rise in the Klamet range, and enter the Sacramento, either by subterraneous mouths, or by percolation. There are others of these subterfluent streams, the waters of which, alternately sink below, and rise to the surface, all of which, enter into the Sacramento, or some lake, either at the surface, or through some cavernous entrance. There are many more of this kind of tributaries on the north, then on the south side of the Sacramento, and however extraordinary they may be, they are found to be most admirably adapted, to the purposes of irrigation.

The first tributary of the Sacramento, on the south side, which I shall notice, is the Feather river, which also rises in the California mountains, near latitude 38° north. Running thence, in a direction nearly northwest, it pursues a very serpentine course, through a most fertile region of country, and finally empties into the Sacramento, at latitude 39° 01' 45" north. Its length is about two hundred miles, fifty or sixty miles of which, will be found to be navigable, for steamboats, of light draught, the greater part of the year. This river, together with its various small tributaries, waters one of the most fertile and admirable regions, in California. It takes its name from the fact, of its being a place of general resort, for the various feathered tribes, which are said to congregate upon its waters, and in its immediate vicinity, in such immense numbers, that one person may, with very little difficulty, kill several hundreds in a very few hours. So numerous are they said to be, in fact, that, in their confused and conflicting bustling, they strew the earth with feathers for many miles up and down the stream, hence the Mexicans call it "rio de las Plumas," the river of Feathers. The next tributary of importance, on this side of the Sacramento, is the American fork, which rises in the California mountains, near latitude 37° north. Its general course is northwest, and its length about one hundred and fifty miles. It empties into the Sacramento at latitude 38° 46' 42" north, about one mile above New Helvetia. This river also waters a large portion of the valley of the Sacramento, as well as a rich, productive region in the vicinity of the mountains, consisting of elevated plains, rolling hills, and small, rich valleys. The American Fork, cannot be said to be navigable for any other crafts then canoes, boats and barges, and for those only during high water, though it is a most beautiful stream.

There is one other tributary emptying into the Sacramento from the south, which I shall notice when I shall have done with the Sacramento and its tributaries. The tributary here alluded to, is called the Tulare, which is the second river in importance, in all the northern portion of the country, and the third river in all California. It takes its rise in the California mountains, near latitude 36° north, and its general course is nearly northwest to its mouth, where it empties into the Sacramento, a few miles above the entrance of that river, into the bay of St. Francisco. Its length is about four hundred miles, two hundred of which, are navigable in ordinary stages of water, for steamboats of light draught, such for instance, as those which ply upon the Ohio and the Upper Mississippi rivers. This river also waters a vast extent, of the great California valley, as well as many rolling prairies, extensive plains, and that hilly and mountainous region, in which it takes its source. It also has numerous small tributaries, which water a great extent of fine, rich country, none of which, are of any importance for the purposes of navigation. Just below the conflux, of this river and the Sacramento, there is a large island, which is formed by the divergence and reunion of these rivers. This island is about four miles in length, and from its peculiar position, especially its contiguity to the mouths, of these great rivers, and the bay of St. Francisco, it will eventually, be found of great importance, although it is now considered entirely valueless.

There are several other streams, which empty into the bay of St. Francisco, both from the north and the south, none of which are navigable, but they are highly important, as they water all the country in the vicinity of that bay, which otherwise would be wholly worthless. There are also, several rivers of considerable importance, in the neighborhood of the coast, and which empty into the ocean, some of which, are also worthy of a brief notice. The principal of these is the Russian river, which has its source in the Klamet range, near latitude 41 deg. north, running thence, in a direction, about west southwest, to the coast, where it empties, near latitude 38° 55' 42" north. Its length is estimated at two hundred and twenty miles, of which, sixty or seventy miles are susceptible of steam boat navigation, the greater part of the residue, is navigable only for canoes and boats. The tide flows up this river about seventy miles, which will very much facilitate its navigation. An extremely mountainous and broken region, is watered by this river, yet there are several very extensive plains, as well as numerous small and fertile valleys, upon the main river and its various tributaries. There is also another river, in this portion of the country, of which, however, I have had occasion to speak, upon a former page, in describing the rivers of Oregon. It is the Klamet river, for a further description of which, the reader is referred to the description before given. The only remaining river in the vicinity of the coast, which I deem worthy of notice, is that which empties into the bay of Monterey, near latitude 37° north. It has its source in the California mountains, near latitude 36° north, thence pursues a course, about west by north, through alternate rolling prairies, fertile plains and valleys. It is about one hundred and fifty miles in length, no part of which can be said to be navigable, for any other crafts then boats, barges and canoes. The flow of the tide extends up this stream, about twenty miles, though not in such manner, as to facilitate its navigation.

The only river which remains to be noticed, is the great Bear river, which, although described as a river of Oregon, is properly, a river of California; but as I have described it sufficiently upon a former page, I shall here give it mere passing notice. It heads near latitude 42° north, and pursues a course, nearly west by south, to the great Salt lake, into which it flows, near latitude 41° north. Its length is about two hundred miles, no part of which, can properly be said to be navigable, otherwise then for boats and canoes. A large portion of the country watered by this river, is extremely mountainous and sterile, but the Bear river valley, through which it lies, is a vastly extensive valley, and many portions of it, possess more then ordinary fertility and productiveness. This river, as well as its valley, derives additional importance, from their proximity, in this great lake, which will, in the course of time, undoubtedly, become the nucleus of an extensive settlement, in the eastern section of both Oregon and California. From the best information which I have been able to obtain, in relation to this lake, its northern extremity extends very nearly to latitude 42° north, but not beyond it, from which it appears, that it is situated entirely in California. It is about two hundred and forty miles long, and averages from forty to sixty miles in width. Its waters are much more highly impregnated with salt, then those of the ocean. The country contiguous to this lake, in each direction, is generally sterile, but the surrounding country, in its vicinity, is usually rich, and highly productive.

The rise in the rivers of this country, like those of Oregon, is at different seasons of the year, in the different streams, depending upon the regions in which they have their sources. Those which rise in the California mountains, have their annual rise in the months of February and November. The rises are generally gradual, but they extend to a very great extent, rising very frequently, eighteen or twenty feet perpendicularly, and submerging much of the low country, in the vicinity of the mouths, of the different rivers, during the continuance of the high waters. The effect of this inundation is, however, rather favorable then otherwise, as all those sections of the country, which have been thus overflowed, produce a much more luxuriant growth of vegetation, than they would otherwise do, which continues perfectly green, presenting a large extent, of springly verdure, even in autumn, when the vegetation of most other portions, is dried and transformed, from the delightful green of May and June, to the natural hay of October. Hence it is, that these portions of the country, are here considered highly valuable, for the same reason, that similar portions of the country, are considered entirely worthless, in Oregon and elsewhere. In those rivers taking their rise in the Cordilleras or Rocky mountains, the overflow takes place here, as in Oregon, during the months of May and June, of each year. The annual rises, of all the rivers of this country, are to be attributed to the same cause, as stated upon another page, in reference to the rise of the rivers of Oregon. The water of all these rivers, like that of those of Oregon, are perfectly transparent, and pure, so much so, in truth, that the bottoms of the rivers, are, not unfrequently, seen thirty or forty feet beneath the surface of the water. They, from their extraordinary purity, possess very little or no fertilizing properties, hence the lands subject to their annual submersions, derive no additional fertility from them; and hence, they are benefited by the overflows, only by the accumulation of moisture, which however, in this arid region, is a very important consideration.

There are but very few islands, in the immediate neighborhood of the coast, yet there are three, which may perhaps, be found worthy of a partial description. St. Catalina is the principal of them, which is situated about fifteen miles from the coast, and near latitude 33 degrees and 40 min. north. Its greatest length is about thirty miles, from east to west and its width twelve miles, from north to south, giving an area of about three hundred and sixty miles. The next of these in importance, is Santa Cruz, which is about sixty miles north from St. Catalina, and nearly the same distance from the coast. Its length being twelve miles, and its width six miles; it has a superficies of seventy-two miles. The other island alluded to, is St. Clement, which is still less in extent, then Santa Cruz, having a surface only, of about twenty four square miles. All of these islands possess a most productive and fertile soil, but they, usually, present an extremely broken, and mountainous surface. They are all said to be most admirably adapted, both to the purposes of grazing and agriculture. Abounding with game of various kinds, and especially the fur-bearing animals, they are places of the annual resort, of hunters and trappers. Each of these has an ample supply of good timber, and fresh water, as well as several very good and convenient harbors. These islands are, as yet, used merely as repositories of smuggled goods, for which purpose, they are most admirably suited, and extensively occupied, but they will, eventually, no doubt, be converted into most delightful, and admirable residences, for retiring Selkirks and broken-down politicians.

As the face of the country is merely alluded to, in the description of the mountains and rivers, it may, perhaps, be advisable here to give a further description of the surface, of each section. The greater part of the Western section, consists of vastly extensive plains and valleys; but it also has many sections of high, rolling hills, and less elevated mountains, besides the main ranges of mountains before described. The principal valley of this section is, the great valley of the Sacramento and its various tributaries: it extends from the base of the Klamet mountains, nearly to latitude 36 deg. north and from an elevated range of country, upon the coast, entirely to the California mountains. This valley, although extending in each direction, as above stated, does not include the entire country, within those limits, but it comprises much the greater part, of all that portion of country. Within the same portion of country, however, there are several ranges of high lands, consisting, in many places, of high swells and hills, and in others, of elevated plains and rolling prairies. About two thirds of all the country, comprised within the above limits, is properly contained, in the valley of the Sacramento, and its tributaries, which is much the most fertile portion, of the same extent, in all California. That portion of this valley, which lies immediately upon the Sacramento river, extends from its month, at the bay of St. Francisco, to the base of the California mountains, a distance of about four hundred miles, and averages about thirty miles in width, on the north side, and about fifty miles on the south side. That portion of it, lying on the Tulare river, generally averages about twenty miles, on each side of the river, to the base of the California mountains, a distance of about three hundred miles, from its confluence with the Sacramento. Besides these great valleys, which constitute the greater portion, of what is called the Sacramento valley, there are various valleys, upon all the different tributaries of the Sacramento, which also form part of that valley. All of these valleys possess a soil, which is scarcely paralleled, for fertility and productiveness, which, however, will more fully appear, from what will be said in reference to the soil, and productions. South of the Sacramento valley, there are also numerous valleys, of very considerable extent, both upon all the various smaller streams, which empty into the ocean, and the various tributaries of the Colorado of the west. All the valleys, in the southern portion of this section, are equally as fertile and productive, as those of the Sacramento. That portion, however, consists chiefly of plains and prairies, which are also very productive, covered with a great variety of vegetation, of extraordinary growth.

The Eastern section also, has several very extensive valleys, the largest of which, are found upon the various tributaries of the Colorado, many of which, average from fifty to a thousand square miles in extent; but the valleys of this section; are comparatively small, though extremely fertile and productive. Through all portions of this section, there is a much greater proportion of elevated and broken country, then in the Western section. High, rolling prairies, elevated plains, and moderately elevated, hilly regions, are found in all the various portions of this section, which yield the greatest variety of vegetation, of most luxuriant growth. The valley of the great Bear river, which is also situated in this section, is a valley of very considerable extent, and of more than ordinary fertility, but that portion of this great valley, in the immediate neighborhood of the great Salt lake, is entirely sterile and unproductive, as is all that portion of the country contiguous to that lake. Upon the coast of the whole extent of Upper California, from north to south, there is an elevated range of country, consisting chiefly, of hills, high rolling, broken prairies, and elevated plains. Both the Western and Eastern sections are, in many places, intersected in various directions, with spurs of the different ranges of mountains, and ranges of elevated, broken and hilly country; but much less of this kind of country, is found in the Western, than in the Eastern section. As to give a particular description, of each portion of this country, would much transcend the limits of this work, and my original purpose, I shall leave this branch of the subject, and proceed to the consideration of those of more practical importance.

The bays and harbors next claim our attention, and that deserving of the first and principal notice, is the bay of St. Francisco, which is situated at latitude 38 deg. north, and

extends about forty miles into the interior, in a direction about
north, north east from its entrance. Its waters are securely
confined within its bed, by an iron-bound coast, which is generally composed of solid basaltic rock. The country adjacent
to this bay, is a very broken and hilly region, but very fertile,
producing oats, clover, and the like, with much profusion.
The entrance of this bay, from the Pacific, is about one mile
wide, upon each side of which, is a high ledge of basaltic
rock, about two hundred feet above the surface of the water.
From these points, on each side of the entrance, the bay gradually expands, to eight or ten miles, in extent, from north to
south, and about twelve miles, from east to west. At the
extreme eastern portion, of this bay, thus formed, its hilly and
rocky banks gradually contract, so as to leave a space, only of
about two miles, between the rocky, hilly shores, which thus,
forms a second entrance, into another bay, of greater extent,
then that just described. At this entrance, the high, rolling,
basaltic banks, again gradually diverge, about ten miles, when
they again contract, leaving a space of about one mile
between them, which is about eight miles from the entrance,
last mentioned, and thus, another spacious bay is formed. A
third and more extensive bay is formed in a similar manner,
the eastern extremity of which, is about forty miles eastward,
from the coast, where it receives the Sacramento. The bay last
alluded to, is twelve miles in extent, from east to west, and
about fifteen from north to south, and like the others
described, it affords the most extensive and secure anchorage.
From this description of the great bay of St. Francisco, it is
seen, that instead of one bay, there are three vastly extensive
bays, which, however, are all connected, forming the bay of
St. Francisco. There are several small islands in this bay, the
largest of which, is situated on the north side of the first bay,
within full view of the entrance, from the ocean. It is about
five miles long, and three in width, and has a very rough and

broken surface, which is covered here and there with timber, of a small growth, and an abundance of vegetation. It is admirably suited to the purposes of grazing, as it not only produces the various grasses, and oats and clover, in great profusion but also, a great abundance of good fresh water. Large herds of fine cattle, are now kept upon it, by a Spaniard, who resides in the lower part of the country.

The next large island alluded to, is located on the south side of the same bay, fronting the town of Yerba Buena. It is also depastured, but by herds of wild goats, which have been placed, upon it, by a foreigner, who resides at Yerba Buena. Besides these islands, there are several others in this bay, which appear to be composed entirely of basaltic rock, and hence, produce no kind of vegetation, but are places of resort for the innumerable fowls of prey, which abound in that region. One of these rocky islands, is situated directly in front of the entrance, from the ocean, and is about one fourth of a mile in diameter. The contiguity of this island to the entrance, and its immediate opposition to that point, renders it very important, as a few guns planted upon it, and well manned, would with all ease, perfectly command the entrance. But facilities for commanding this entrance, are not wanting, for a few guns upon either side of it, would sink a whole fleet, that should attempt a hostile ingression. Outside of this bay, also, and within a few miles of the entrance, is another vast rocky island, rearing its ancient and majestic head, several hundred feet above the lashing surf, and roaring billows below, as if designed by nature, to point out the entrance, into that great bay of bays. A more admirable and advantageous position, for a light-house, can scarcely be conceived of, and there is but little doubt, but that those who visit St. Francisco, two years hence, instead of seeing a massive, dark rock looking out upon the mighty deep, at the month of that bay, they will there behold, a brilliant luminary of the ocean. From what has already been said, it must be apparent to all, that there are few bays, if any, in any part of the world, which surpass this, for security of harbor, and extent of anchorage. It has been well said, that "in this bay, all the fleets and navies of the whole world, could ride, in perfect safety." This bay alone, would answer all the commercial purposes of California, in all time to come. There is ample water at the·entrance, for vessels of the largest class, whether during the ebb or flow of the tide, which, in this bay, rises about eighteen feet perpendicular. All things being considered, I am of the opinion, that a harbor can not be found, equal in all respects, to that of the bay of St. Francisco. It is of the greatest importance, not only to California, but also to all commercial governments of the world, whose ships of war, merchant ships, or whalers, cruise in the Pacific, as it affords them the most extensive anchorage, and secure harbor, which is surrounded by one of the most fertile countries, in the known world, where all necessary ship supplies, may be obtained, in any abundance, and upon the most favorable terms.

The bay of Monterey is the next in importance, but its chief importance is derived from its central, and otherwise peculiarly advantageous position, and not from its extent of anchorage, or security of harbor. It is situated at latitude 37 deg. north and is about twenty miles in extent, and semicircular in form, affording tolerably extensive anchorage, and secure harbor against all winds, excepting those from the west, and north east which drive almost directly into the bay, rendering the harbor very insecure, as against those winds. As an evidence of this fact, a vessel was stranded there, a few years since, and the wreck now lies upon the beach, within a few hundred yards, of the ordinary anchorage. I was informed that the captain of this vessel, finding a wreck inevitable, headed directly upon the beach, under full sail, which, of course, had a tendency to decide the matter as to a wreck, as well as to produce some rather unpleasant concussions. In this bay, as in St. Francisco, the tide rises about eighteen feet, and there is also ample water, at the entrance of this bay, as at that for the reception of vessels of any class, either during the ebb or flow of the tide. The entrance is also, very easily commanded, but it is by no means as advantageously situated in that respect, as that of the bay of St. Francisco. It is the opinion, however, of many, that the entrance of this bay, can be as effectually fortified, as that of any other, with the appropriate expense. The chief importance attached to this bay is derived from the tact, of its being contiguous to the seat of government, which will undoubtedly be the case, until there shall be some enlargement of the state, either upon the north or the south. The bay of St. Diego is also, a bay of very considerable extent, which is situated near latitude 33 deg. north, affording very commodious, and safe anchorage. It is about twenty miles in extent, from its entrance to its extreme eastern portion, and it affords extensive anchorage, and safe harbor, against all winds, excepting those blowing from the south, and the southwest. This bay is also vastly important, from its local position, being in the extreme southern portion of the country, for without it, all that part of the country would be entirely excluded, from all commercial advantages. Besides the principal bays here described, there are several others, which, however, are of much less importance, though perhaps, of sufficient importance, to require a brief notice. Of these there are but two, which I shall notice, the one of which, is situated in the extreme northern, and the other in the extreme southern portion, of the country, the former is called Bodago, and the latter Colorado. Bodago is near latitude 40 deg north, and is about twelve miles in extent, but the entrance is rather difficult, and the anchorage unsafe, and, at times, dangerous in the extreme. This bay, however, together with the harbor, formed at the mouth of the Klamet river, before described, will afford ample commercial facilities, for the extreme northern portion. The Colorado is situated at the mouth of the Colorado of the west, near latitude 32 deg. north; it is very spacious, affording extensive and secure anchorage for ships of any class, sheltering them, perfectly, against all winds, excepting those which blow directly from the south. This gives a brief view, of the facilities for extensive commerce, in Upper California, which are seldom, if ever, surpassed.

Chapter 9

A DESCRIPTION OF WESTERN CALIFORNIA

The soil is extremely varied, not only in the two sections, but also in the different portions of each section; the hills and mountains being entirely sterile and valleys and plains extremely fertile. That of the valleys is vastly rich and productive, so much so in fact, that I think, I venture nothing when I say, that it is not only not surpassed, but that it is not even equaled. The deep, rich, alluvial soil of the Nile, in Egypt, does not afford a parallel. Remarks like these, I am aware, are apt to be considered as mere gratuitous assumptions; but to ascertain how far they are sustained by fact, the reader is referred to the sequel, especially that part of it, which treats of the productions, which it is believed, will not only convince him of their truth, but may, perhaps, induce him to indulge in assumptions and speculations, even more enlarged. The soil of the various valleys of the Western section, varies from a rich alluvial, to a deep, black, vegetable loam, upon strata of sand, gravel, clay or trap rock. That of the plains, is, principally, a deep, brown, vegetable loam, or decomposed basalt, with a substratum, of stiff clay, or gravel and sand. And that of the hills, is chiefly, a brown, sandy loam, or a loose, gravelly soil. The mountains and most of the more elevated hills, are generally entirely barren, and consist principally of primitive rocks, such as talcon slate, and other argillaceous stone, with hornblend and granite. The less elevated hills consist, chiefly, of basalt, slate and marble. Gypsum and a kind of white clay, are also found, in many places; the latter of which, is very abundant, and which is used extensively by the inhabitants, for the purpose of whitewashing their dwelling houses, both externally and internally. It is also used for the purpose of cleansing, as a substitute for soap, and for this purpose, it is found to be most admirably adapted. It may be estimated, that about two thirds, of all the Western section, are cultivable lands, and that three fourths of it, including the arable lands, are pasturable lands, to each of which purposes, the whole section, to the extent, and in the proportions stated, is peculiarly suited. The remaining of sand or clay; and that of the hills, is usually, a light, brown, vegetable earth, having a substratum of gravel, sand or clay. The mountains, and hills, like those of the Western section, are for the most part, entirely sterile, yet as before remarked, there are many portions of the hills and mountains even, that are tolerably productive. There is a much greater variety of soil in this, than in the Western section; in one day's ride, you may pass over every possible variety of soil, from the most fertile, to the most barren and unproductive. The mountains are, generally, composed of talcon slate, granite, hornblend and other primitive rock, and the hills are, principally, composed of marble, limestone, basalt and slate. The white clay before spoken of, is also found in this section, in great abundance. The proportion of barren land, is much greater in this, than in the Western section. As nearly as I could ascertain, about one third, of the whole section, is susceptible of cultivation, while about two thirds, including the arable lands, are well suited to grazing purposes, and the remaining third, for extraordinary unfruitfulness, and entire destitution, of all fecundity, can be surpassed, only by some portions of Oregon, which are seldom, if ever, surpassed in worthlessness.

The information which I was able to acquire, does not afford me sufficient data, upon which to predicate any very accurate conclusions, in reference to the mineral resources of California; but sufficient investigations have been made, to determine that many portions, of the mountainous regions, abound with several kinds of minerals, such as gold, silver, iron, lead and coal, but to what extent, the extreme newness and unexplored state of the country, utterly preclude all accurate determination.

It is, however, reported in the city of Mexico, that some Mexicans have, recently discovered a section of country, in the extreme interior of California, which affords ample evidences, of the existence of both gold and silver ore, in greater or less quantities, for thirty leagues in extent. Since this report is so very extraordinary, and since it originated as above stated, the safest course would be, to believe but about half of it, and then, perhaps, we should believe too much. Dr. Sandels, a very able mineralogist, who had for some time been employed in his profession, by the government of Mexico, spent four or five months, in mineralogical investigation, in upper California. It was from this gentleman, that the above information was derived, hence it is entitled to implicit reliance.

The climate of the Western section, is that of perpetual spring, having no excess of heat or cold, it is the most uniform and delightful. The mean temperature, during the year, is about 61° Fahrenheit; that of the spring is 66°; that of the summer 70°; that of the autumn 67°; and of the winter is 61° Fahrenheit. The mean temperature of the warmest month is 74°, and that of the coldest month, is 48° Fahrenheit. This statement is not designed to apply to the entire Western section, for in the extreme northern portion, snow sometimes falls, but it very seldom lies more then two or three hours, always disappearing at the rising of the sun; but even here, running water never freezes, nor does standing water ever freeze, thicker then common window glass. In the southern portion, and even as far north as latitude 38° north, snow, frost and ice are unknown. An equability of temperature is found, in all portions of this section, which very few portions of the world afford, none, perhaps, unless it be some portions of Italy. In many portions of this section, immediately upon the coast, it is warmer in the winter season, than in the summer. This is attributable to the fact, of the winds blowing regularly from the north or northwest, during the summer, and from the south, southwest or southeast, during the winter, which also accounts for the extraordinary mildness of the climate, during all seasons of the year. Compared with the climate, in the same latitude, on the east side of the Rocky mountains, the difference is almost incredible. It is milder on the Pacific coast, in latitude 42° north, then it is in 32° north on the Atlantic coast, being a difference of more then ten degrees of temperature, in the same latitude. No fires are required, at any season of the year, in parlors, offices or shops, hence fuel is never required, for any other than culinary purposes. Many kinds of vegetables are planted, and gathered, at any and every season of the year, and of several kinds of grain, two crops are grown annually. Even in the months of December and January, vegetation is in full bloom, and all nature wears a most cheering, and enlivening aspect. It may be truly said of this country, that "December is as pleasant as May." The remarks here made, in reference to the mildness, and uniformity of the climate, are applicable only to the valleys and plains, for the mountains present but one eternal winter. Hence it is seen, that you may here enjoy perennial spring, or perpetual winter at your option. You may in a very few days, at any season of the year, pass from regions of eternal verdure to those of perpetual ice and snow, in doing which, you pass through almost every possible variety of climate, from that of the temperate, to that of the frigid zone.

Here it is rather colder than would appear from this, while in the extreme southern portion, it is rather warmer. It is applicable particularly, to the latitude of 37° north, though very little difference will be found, in all the various portions of this section, which will be seen from the following statement. In the extreme northern portion, part of this section, which is the extremely mountainous portion, is noted for its extraordinary barrenness and sterility. The soil of the valleys of the Eastern section, is in all respects, similar to that of the valleys, of the Western section; that of the plains is a deep brown loam, with a subsoil.

The rainy season is, generally, confined to the winter months, during which time, rains fall very frequently, though not incessantly. During all this season, the weather is alternately rainy and clear; one third, perhaps, of the whole season is rainy, and the residue is clear and delightful weather. The rainy season here, although it is confined to a portion of the same season of the year, as that in Oregon, yet it differs, in many respects, from the rainy season, in that country. There, the rains are almost incessant, but slight, while here they are much less frequent, but pour down in torrents. The only rain, which falls in this country, is during the rainy season, during the residue of the year, scarcely a drop of rain ever falls; but there have been a few instances of its falling, as late as April and May, though this is very seldom. In addition to the moisture accumulated by the earth, during the winter season, the vegetation always receives additional moisture from the dews, during the summer. It would seem that the inhabitants of a country, watered only by the rains of three months, and the dews of the residue of the year, must suffer intensely, from the effects of such continued drought, but such is not the case in this country. The extraordinary mildness of the climate, together with the falling of the rains, causes the vegetation to put forth early in the month of December, and to mature in the spring, or very early in the summer. So it is of wheat, and other grains, being sown in November or December, they are matured in the spring, or early in the summer, and before they are affected by the drought. In many portions of the country, the vegetation, so far from being injuriously affected by the drought, is seen in full bloom, during every month of the year. This remark, however, only applies to a certain species of vegetation, which perhaps, derives a sufficiency of moisture from the dews. It is true, that crops of wheat, corn, and the like, are much effected by the drought, whenever there has been a deficiency of rain, during the previous rainy season. When rains fall in abundance during the winter, it is held as a sure prelude, and in fact, an assurance, of an abundant crop, the ensuing summer; but, if there is an insufficiency of rain, crops are less abundant. Seasons which are preceded by a rainy season, which produces a deficiency of rain, are called dry seasons. These are said to occur, generally, once in four or five years, yet latterly, two dry seasons have occurred, in succession. Although the crops of the dry seasons, are much less abundant than those of the ordinary seasons, yet, as will more fully appear, upon a subsequent page, the crops even of a dry season, are much better here, than they are at any time, in Oregon, or even in most of the States.

The climate of the Eastern section is much more variable, than that of the Western section, and is subject to much greater excesses, of both heat and cold. This is attributed to its contiguity to, and its being surrounded almost entirely by, the various mountains, many of which are covered with perpetual snows. A further reason is found, in the fact of its being cut off almost entirely, from the pacific influence of the ocean. The mean temperature of this section, is about 58 deg. Fahrenheit, judging from such facts as I was able to collect, upon this subject, for we have not the same data, in reference to the climate of this section. Snow sometimes falls in some portions of this section, especially in the vicinity of the mountains, but it very seldom lies, more than two or three days. Running water never freezes, only in the immediate neighborhood of the mountains, nor does standing water ever freeze, in portions remote from the mountains, more than the eighth of one inch in thickness. There are numerous valleys in this section, which have as mild winters, as do any portions of the Western section. Many portions are also found here, as in the Western section, where snow, frost, and ice, have never been known. These facts are ascertained, from the Indians and trappers, who inhabit those regions. This section is also, subject to the influence of the southern winds, which prevail during the winter, as its southern extremity, is not entirely walled in by mountains, as it is elsewhere, but it is much lees affected by either, the southern or northern winds, than the Western section. The excessive heat, which would otherwise prevail here, is vastly diminished, by the strong north and north westerly breezes, which pour in the cold atmosphere from those regions, and thereby supplying the vacuum, which is created by the heated prairies and plains below. The snowy mountains also, have a great tendency to diminish the heat of summer, and they also, vastly increase, the cold of the winter. The rainy season of this section, is not unlike, that of the Western section, in any other respect, than perhaps, that of its being of longer continuance. During this season, however, it rains much more frequently here, than in the Western section. It is true, that this section does not possess as mild and uniform a climate, as the Western section, but it possesses a much greater variety of climates, and temperatures. In the lower valleys is summer, in the more elevated valleys is spring; upon the elevated plains and prairies is autumn; and upon the mountains is winter. There are many portions in which, at any season of the year, you may travel in one day, through every degree of temperature, from 120 deg. to minus 18 deg. Fahrenheit. Here, perpetual summer, is in the midst of unceasing winter; perennial spring, and never failing autumn, stand side by side; and towering snow-clad mountains forever look down upon eternal verdure.

From what has been said, in reference to the climate, very correct conclusions may be readily drawn in reference to the adaptation of this country, to the promotion of health. There are few portions of the world, if any, which are so entirely exempt from all febrifacient causes. There being no low, marshy regions, the noxious miasmatic effluvia, so common in such regions, is here, nowhere found. The purity of the atmosphere, is most extraordinary, and almost incredible. So pure is it, in fact, that flesh of any kind may be hung for weeks together, in the open air, and that, too, in the summer season, without undergoing putrefaction. The Californians prepare their meat for food, as a general thing, in this manner; in doing which, no salt is required, yet it is sometimes used, as a matter of preference. The best evidence, however, that can be adduced, in reference to the superior health of this country, is the fact, that disease of any kind is very seldom known, in any portion of the country. Cases of fever, of any kind, have seldom been known, any where on the coast, but bilious intermittent fevers, prevail to a very small extent, in some portions of the interior, yet they are of so extremely mild a type, that it is very seldom found necessary, to resort to medical aid. Persons attacked with these fevers, seldom adopt any other remedy, then that of abstaining a short time, from food, or going to the coast. The latter remedy is said to be infallible, and I am inclined to that opinion, from the fact that fevers are so seldom known, any where on the coast, and from one or two cases, that came under my own observation. The extraordinary health upon the coast, is, perhaps, attributable, in a great measure, to the effect of the exhilarating and refreshing sea-breezes, which, at all times, prevail in that vicinity. All foreigners, with whom I conversed, upon this subject, and who reside in that country, are unanimous and confident in the expression of the belief, that it is one of the most healthy portions of the world. From my own experience, and knowledge of the country, especially, of its entire exemption, from all the ordinary causes of disease, and the extraordinary purity of its atmosphere, I am clearly of the opinion, that there are very few portions of the world, which are superior, or even equal to this, in point of healthfulness, and salubrity of climate. While all this region, especially on the coast, is entirely exempt, from all febrific causes, it is also entirely free, from all sudden changes, and extreme variableness of climate, or other causes of catarrhal, or consumptive affections; hence, I cannot but think, that it is among the most favorable resorts in the known world, for invalids.

The productions will next engage our attention; and here, such facts will be adduced, as will, to some extent, at least, sustain the view taken upon another page, in reference to the extraordinary fertility of the soil. The productions of the Western section, will be found to differ very materially, from those of the Eastern. I shall first notice those of the Western section, at some length. The timber of this section is, generally, confined to the coast, the rivers and mountains; but there are many portions of the different valleys, off the rivers, which are well supplied with good timber. The largest and most valuable timber is found, upon the coast, where dense forests, in many places, are found, consisting of fir pine, cedar, "red wood," (a species of cedar,) spruce, oak, ash and poplar. Much of this grows to an enormous size, especially, the "red wood," fir and pine, which are frequently seen two hundred, and even two hundred and fifty feet in height, and fifteen or twenty feet in diameter. This timber makes excellent lumber, but its vast size, renders it extremely difficult, either to chop or saw it, with any degree of facility. The timber in the interior, both on the rivers, and in the valleys remote from the rivers, consists chiefly, of oak, of almost every variety, including red, white and live oak, ash, poplar, cherry and willow. It consists chiefly, however, of the different varieties of oak and ash. The timber of the mountains consists of pine, fir, arbor vitro, cedar and spruce. Besides the varieties of timber, here mentioned, in many portions of the country, there is a dense undergrowth of thorns, hazels, briers, roses and grape vines, both upon the coast, and in the interior. The timber of the Eastern section, is much the same, as that of the Western section. Here, as in that section, it is chiefly, confined to the mountains and rivers, but it is, generally, of a much smaller growth, than the same species found in that section. It consists, principally, of pine, fir, spruce, cedar, ash, poplar, cherry and willow. The oak, ash, cherry, poplar, and willow, are generally, found upon, and in the vicinity of the streams, while the fir, pine, spruce and cedar; are found, mostly, upon, and in the neighborhood of the mountains, and the more elevated regions. The undergrowth of this section, also, consists, principally, of hazels, thorns, briers and grape vines. As before remarked, there are some portions of this section which produce scarcely any vegetation besides the wormwood, or properly, artimesia, and the prickly pear. It is frequently asserted that there is a very great deficiency, of timber in this country, but such truly is not the case; there is ample timber, in both sections, and in all the various portions of each, for all useful purposes. It is true that there is not the same quantities of timber here, as are found in some portions of Oregon, or in some parts of the States, yet, the same quantity is not required, in a climate of such extraordinary mildness and uniformity.

Both the climate and the soil, are, eminently, adapted to the growing of wheat, rye, oats, barley, beans and peas, hemp, flax, tobacco, cotton, rice, coffee, corn and cane, as well as all kinds of vegetables, and especially, such as potatoes, turnips, beets, carrots, onions and the like. And both the soil and climate are no less adapted to the growing of the greatest variety of fruits; among which are apples, pears, peaches, plums, cherries and grapes, as well as most of the tropical fruits, particularly such as oranges, lemons, citrons, dates, figs and pomegranates. It is rather surprising, that almost all of the tropical and northern grains and fruits, should be produced here, in conjunction, in the same latitude; but it is no more surprising, than it is to find a southern climate, in a northern latitude, as is the case, everywhere upon the Pacific coast, and which is clearly attributable to the causes stated upon a previous page. There are other mediate causes which might be assigned, but the above is, manifestly, the proximate cause; yet, accounting for a northern latitude's possessing a southern climate, is, after all, much like accounting for a northern man's possessing southern principles; many circumstances, in either case, must be taken into the account. Without attempting to assign any further reasons, however, I will proceed; for, perhaps, it is sufficient for the present purpose, to show that such is the fact, for which each can account, at his leisure, and in his own way. Many kinds of the grains and fruits above enumerated, are indigenous, for instance, the oats, wheat, rye; many of the tropical fruits, and a great variety of grapes; flax, a kind of hemp, and red and white clover, are also indigenous productions. The oats here alluded to, have precisely the external appearance of our common oats; but, upon examination, it will be seen that the grain differs slightly from that of ours. It is rather smaller, and is covered with a kind of furry integument; otherwise, it is precisely similar to that of our common oats. They, generally, grow much higher than ours, and the stalk is much larger, but this is attributable to the superior fertility of the soil, and the greater generative influence of the climate, and not to the difference of the species. Their usual height is about two or three feet, and the stalk is, commonly, about the size of that of our ordinary oats; but they are frequently found, even eight feet high, having a stalk half an inch in diameter. Several of the farmers here, informed me, that they had often seen many thousands of acres in a body, which were higher then they could reach, when on horseback. They only grow to this enormous height, during those seasons, which have been preceeded by the falling of an abundance of rain during the rainy season. The season which I spent in this region was a dry season, that is, comparatively little rain fell during the previous rainy season; but, upon several occasions, I measured the stalks of oats, which were six feet long, and nearly half of an inch in diameter. In traveling through the various sections of the country, I have passed through thousands of acres, which were from two to five feet in height, and as dense as they could possibly stand: when, at the same time, I almost hourly saw the old stalks, of years previous, which were seven or eight feet in length, and sufficiently large and strong, for walking sticks. It is not uncommon, either in a dry or wet season, to see continuous plains and valleys, of thousands of acres in extent, which are thickly, and almost entirely clad, with oats of two or three feet in height, which would produce much more abundant crops, than our cultivated oats. In many portions of the country, in the interior, the Indians subsist almost wholly upon them, and in other portions, if a farmer wishes to grow a crop of oats, he has nothing to do, but to designate a certain tract as his oat field, and either fence it, or employ a few Indians, to prevent the herds from grazing upon it; which being done, in May or June, he reaps a much larger crop, then we are able to do, in any of the States, with all the labor and expense of cultivation.

The clover, of which I speak, is in all respects, like our ordinary red, and white clover, grown in the different States, with the exception of its growing much larger. Its usual height is about two or three feet, but vast bodies of it, are, frequently found, four or five feet in height, and as dense as it can possibly grow. It is chiefly confined to the valleys, contiguous to the rivers, but it is also, sometimes found, in large bodies, in many of the plains, and upon the hills. All of the bottoms and valleys, as well as many of the plains and hills, abound with this clover, which, when matured, affords a most excellent natural hay, of which, all kinds of stock, are extremely fond. The flax found among the spontaneous productions, is in all respects, like that grown in the States. Its general height is two or three feet, though it is frequently found much larger, Unlike the oats and clover, it is chiefly confined, to the northern portion of the country, and is seldom found in larger tracts than five or six hundred acres in a body, but wherever it is found, it grows very densely and luxuriantly, even more so then that grown in the east. The fibres appear to be equally as strong, as those of the ordinary flax, and it is, in truth, the same species. It is used by the Indians, to a very large extent, for the purpose of making seines and ropes, to which purposes it is found to be admirably suited. The hemp here found, does not resemble ours, nor is it properly hemp, although so called; it is properly a species of the spurge, commonly called milk-weed, but there called hemp. Like the spurge, it emits a milky juice when wounded; grows about three feet high, and has a tough fibrous bark, which is used by the Mexicans and Indians, in large quantities, for making ropes, seines, and for various other purposes. Comparatively, it grows in very small quantities, as you very seldom see more then fifty or a hundred acres of it together. Wheat and rye are also, said to be indigenous growths, but I am not of that opinion, although I have seen wheat, rye, oats, clover and flax, all growing together, more then three hundred miles, from any settlement. But upon a close observance, I perceived, that the wheat and rye, were found only, in the immediate vicinity of the encampments, of the traders and trappers, who have, for years, traversed that country. Upon inquiring of those, who have resided in that country, for many years, I ascertained, that the traders and trappers, in passing through the interior, frequently take both wheat and rye with them, as food for themselves and their horses. These facts, were fully convincing, to my mind, that the wheat and rye had been introduced, into the interior, in that manner. Other persons informed me, that they had, very frequently seen, both wheat and rye, far in the interior, and in portions of the country never visited by the traders and trappers, but still, I am of the opinion, that if not introduced in the above manner, they must have been introduced by the Indians, or fowls, and hence, that although they are spontaneous, yet, they are not indigenous productions. The various grasses found here, are much like those found in Oregon, and in many of the States. That common to the lower valleys and bottoms, is much larger and coarser, than that which grows upon the more elevated valleys, plains and hills. The former usually grows, about two or three feet high, while the latter grows, but about six inches or a foot high. The short grass is much the finest and sweetest, and is always sought after, in preference by all herbivorous animals. Both kinds here alluded to, form a very excellent quality of natural hay, during the summer, of which the herds are very fond, and which is sought by many grazing animals, in preference to the green herbage, which is found at every season of the year. Thus, it is seen, that the various grasses, the oats and clover, all of which are indigenous productions, not only afford inexhausted pasturage, during the growing season, but also, inexhaustible provender, during all the residue of the year.

Thus far, I have only spoken of the indigenous productions, those which are produced by tillage, will next be considered. The wheat will receive our first, and most particular attention, as it is the principal grain grown in this country, as yet, and as it will undoubtedly, always constitute one of the principal staples of the country. There are several kinds of wheat grown here, among which, are all the common varieties, grown in the States, as well as several varieties, which are unknown in the States. The wheat most commonly grown, however, is that which is called the wheat of Taos, which grows here, about three or four feet high, and bears seven distinct heads or ears, each of which, is equally as large, as those of the common variety. One head is situated upon the stalk, precisely as that of the ordinary wheat, and upon each side of this head, there are three others, putting out from the main stock, about three fourths of an inch, below each other. The berry is equally as large, as that of the ordinary kind, and it is said to weigh, about four pounds to the bushel heavier. This wheat produces very abundantly, as also, do the various other kinds, as far as they have been tried. The average crop is from thirty to forty bushels to the acre, or to one of sowing; but as average crop of fifty, sixty, and even seventy bushels, to the acre, is frequently received. Several very respectable and credible gentlemen, informed me, that there had been an instance, within their own knowledge, of a farmer's having received one hundred and twenty bushels to the acre; and that, the next year, from a spontaneous growth, upon the same ground, he received sixty-one bushels, to the acre. To many it will appear impossible, that one acre of ground, should produce that quantity of wheat, and hence, to them, the above statement will appear incredible; but I have not the least doubt, of its entire correctness. This is no more extraordinary, then it would be to see oats growing spontaneously, four, or even five or six feet high, over thousands of acres; nor is it farther removed from the common order of things, than it would be to see spontaneous growths of flax and clover, of three or four feet in height, covering vast plains and valleys, as far as vision extends, yet these things are true. Wheat is generally sown, from the first of November, to the first of March, and is harvested in May or June, depending upon the time of its being sown, which is usually deferred, until the commencement of the rainy season. This course is pursued, because of the greater ease with which the lands are ploughed, after the falling of the rains. Rye, barley, and cultivated oats, hemp and flax, have not, as yet, been tried, but they will all, undoubtedly, produce extremely well, judging from what has been previously said, in reference to their spontaneous productions. Corn is not grown to much extent, but wherever it is grown, it yields extremely well, giving an average crop, of about fifty or sixty bushels to the acre. It is proper, however, here to remark, that the corn grown here, at this time, is what is called the Spanish corn, which is a much smaller kind, than our common Indian corn, and produces much less abundantly; and that, after it is planted, no further attention is paid to it, until it is matured. With ordinary cultivation, even this kind would, undoubtedly, give a much more plentiful return. It is commonly planted, in February and March, and is harvested, any time after the last of June, by which time, it always matures. The climate and the soil are both, peculiarly adapted, to the growing of tobacco, cotton, rice and cane. Tobacco has already been tested, with eminent success; it is said to grow with as much luxuriance, and to yield as plentifully, as it does in Cuba; and the quality is thought not to be inferior, to that grown in Cuba, or elsewhere. Rice, cotton and cane, have not, as yet, been tested, but the probability is, that they will succeed admirably. It is said, by some, that cotton, can not be grown, even with ordinary success, where there is no rain during the summer; but experience controverts this view; for it is grown with eminent success, in other portions of Mexico, which have a similar climate, and which have not a drop of rain, during the entire summer. All kinds of garden vegetables, are grown here, with extraordinary success, many kinds of which, are planted and gathered, at any, and every season of the year. Melons of all kinds, produce extremely well, in all portions of this section, much better, in fact, then they do in any portion of the States.

The various fruits which are here produced, have been enumerated upon a former page, including both those which are indigenous, and those which are cultivated, as well as all of the northern and the tropical fruits. The latter are chiefly confined to the southern portions of this section, while the northern fruits abound, in all the different portions, both in the north and the south. The same variety, of the ordinary cultivated fruits, of the north, is not found here, as exists in many of the states, but several varieties have been introduced, and they have been found to yield most plentifully. Even in the most northern part, of this section, the peach trees, and various other fruit trees, bloom in January and February, and in the southern part, as early as December. The cultivated grape grows most luxuriantly, and produces very abundantly; and when ripe, it is among the most delicious and grateful fruits, that ever grace the festival board. There are many vineyards here, of ten or fifteen acres in extent, where the grape is grown in large quantities; and prepared and preserved, in all the various manners, know elsewhere. At these vineyards, raisins are made in sufficient quantities, for home consumption, and may, undoubtedly, be made in large quantities, for exportation. They are usually prepared either by partially cutting the stalks, of the branches, before the grapes are entirely ripe, and allowing them to remain upon the vine, until they are perfectly dried; or by gathering them, in their matured state, and steeping them, for a short time, in an alkaline lye, previous to their being dried. Those which are cured by the first method, are the most delicious, and are much preferred; and they are, perhaps, not inferior to the Malaga raisins, which are imported from Spain. Besides the delicious fruits, which they afford for the table, they also afford a most generous wine, which always constitutes, one of the grand essentials of a California dinner. Here I must confess, that my temperance pledge, although formerly including all alcoholic, intoxicating and vinous liquors, did not extend to the latter, in California; and I am inclined to believe that old father Mathew himself, however far he might be from doing so in the north, would drink wine in California; I know old Bacchus would.

A great variety of wild fruits, also abound, in all the different portions, of this section, among which, are crab-apples, thorn-apples, plums, grapes, strawberries, cranberries, whortleberries, and a variety of cherries. The strawberries are extremely abundant, and they are the largest, and most delicious, that I have ever seen; much larger, than the largest, which we see in the various States. They bloom in January, and ripen in March, when they are gathered and dried, in large quantities, by the settlers and the Indians. The grapes are also unusually plentiful, especially, in the vicinity of the rivers, creeks and lakes, where the greatest variety is found. They are gathered in great quantities, by the various tribes of Indians, not only for their own consumption, but for that of the white settlers. I have not unfrequently seen the Indians, arrive at Capt. Sutter's fort, with thirty or forty bushels at a time, which being measured, the Capt. would pay them, some trivial compensation, when they would depart for their villages, with the view of returning the next, and every succeeding day, while the grapes were to be obtained. The grapes thus obtained by the Capt. were designed either for the table sauce, or distillation. The mast of this section, is also extremely plentiful, in all the different valleys, and other timbered lands, especially the acorns, which I have observed here, in much greater abundance, then I have ever seen them elsewhere. All the common varieties, found in the States, are also found here, and in quantities sufficient for all the swine, and all the other animals, which subsist upon mast, as well as the various tribes of Indiana, many of whom, subsist almost entirely upon them, the greater part of the year. Large, spreading, white oaks, are often seen, which produce thirty or forty bushels, to the tree; under many of which, the ground is literally covered with them, several inches in thickness.

The grain and fruits, of the Eastern section, differ somewhat, from those of the Western section, which is attributable, to the great difference of soil and climate. Many of the spontaneous productions are, however, the same, in many portions of this section, for instance, the oats, clover, flax and hemp, many of the wild fruits, and various grapes, all of which, grow here also, with the greatest luxuriance, and in the largest quantities. The cultivated productions will, from the peculiarity of the soil, and climate be confined to wheat, rye, oats, flax, hemp, tobacco, corn, rice, beans, peas, the various vegetables, apples, pears, peaches, plums, grapes and cherries. Cotton and corn, can not, perhaps, be grown with any degree of success, in any portion of this section, nor can many, if any, of the tropical fruits. Nothing can be said with certainty, in relation to the yield of the various cultivated grains and fruits, which may be produced in this section, as all agricultural experiments, have, thus far, been confined, entirely to the Western section; but judging from the peculiar adaptation, of the soil and climate, to their production, there is no doubt, but that, many of the various productions, above enumerated, may be produced here, with the same cultivation, equally as abundantly, as they can be in the Western section. This view is strengthened, when we reflect, that all the various indigenous grains and fruits, grow equally as luxuriantly, and produce, with equal profusions, here, as in that section.

Chapter 10

TYPES OF ANIMALS

Stock of all kinds, succeed most admirably, in all portions of the Western section, which, however, would be inferred, from what has been previously adduced. Immense herds, of all the various domestic animals, are reared, with little, or no expense. They require neither feeding nor housing, and are always sufficiently fattened, for the slaughter-house. Instead of becoming lean and meager, during the winter, as our herds do, they are always much the fattest, and in the best condition, during that season. Horses are here found, in herds almost innumerable, and they are always in the best condition, for active and laborious service. Although they are rather smaller than ours, they are much more hardy and fleet, and equally as well, if not better proportioned. They endure fatigue much better, than any horses with which I am acquainted; it is not uncommon to ride or drive them, for several days in succession, without either food or rest. It is the practice of the Mexicans to tie them up, without food or water, for several days previous to using them; this course, however, is only pursued, when some extraordinary feat is to be performed; as that of riding the same horse a hundred miles in ten hours, which is not unfrequently done. For a Mexican to ride a hundred miles in one day, is not uncommon, nor does it appear to require any extraordinary effort. One hundred miles a day, are as frequently driven by the Mexicans as fifty are by our people, in truth, with them, it is but an ordinary day's ride, which, however, is generally performed with two or three horses, which are alternately ridden, as circumstances require, The usual gait at which those horses are driven, is a fast gallop, at which gait they are frequently kept, for many hours in succession, with very slight intervals of rest, of five or ten minutes, and that too, without food. I have frequently ridden those horses, over the plains of California, upon a fast gallop, for five or six consecutive hours, without the least intermission. This will enable the reader to arrive at a tolerably correct conclusion, in reference to the hardiness, and durability of the California horses, which, although they are rather smaller, are, I think, in many respects, superior to our own. They are, generally, better formed, and much more fleet, then our common horses. Among them, you will see every variety of color, imaginable, from a jet black, to a snow white. All the varieties of colors found among our horses, are found among them, besides many varieties which are never found among ours. Many are roan, with the exception of their manes, tails and ears, which are black, brown or bay; others are white, with the exception of their manes, tails and ears, which are cream-colored, tipped with bay or black; and others are lead, copper or cream colored, with bay, black or brown ears, manes and tails. Perhaps the description given of Jacob's cattle, would be as expressive of the variety of colors, of the California horses, as any that can well be given. They are much better trained for the saddle, than ours, and generally, much better gaited, and more gentle and kindly disposed when broken.

The different farmers always keep a number of herdsmen, whose business it is to drive the horses, from place to place, as it becomes necessary, to seek additional pasturage, and who are, usually, Indians or Mexicans of the lowest grade. One of these herdsmen, wishing to catch any horse which he may desire, mounts one of his most fleet horses, which he always keeps under the saddle, for that purpose, and rushes into a band with a "lasso," which, when he has approached within twenty or thirty yards, of the designated steed, he throws, with surprising accuracy, around his neck, and thus he is noosed and secured. They are either taken in the above manner, or they are driven into a "caral," where they are taken, in the manner just described. The "lasso," is a very strong rope, usually made of raw hide, and is about sixty feet in length, at one end of which, there is a noose, which is thrown upon the neck of the horse, as before stated, while the other end, is firmly attached, to the pommel of the saddle. As soon as the "lasso" is thus thrown upon the neck of the horse, designed to be taken, the saddle horse, being properly trained, immediately braces firmly, in order to guard against the frightful efforts, of the plunging and snorting steed; and from the decided advantage, which he has, in pulling by the girth of the saddle, while the other pulls by his neck only, he invariably succeeds in resisting every effort, of the wildest and most powerful. These horses are but slightly smaller then ours, which may, perhaps, be attributed to the entire inattention, to their rearing, which may be seen from the following facts. Many of the farmers have as many as fifteen or twenty thousand head, which are all permitted to range together, with very little notice or attention, other then that of branding them when young. So numerous are they, that they have frequently been killed by thousands, in order to preserve the vegetation for the cattle, which are considered much the most valuable. Instead of this inhuman and destructive practice, how easily could those indolent beings, drive their horses into the interior, which extends almost a terra incognito, and which everywhere, abounds with spontaneous and inexhaustible vegetation? By this course, they would not only preserve and increase their stock, but they would also preserve a character, for propriety and humanity; but inherent indolence forbids any course which requires any active exertion. A Mexican always pursues that method of doing things, which requites the least physical or mental exercise, unless it involves some danger, in which case, he always adopts some other method.

The cattle are much more numerous then the horses; herds of countless numbers are everywhere seen, upon all the different valleys and plains, throughout this entire section. It is said that many of the farmers have, from twenty to thirty thousand head. In whatever district you travel, you see many thousands of large fine cattle, which, in herds innumerable, are traversing those unbounded plains, of oats, clover and flax, of unparalleled growth. These cattle are undoubtedly superior to ours, especially for the yoke, as they are much larger, and they are equally as valuable for their milk, and much more valuable for their beef, which is always much fatter and more tender, then that of our cattle. When domesticated, they are equally as gentle and as tractable as ours, but before they are domesticated, they are as wild, as the deer or elk. Each farmer however, usually has as many of both oxen and cows, as are required upon his farm, which are fully domesticated, but as a general thing, they are not only as wild as the deer and elk, but they are as ferocious as tigers. Such is their ferocity, that it is extremely unsafe, to venture among them, otherwise than on horseback, in which manner, persons not only go among them, with perfect safety, but a few persons may thus drive and herd them, with the same facility, that they could our cattle. Should a person venture among them on foot, when they are collected in large herds, he would be instantly attacked and slain, unless he should find refuge, in some position which would prove inaccessible by them. As a general thing, the farmers herd them regularly, and occasionally drive them into a "caral," or inclosure, when their timidity is so increased, and their ferocity is so diminished, that they are caught and branded, with much facility. They are taken, when driven into these "carals," in a manner, similar to that in which the horses are taken, as before described, but with a slight difference, which I will here notice. The "lasso," instead of being thrown upon their necks, is thrown upon their hindmost legs, when the other end of the "lasso," being firmly attached to the pommel of the saddle, the rider plies the spur, to his horse, and in the twinkling of an eye, the captured bullock, is prostrated upon the ground, plunging and leaping, with desperate effort, to acquire an upright position, but all to no purpose. Now the red-hot iron is applied, as the owner directs, giving such impress as he may have selected as his brand, when the "lasso," is detached from his legs, by an Indian, who is very cautious to secure a safe retreat, before the infuriated animal, again obtains footing. There are stated times, at which the different farmers, thus collect their cattle, for the purpose of branding them, when the various farmers in the same neighborhood, always convene, at each point designated, for the purpose of ascertaining, whether their cattle are intermingled with those of their neighbors. Cattle were reared, formerly, for their hides only, but latterly, they are reared for their hides, tallow and beef. Several respectable gentlemen informed me, that formerly, it was very common for persons to kill hundreds and thousands of their cattle merely for their hides, leaving the beef of innumerable, fine, fat cattle to the wolves and buzzards. The same gentlemen also informed me, that in traveling through the plains of the interior, they had often seen the ground strewed, with many hundreds, of large, fat cattle, which had been killed, merely for the hides and that the bodies being thus exposed to the rays of the sun, the tallow was actually exuding from them, to such an extent, that the surface of the ground was actually saturated with it, for several feet, around each. This affords another instance, of the destructive prodigality of the Mexicans, which, however, is not latterly pursued, but the course pursued by them now, would not be considered sufficiently frugal by an Americas, as many of them weekly kill, three or four calves, which are either used or thrown away, by themselves, or their servants. As has been before remarked, both cattle and horses are now driven, in large numbers, to Oregon, and the presumption is, that the increasing emigration, to that country, will render it an extensive market, for the various herds of this country, for many years to come.

Much attention is latterly paid to the rearing of sheep, which are now found in great numbers, and which are of a very superior kind. They thrive extremely well, in all the venous portions of the country, but more particularly, in the more elevated and mountainous regions. They are equally as large, and produce quite as much wool as ours, but it is of rather a coarser quality; which fact is, perhaps, partly attributable to the climate, but mostly to a total neglect in reference to their improvement They produce their young twice annually, and many of the males have two distinct pairs of horns, or four horns, two upon each side of their heads, each coiling repeatedly around, as do those of the ordinary sheep. Many of the farmers have as many as ten or twelve thousand, of the wool of which, various kinds of coarse cloths and blankets, are manufactured. Sheep are also now driven to Oregon, in numbers sufficient to supply all the different settlers. The Hudsons' Bay Company has, latterly, driven many to that country, with which, all its various forts and settlements are supplied. Hogs are now reared, by the Mexicans, in all the different settlements, but not with a view of making pork; for, from some religious scruple, or some other scruple, or perhaps, from a dislike to eat his kind, a Mexican will not eat pork. Hogs are, therefore, reared by them, merely for the purpose of making soap, of which, by the by, they require large quantities. From the extraordinary abundance of mast here found, the hogs are always fat, so that they require no feeding, at any season of the year. Besides the various fruits upon which they subsist, there are also, very great quantities of edible roots, upon which, as well as upon the oats, clover and the like, they subsist previous to the falling of the mast. Hogs, like all other animals here, increase to an extent, almost unparalleled, but they are rather inferior to ours, yet they are equally as large, weighing, usually, from one hundred, to six hundred pounds. Herdsmen are always employed, by the different farmers, to take charge, not only of the herds of horses, but also of the cattle, sheep and hogs. These herdsmen always remain with, or in the immediate vicinity, of the different herds, driving them from place to place, as circumstances may require, with a view of protecting them from the incursions of the Indians and wolves. The herdsmen thus employed, are either, Indians, or the lower order of Mexicans, who are well skilled in their particular business, to which, they are very attentive, and in which, they appear to enjoy, almost infinite delight. The Eastern section is also well adapted to the rearing of herds of all kinds, though as before remarked, it is not as eminently suited to this purpose, as the Western section. That this section is suited in more than an ordinary degree, to grazing purposes, will be readily collected from what has been said, upon the former pages, in reference to its climate and productions, but, as no experiments have been made, in this respect, nothing can be said with definite exactness; enough, however, has been said to enable each, to draw his own conclusions, with some degree of correctness.

The game of the Western section, consists, for the most part, of elk, deer, antelope, bear, wolves, goats, foxes, squirrels, raccoons, martens, muskrats, beavers, otters and seals. The most numerous of these, are the elk and antelope, which are found in immense numbers, in all the various plains and valleys, and upon the hills and mountains. It is very common to see herds, of five or six hundred elk, ranging from vale to vale, amid the oats, clover and flax, with which, the plains and valleys everywhere abound. I remember to have been riding through these plains, with a countryman of ours, when, just as we passed a point of timbered country, near the river, about four or five hundred elk emerged from the woods. As they were passing, score after score, in quick succession, I suggested to my companion, the propriety of shooting one of them, to which he replied, that he "intended to do so," but made no other arrangements, than to dismount. Now, fearing that he would not shoot, until they had all passed, I inquired why he did not shoot. He replied, that he "would in a moment," but he permitted them all to pass, excepting the very last, which he shot, as soon us it came opposite to him, when it ran a short distance, but soon fell. We were instantly at the spot, when the California hunter commenced to divest our victim, of its outer garment. During this process, I inquired of him, why he did not shoot before, when they were much nearer him, and the opportunity was so much more favorable. He replied, that he saw I was no hunter. "The one behind," said he, "I selected because it was the fattest, and 1 knew it was the fattest because it was behind, for the fat ones cannot run as fast as the lean ones." This view I found to be correct, for a fatter animal, I never saw, in California or else-where. In every part of the country, through which I passed, I found them equally abundant. Many of the farmers, instead of killing their cattle, go, or send their servants out, whenever they wish to secure a supply of meat, and kill as many as they may require, for their families, and the Indians in their ser-vice. Several of these gentlemen informed me, that they had, very frequently, killed seven or eight each morning, end in less time then one hour. The elk here, are always very fat, and they make the very best of beef, which is, in fact, much ten-derer and sweeter, than that of our common cattle. They are much larger than those which are found on this side of the mountains, weighing usually from three to six hundred pounds. They can be as certainly relied upon, for their meat, as the common cattle, for they are very nearly as domestic. They are very easily domesticated, in which state, they are even now found, in various portions of this section, and are seen intermingling with other domestic animals upon the farms. The antelope are equally as numerous as the elk, and are much more domestic. In whatever direction you travel, you will see many hundreds of them, either grazing upon the plains, or collecting in large flocks, in the shades of the scattering pines, throughout the plains. They are beautiful animals, but neither their skin nor flesh, is as valuable as that of the elk. Their skins are much less valuable, because of their thinness, and hence, inadaptation to the making of leather. In this respect, they very much resemble the skin of the deer, as which, they are equally as thick and valuable. Their flesh is much tenderer, then that of either, the elk or deer, but it is also much leaner, and consequently, much less nutritious. These animals have many peculiarities, some of which are, perhaps, worthy of a partial notice. They are extremely domestic, so much so, that they will, at times, remain in the shades of the trees, until you approach within a very few rods of them, when they will bound off slowly, occasionally stopping, and turning towards you, then again, leaping slowly away. Large numbers of them, will very often, trot directly towards you, and gazing intensely at you, they will thus approach, within eight or ten rods of you, when they will leap frightfully away, a distance of several rods, then turning towards you again, they will, with a fast pace, approach very near to you, as before, then standing and looking eagerly at you, they remain until their timidity is again aroused, when they again bound swiftly away. They thus approach, and re-approach, very frequently, and until their curiosity is satisfied, or their fears are aroused, when they leap and bound away, with the velocity of light, and are soon lost in the stallworth vegetation, of the vast valleys. Their curiosity is evidently excited which is the cause of their thus, approaching and re-approaching. Those who are acquainted with their peculiarity, in this respect, are frequently, able to kill many of them, merely by distending a red handkerchief, or any red cloth, which will so attract their attention, that they will, immediately advance, within a few rods of them, where they will stand, gazing upon the cloth, until they are fired upon, when those which are not affected by the fire, gallop slowly away a few rods, when they again advance as before. This is frequently repeated, until dozens of them have fallen victims, to their inherent curiosity. The deer are much less numerous, than either the elk, or antelope, but they are much more plentiful, than they are in the States. There are various kinds of the deer, found in this section, such, for instance, as the white tailed, the black tailed and the moose deer. All of these abound in every part of this section, but because of their comparative wildness, and the great abundance of preferable game, they are very seldom hunted.

Several kinds of bear are also found, such as the black, brown and grizzly bear, all of which, are found in great abundance, especially, the brown bear, which are, frequently seen in herds, of fifteen or twenty in number. Their flesh is much admired by the Mexicans, as food, consequently, they are much hunted; and those are often found, that weigh twelve or fifteen hundred pounds. It is very difficult to distinguish them from the buffalo, when at a distance, for they very much resemble them, both in color and size. They are ferocious, only when attacked, when they will readily give battle, which they conduct with almost unparalleled fury and success. Upon being attacked, they stop a few moments, and until they have successfully repelled every assault, of either man or dog, when they again move swingingly on, until they have secured a safe retreat. The rifle and the "lasso" are, the only weapons, against which, they can not successfully contend. When a foreigner, with a good rifle, carrying about eighteen balls to the pound, happens to come in contact with one of them the contest is soon over; the king of the forest is slain. The "lasso" of the Mexicans, is a weapon, which is also found, too formidable for his majesty, under the repeated assaults of which, he is very readily made to recoil. The process by which, the Mexicans thus take them, is very interesting, especially to those who are unacquainted with Mexican manners and customs. When they wish to capture one of these formidable animals, five or six of them, with chosen, and trained horses, sally forth, to his usual haunts, where, at any time, large numbers are found. Each being supplied with a strong "lasso," and an abundant supply of knives, swords and the like, the battle now commences; *one* party having a decided advantage, in the multiplicity of weapons, and speed, and the *other*, having vastly the advantage, in physical strength and courage. The assault, is generally, first made by the Mexicans, who commence a most furious, running charge, both from the front and rear. Seeing his precarious predicament, the bear meets the charge from the front, with such accumulating ferocity and violence, that his assailants are soon put to flight, when he shakes his ponderous head, utters a most terrific growl, and commences a hot pursuit; but soon, the Mexican forces, are brought to bear upon his rear; his hindmost legs are entangled in the "lasso;" and he is prostrated upon his back, uttering most piteous, growling cries. The forces of the assailants, are now united, and a lasso is also thrown upon his neck, when the spurs are rapidly plied to the horses, which now exert every energy, every nerve, and soon, the powerful victim is distended upon the ground, in an entirely defenceless condition. As their victim is now completely in their power, they proceed to attach a "lasso" to almost every limb, which being done, they move off, either rapidly or slowly, as their preference and the weight, of their victim, may happen to suggest. Bear are taken in this manner, only when it is desired to take them alive, for the purpose of bear-baiting. The black and grizzly bear, are not as numerous as the brown bear, yet when compared with those of any other country, with which I am acquainted, they may be said to be very numerous. In almost every direction, in which you travel, through the plains and mountains, you will very frequently see, herds of ten or fifteen in number, many of which, are equally as large as the brown bear, but they are generally much smaller, weighing from five, to twelve hundred pounds. These are also taken by the Mexicans, in the manner above stated, but in much less numbers, then the brown bear. Capturing the bear, in this manner, is one of the chief amusements of the Mexicans, and they really evince an energy and bravery, in this kind of conflict, to which they are entire strangers, when in conflict with men, and especially Texans.

Wolves are very numerous in all portions of this section, among which, are the black, gray, and the prairie wolves; the latter of which, are very small, but they are much the most numerous and troublesome. Of the former, the gray wolf is much the most numerous, but the black wolf is much the largest, being generally about the size of our common large mastiffs. All the different kinds of wolves, are very troublesome in all the various settlements, into which they make very frequent inroads, not only destroying the hogs and sheep, but also, frequently attacking and destroying even the grown cattle. The cause of there being such an abundance of all the different kinds of wolves, is, perhaps, that they are never killed, either by the Mexicans or foreigners. They do not kill them, because they are entirely worthless, and because the people in that country, have not a superabundance of ammunition. In traveling through the valleys of this section, you will pass many hundreds of them, during the day, which appear to evince no timidity, but with heads and tails down, in their natural crouching manner, they pass within a very few rods of you. As shooting them would be a waste of so much ammunition, you allow them to pass unmolested, and thus, their timidity is diminished, and their familiarity and numbers are increased. The fur-bearing animals are much more numerous in this section, than in any other portion of the country, west of the Rocky mountains, especially the beavers, otters, muskrats and seals. Besides these, there are all those, enumerated upon another page, which, however, are much less numerous. There are many persons here who follow trapping as a business, and who succeed extremely well. The Hudsons' Bay Company extends its operations, to this country also, where in fact, it obtains a greater portion, of its annual collections of peltries. An edict was recently issued by the government of California, which required that company to discontinue the business of trapping in that country; so far, however, it had proved entirely inoperative. The trappers, of that company, were still trapping, in that country when I left, and their labors were attended with extraordinary success. Much more regard is here had, to the preservation of the fur-bearing animals; a governmental regulation exists which requires the trappers to take them, with strict reference to the proper season, which has tended very much, to prevent their diminution. The game, of the Eastern section, is very much the same, as that in the Western section, with very few exceptions, all the different species found in that, are also found in this section. In addition, however, to the game found in that section, the white bear, the mountain sheep and the buffalo, are also found, in this section. The latter of which, are here found in much greater numbers, than in any other portion of the country, west of the Rocky mountains. In many portions of the country, the plains and hills are literally covered with them. Sev-

eral tribes of the Indians here, as in Oregon, subsist almost
entirely upon the beef of the buffalo, which they are enabled
to obtain, in any desired quantities.

The feathered animals, of the Western section, consist
chiefly, of geese, ducks, brants, cranes, gulls, pelicans, plo-
vers, eagles, hawks, ravens, woodpeckers, pheasants, partridges, grouse, snow-birds, blue-birds, blackbirds, and
robins, with a great variety of other birds, common in the
States. The former of these, and especially the water-fowls,
are vastly numerous, particularly upon the coast, and in the
vicinity of the rivers, bays and harbors. During the winter and
spring seasons, all the various lakes, bays and rivers, as well
as the low lands, and wheat fields, throughout the whole
country, are literally covered with the various water-fowls,
which appear to have convened here from all the northern
world. In many portions of the country, during these seasons,
they congregate in such immense numbers, that their unceasing confusion proves noisome in the extreme, to the settlers.
The wheat fields and the low lands are their usual haunts, during the winter, when hundreds of them, may be killed, in a
few hours. I was informed that one man, could at any time,
during the winter, obtain feathers sufficient for a feather-bed,
from those which he could kill in a very few hours. When
passing down the Sacramento river, and crossing the bay of
St. Francisco, I have frequently been greatly annoyed, by the
almost deafening, tumultuous and confused noises, of the
innumerable flocks, of geese and ducks, which were continually flying to and fro, and at times, blackening the very heavens with their increasing numbers, and making the aerial
region ring, with their tumultuous croaking and vehement
squeaking. During the winter season, California is truly, a
noisy, turbulent region; all the northern world, seems to have
given up, its millions of the feathered tribes, which are here in
universal convention, having complete possession, of the

entire country. However noisome the increasing numbers, and the confused noise of these multifarious proprietors of California, may be to the settlers, there is no prospect of any diminution of either, for they are assembled here, by millions, merely to propagate their kind, and to teach their squeaking young, the art of noisy clamor. The fowls of the Eastern section, are, with very few exceptions, the same as those of the Western section; yet many kinds found in that section, are found in much less abundance in this, especially the various water-fowls, but compared to any portion of the States, they would be called very abundant. As they congregate in this region, merely to enjoy its delightful climate, and propagate their kind, it is said, that there are numerous places, where many bushels of their eggs, may be obtained in a few hours. This, however, is the case only in the Western section, where I have no doubt, but that it occurs, for to my own knowledge, as before remarked, there are many places, where the ground is literally covered, and the whole heavens completely blackened, with innumerable flocks, of countless numbers, of geese, ducks, brants, cranes and all the various noisy tribes, of all the feathered creation.

The fish and fisheries, of this country, will next, receive a passing notice, the former of which, are unusually plentiful, in the Western section, consisting, chiefly, of salmon, salmon-trout, cod, sturgeon, flounders, carp, perch, ray, lampreys, smelt and eels. A very great variety of shell fish, such as clams, oysters, crabs and muscles, abound, in all the various bays and inlets in the greatest profusion. Whales are also very numerous, everywhere upon the coast, and even in many of the different bays. There are various kinds of the salmon, which are the most numerous, and much the best fish, found in this country, or perhaps in any other country, for I am of the opinion, that they are much the finest fish, any where taken. They are much superior to the salmon of the States, both in flavor and size. Their usual weight is from ten, to fifty pounds, and their length from eighteen inches, to four feet. These, as well as the various other kinds enumerated, abound in all the various rivers of the interior, and in all the different inlets and bays, where they are taken at any season of the year, but they are much more abundant, during the spring and autumn, at which seasons, all the waters are literally full of them which is evinced by their incessant leaping and plunging. They commence to run in April and October, of each year, each run continuing about, two months, during all which seasons, both Indians and whites are more or less employed, in securing their supplies for the residue of the year, but they are taken chiefly, by the Indians, who here, as in Oregon, take them by a great variety of methods. They take them chiefly, however, with seines, which they manufacture, and which are of a very good kind, answering all the purposes of the ordinary seines, used by our people. With these, they are able, at certain times, to take fifteen or twenty barrels, at a single draught, which they repeat with surprising rapidity. Many of the Mexicans subsist almost entirely upon them, while many of the Indians, live wholly upon them, especially, during the seasons of their greatest abundance. They are used by the whites in their fresh, dried, or pickled state, while the Indians use them, in their fresh or dried state only. They are dried and prepared here, as in Oregon, merely by exposing them to the rays of the sun, without the aid of salt, or any other preservative, as ample preservative properties are found in the extreme purity of the atmosphere. The oysters are rather smaller, than those found upon the Atlantic side, but they are of a very excellent kind, being inferior in flavor and in deliciousness to none. They also, as well as the clams and muscles, are taken both by the Mexicans and Indians, in very great quantities, which also form a principal item of their food. Whales are also vastly numerous, not only in the ocean, but also in most of the bays and inlets, and especially, in the bay of Monterey, where many are very frequently seen, even from the streets, alternately leaping and plunging, in the different portions of the bay; first exhibiting their ponderous heads, throwing up vast torrents of water, which are falling in misty spray, then plunging and sinking slowly away, displaying their protracted hacks, and flirting their tails, amid the convulsed waters, they disappear. While some are plunging, others are leaping, as some appear, others disappear, and thus, is the otherwise calm and *Pacific* ocean, kept in incessant commotion. What adds the greatest importance to these scenes, is the fact, that they are constantly being enacted, and that too, in the very midst of the ships, barques and brigs, in harbor, and in full view of the gentlemen in their offices, and the ladies in their parlors. A strange commingling of oceanic and terrestrial beings! The fish of the Eastern section, are not as numerous as those of the Western section, nor is there the same variety in that section, yet, all the rivers of that section, also abound with several kinds of the salmon, salmon trout, carp, herring, perch, ray and flounders. The great salt lake, of that section, is also, said to abound with a great variety of excellent fish. The fisheries of the Western section, are innumerable, and inexhaustible, and they are found in every portion of the country, both upon the coast, and in the interior, but from the very partial demand for the fish, the various fisheries, have not been brought into requisition. The principal fisheries, which are now used, to much extent, are those upon the different rivers, and which are usually possessed, by the various tribes of Indians. It is thought that the fisheries of this country, will not be found inferior to those of Newfoundland, and they certainly will not, in reference to their numbers, the quality of their fish, or their inexhaustibleness.

Chapter 11

SETTLEMENT AND IMPROVEMENT IN CALIFORNIA

The settlements and improvements are, chiefly, in connection with the different forts, military posts, and missionary stations, and at the various towns, all of which are confined entirely, to the Western section. Of these, I shall first notice, the forts and military posts, of the former of which, there are but two, one of which, is called New Helvetia, and the other is called Ross. Both of these are now in the possession of, and owned by, Captain Sutter, the former of which he built, and the latter he purchased of the Russians. New Helvetia, the most important of these, is situated in a well chosen position, on the south side of the Sacramento, about one mile from its south bank, 100 miles, east by north, from Yerba Buena, at latitude 38° 45' 42" north. In form, it is a sexangular oblong, its greatest length being 428 feet, and its greatest width, 178 feet; 233 feet of its length being 178 feet wide, and the residue but 129 feet wide. It is inclosed by permanent "adobie" walls, which are 18 feet high, and three feet thick, with bastions at the corners, the walls of which, are five feet thick. It is entered by three large swinging gates, one of which, is on the north, another on the south side, and the third at the east end. The first of these, is entirely inaccessible from without, because of a deep, and impassable ravine, which extends the whole length of the fort, on the north; on each side of the second, is a platform, upon each of which, a nine-pounder is planted, and the third is completely commanded, by one of the bastions. There are two bastions, each of which has four guns, two nine-pounders, and two six-pounders; and in all, there are twelve guns, of different caliber. The inner building of this fort, consist of a large and commodious residence, for the various officers, in connection with which, is a large kitchen, a dining room, two large parlors, the necessary offices, shops and lodging apartments. Besides these, there is also a distillery, a horse-mill and a magazine, together with barracks, for the accommodation of, at least, one thousand soldiers. In connection with the fort, there are one thousand acres of land, under a good state of cultivation, and upon which are all the necessary buildings, together with an extensive tannery. Of this fort, Captain Sutter has charge, in person; he has about one hundred men, constantly in his employment, who annually sow one thousand acres of wheat, and have charge of his numerous herds, which, in all, amount to about twenty thousand head. Those, having charge of the various herds, are, generally, Indians, but his building and farming, are superintended chiefly by foreigners. He also has a large number of experienced trappers, in his service, who have charge of about one thousand traps, and from whose services, he annually realizes several thousand dollars.

Besides the business thus carried on, by the Captain, he is also doing a very extensive business, in a military way. All the usual military formalities, are regularly observed; sentinels are always kept out, day and night, who invariably give the captain, timely notice of the approach of persons, during the day, or of the slightest movement, of any thing, in the human form, during the night. Here too, the natives are being instructed, in the art of war; forty or fifty of them, are taken and instructed, for several months, and until they have acquired, a general knowledge, of military tactics; when they are turned off, and forty or fifty others are taken, who are drilled and trained, in the same manner, when they are also dismissed, and others taken in their stead, and so on continually.– The Mexicans, not being able to divine the cause, of all this military parade, at one time, became very suspicious, that all was not right; and finally, their suspicions were increased to such an extent, that they determined to effect the captain's unceremonious expulsion, from the country, of which determination, he was duly advised. The captain took the matter under consideration, and soon determined, to resist any attempted encroachment, upon his rights, and accordingly, informed the government of his determination. The government, however, proceeded to make its preliminary arrangements, for his expulsion, preparatory to which, a spy was sent, in the disguise of a friend, to the captain's fort, in order to ascertain his true position, as to vulnerableness, and means of resistance.– Upon the arrival of this mysterious visitor, an enemy in disguise, "a wolf in sheep's clothing," or a *Mexican in man's clothing*, the captain soon suspected his object, and informed him, that he must immediately depart, or he would, at once, order him to be put in irons, and, at the same time, informed him, that if the government, whose spy he was, thought proper to attempt his expulsion from the country, he was perfectly willing, at any time, to test its ability to accomplish that object.– This hypocritical visitor, now made rather an irregular disappearance, amid the jeers, taunts and threats, of the captain's men, and if he was not prepared to report to his *owners*, that the captain was invincible, he was fully prepared to report, that the captain *thought* himself invincible, which would be precisely the same thing, as far as Mexicans were concerned. The government, finding, that the captain was not to be deterred, and that an attempt to effect his expulsion, would be attended with *dangerous* consequences, *of course*, abandoned the undertaking. Ever since that time, the government has treated the captain with extraordinary kindness, bestowing upon him, the office of alcalde, and other little governmental favors, designed to repair the cloak of hypocrisy, which had been to seriously lacerated, in the above transaction. The truth, however, is that the Mexicans look upon the captain, with much more than ordinary suspicion, notwithstanding their pretended friendship; but whether they are justified, in viewing the captain, with some little suspicion, I do not pretend to say, as to that, each will judge for himself. Having heard thus much, in reference to this gentleman, many might be led to inquire more particularly, as to the captain; I will therefore remark, that he is a Swede by birth; he emigrated, at an early day, to the United States, where he resided for several years, residing most of the time, at St. Louis and St. Charles, in Missouri, and in 1839, he emigrated to California, where he has since remained. His military taste, as well as his military title, was derived from his service in Bonapart's army, to which he was attached, for several years. A more kind and hospitable gentleman, it has seldom been my fortune to meet. Such is his treatment of all foreigners, who visit him, that when they leave him, they are compelled to do so, with much regret, and under many obligations, for his continued, untiring and gentlemanly attentions.

Ross is the other fort, to which I have alluded, as belonging to Captain Sutter; it is situated on the coast, near the bay of Bodaga, at latitude 38° 55' 42" north. It is about sixty rods square, and is inclosed by a strong, wooden wall, which is two feet thick, and eighteen feet high. The interior buildings consist of two large and commodious dwelling houses, for the officers, two magazines, store-houses, a prison, a chapel, shops for the various mechanics, and barracks for several hundred soldiers. In connection with the fort, there is a large farm, about two hundred acres of which, are in a good state of cultivation, and upon which, there is a good orchard, a vineyard, a horse and wind-mill and several dwelling-houses, stables and barns. Agricultural pursuits, and the rearing of herds of cattle, horses and sheep, are the chief objects of attention, at this establishment. Such persons are in charge, from time to time, as the captain designates for that purpose. Here as at New Helvetia, large numbers of Indians are also employed, who conduct the agricultural operations, and who have charge of the various herds. A great abundance of fruit, such as apples, pears, and peaches, is here, annually produced, and perhaps, in greater quantities, then in any other portion, of the country.

The military posts, which belong to the government, I will now merely enumerate, without giving a description of each, for to do which, would extend these pages far beyond their present limits, and would, perhaps, convey no very important additional information. All that is deemed necessary, then, will be merely to give the names, of each post, together with the number of soldiers and cannons at, and in connection with each. At Paobalo below, there are thirty soldiers, and twelve cannons; at St. Diego, there are twelve soldiers, and two cannons; at Santa Barbara, there are twenty soldiers, and six cannons; and at Monterey, there are two hundred soldiers, and twelve cannons; at Santa Cruz, six soldiers and two cannons; at St. Joseph, six soldiers, and two cannons; at St. Francisco, fifteen soldiers, and six cannons; and at Sonoma, thirty soldiers, and five cannons. None of these are forts, nor are they properly, military posts; they consist in nothing more, than a few men being stationed, at the different towns, and missions above enumerated, with a few guns at each, which, however, are never in order for use, nor are they designed for use. The object of these posts, as they are called, appears, merely to be, to awe the lower order of Mexicans, into submission to the law, and the observance of order, and an empty gun, answers that purpose, as well as a loaded one. As an instance of the inaptitude, of these posts, for the prosecution of successful warfare, either offensive, or defensive, I will relate an occurrence, which was narrated to me, by a gentleman at St. Francisco. Upon the arrival of an American man of war, into the bay of St. Francisco, a messenger was dispatched, from on board, to the military post at that place, for the purpose of ascertaining, whether the officer in command, would return a salute, if fired from the ship. The officer hesitated for a moment, but finally replied, that he was entirely out of powder, but that he would endeavor to get some, and return the salute. He made several unsuccessful efforts, at the different stores, where it appeared that neither himself, nor his government, had any credit, but finally, my informant furnished him with the powder, upon a credit, when the officer repaired to his post, and after working with an old, rusty cannon, a few hours, he informed the commander of the ship, that all was in readiness. But upon attempting to return the salute, the officer found that all was not quite ready, for it was with the greatest difficulty, that he could succeed in discharging the rusty gun, but he did finally succeed, and thus, the *honor* of the nation stands unimpaired, but its *credit* is much impaired, for the powder was not paid for, up to the last accounts. From the foregoing, the actual military strength, of California, is seen to be, three hundred and nineteen *Indian* soldiers, forty-seven *rusty* cannons, and *no ammunition*. In addition to the military force, above enumerated, about six or seven hundred troops might, possibly, be raised in an extreme case, which would make the entire force of this country, about one thousand *Mexican* troops. The soldiery of this country, like that of all other parts of Mexico, consists of the very lowest order of Mexicans, who are, in fact, nothing more nor less, then the most degraded and wretched, of those timid and inert aborigines.

The missionary stations will next, receive a passing notice, which will consist, merely of a statement, of their number, and a general description of them, collectively. In all, there are twenty missionary stations, ten of which, are very valuable in lands, horses, cattle and vineyards, the residue of which, are valuable only in lands and vineyards. These are all, extensive establishments, which are occupied by the catholic priests, and others, ostensibly for the purpose of christianizing the Indians, immense numbers of whom, are connected with each station, and who are under the absolute control, of the most despotic and inhuman priesthood. The practical effect of these establishments has, thus far, been, to crowd those vast plains and valleys, in their vicinity, with countless herds of large, fine cattle, horses and sheep, to plant and grow extensive vineyards, of those delicious grapes, and to erect spacious, and palace-like edifices, for the accommodation of those religious oppressors, who are there thought to be, the authorized keepers, not only of the consciences of men, but also of the keys of both heaven and hell. A further effect of these establishments has been, not only to enslave and oppress, thousands of these timid and unsuspecting aborigines, but also to reduce all the common, and lower orders, of the people, to a most abject state of vassalage, and to stamp indellible ignorance and superstition, upon their imbecile and uncultivated minds. In order to show more fully, the vast amount of menial servitude, which has been, from time to time, thus forcibly imposed upon, the various weak and inoffensive tribes of Indians, whom fortune, or rather *misfortune*, has thus exposed, to the absolute despotism, of a monarchal priesthood, I will here, give a brief exhibit, of the extraordinary wealth and power, of these *very devoted* and *praiseworthy* religious instructors. At many of the different stations, they frequently have from five, to fifteen thousand head of horses, and from ten, to thirty thousand head of cattle, besides many thousands of sheep, and hundreds of hogs, all of which, are reared by those Indians, most of whom, have been dragged, forcibly into their service. So numerous are the herds, reared at many of these stations, and so little do these profligate priests, regard the toil and labor, which their rearing has cost the poor, and oppressed natives, that they have, in many instances, required the Indians to kill many thousands of them, merely for their hides. I was informed by several respectable foreigners, that there was an instance, but a few years since, of one of those priests' causing twenty thousand head, of large, fine cattle to be killed for the hides only, leaving their tallow and beef, at the disposal of the various carnivorous animals, which there abound, in countless numbers. In connection with most of these stations, there are also, large vineyards, containing from five to fifteen acres of thrifty vines, producing a superabundance of large and delicious grapes, from which vast quantities of the most excellent wine are extracted, and always kept on hand, for the use and benefit, of the more than regal priesthood. Buildings of various kinds are erected in connection with each of these stations, among which, are not only the magnificent residences of the priests, but also all other buildings, the erection of which, either the convenience or the pride of the priests, happens to suggest. Among those, the erection of which, is suggested by their pride, are of course, many magnificent, and vastly expensive churches, which are well supplied with golden images, which are held by many, as the mere insignia of the Divine presence, while many others, who are the more ignorant, view them not as mere images, but as so many Gods in reality. It is estimated, that the entire wealth, of all these missionary settlements, including the herds and lands, together with all the various improvements, amounts to about four hundred thousand dollars, which immense amount, has been extracted, either from the helpless and defenceless aborigines, in forced labor, or from the ignorant and superstitious Mexicans, in the exaction of unholy tithes.

There have been numerous instances, of those missionary *generals*, having armed companies, of Mexicans and subdued Indians, whom they have sent out, for the purpose of dragging the defenceless, naked natives to the missions, with no other view, than that of enslaving them, but ostensibly with the laudible view of christianizing them, which, by the by, affords them a very plausible pretext, for the accomplishment of their inhuman purposes. These companies meeting with the least resistance, have, frequently, fired upon their unoffending victims, and slain them by scores, and thus, in the extreme anxiety of these priests, in reference to the future welfare, of these poor and benighted beings, and in their most divine and christian determination, to save human souls, they, as far as they have the power, destroy both soul and body. To quiet the consciences of these bloody tyrants, religion is brought to their aid. They insist, that, notwithstanding all the apparent oppression, outrage and death, which they are daily inflicting upon the natives, yet it is a great blessing to them, for the sooner the finally obstinate are cut off, the better for them, as their longer continuance on earth, only enhances their guilt here, and increases their punishment hereafter; and the converted are paid, more then a hundred fold, for all their sufferings and deprivations, by being permitted to share the never-ending joys of heaven, with their cruel oppressors. These are some of the many blessings, resulting to those whom they *convert*; and they do really *convert* them, but not to christianity; *they convert them to their own use*; a clear case of *trover and conversion*. These flagrant oppressions are not confined to the Indians, but they are extended, in a greater or less extent, to all the Mexicans, which may be seen, from an occurrence which I will now relate. Upon the decease of a very elderly, and extremely wealthy farmer, in the northern part of California, the priests applied to the heirs, for an appropriate dividend of the property of the deceased, which was one tenth of the entire estate. The deceased had for several years, refused to pay tithes to the priest, and his heirs followed his example, and also refused to pay the tithes, because of which, the priests became so highly offended, that they refused absolutely, to perform the ordinary religious rites, or to permit the friends of the deceased, to inter the corpse within the consecrated grounds. According to the superstitions, of these people, to inter the corpse elsewhere, and especially, "without the benefit of the clergy," would be tantamount, not only to excluding the spirit of the deceased, from the joys of heaven, but also, to heaping upon it, all of the woes of hell. This thought, the friends of the deceased, could not, for a moment, endure, consequently, they at once, proposed to pay the tithes, and thereby, secure the immediate interment of the body, and ultimate happiness of the spirit of their deceased friend; but, as astonishing as it may appear, the priests now refused to receive a tenth, but demanded one fifth of all the property of the decedent. With this most unreasonable, and unjust demand, the heirs of the deceased, of course, refused to comply, but embalmed and preserved the body, as they best could, until they could apply to the governor, who was then, about four hundred miles from that place. A courier was accordingly dispatched, to the residence of the governor, where he arrived in a few days, when all the facts, and attending circumstances, having been made known to the governor, he immediately, issued his edict, requiring the priest, who resided in the neighborhood of the deceased, not only to yield his assent, to the interment of the corpse, in the consecrated ground, but also, to perform the accustomed saving rites, and that too, in his own proper person. This edict reached the obstinate divine, in a very few days, who upon receiving which, immediately, though very reluctantly, proceeded to the discharge of the important duty, imposed upon him by the *governor*, not of the *universe*, but of *California*. Notwithstanding three weeks had elapsed, since the death of the deceased, the burial now took place, within the consecrated grounds, and under all the clerical pomp and parade, which are customary, upon such occasions. Thus the blessings of heaven were secured; the woes of hell averted; the heirs were permitted to retain, their rightful property; and, for once, the priests in all their might, were subjected to an inglorious defeat, even in California. The Mexicans are now discovering that no good, but much evil is arising from, those missionary establishments, consequently, they have determined to convert them to their own use, which in truth, they have absolutely done, in one or two instances. A large majority, of all the Californians, are much opposed to the existence of these institutions, the consequence of which, will eventually be, that, as they are public property, they will be made available, and *converted* to the public good, golden images and all. This would, undoubtedly, be perfectly right, for they are now, nothing more nor less, then powerful engines, of high-handed oppression, relentless cruelty, and unremitting sinfulness.

There are but five towns this country, all of which are situated upon, or in the vicinity of the coast. The largest of these is called Poabalo, which is situated near latitude 33 deg. north, a few miles east from the coast. It contains a population, of about fifteen hundred, consisting chiefly of Mexicans and Indians. There are very few foreigners at this place, even fewer than there are at several of the smaller towns. It contains about two hundred buildings, which are small, and otherwise inferior, the walls of which, are generally, constructed of "adobies;" which are large dried brick, and the roofs chiefly of tiles; they are but one story high, though many of them are very convenient. Although this town is the largest found in this country, yet from the fact of its being situated in the interior, it is of much less importance, than those which I shall subsequently describe. In point of population, Monterey is the second town, but from its situation upon the bay of Monterey, and from its being the seat of government, it is a much more important town then any other in the country. It is situated on the south side, of the bay of Monterey, in full view of the ocean, and near latitude 37 deg. north, containing a population of about one thousand, which consists, principally, of Mexicans and Indians. Including those within its suburbs, it contains about one hundred buildings, the walls of which, are also chiefly constructed of "adobies," and the roofs of tile. These building, like those of Poabalo, are also very cheaply constructed, and are, generally, but one story high, yet the governor's house, and those of several of the foreigners, are exceptions to this; that of the governor, especially, is rather a spacious and convenient dwelling. There are many more foreigners at this place then at any other town in the country. They consist of Americans, Englishmen and Frenchmen, but they are chiefly Americans. This town is situated upon one of the most beautiful sites for a town, or even for a city, that I have ever beheld; being a gently undulating plain, with a single, small pine or oak, interspersed here and there, without any undergrowth, surrounded by a vast interior, of fertile plains and valleys, and in full view of rolling billows, and the lashing surf, of that unbounded ocean; it wears a most picturesque and grand appearance. This is, in all respects, a most delightful and favorable site, for a great commercial emporium, as which it is undoubtedly, destinated ultimately, to be occupied. The third town, in point of population, is Poabalo, which is the same name as that given the first town mentioned; they are distinguished, however, by the addition of above and below, that being called Poabalo below, and this Poabalo above. It is situated about four leagues from the coast, north northeast from Monterey, and near latitude 37 deg. and 20 min. north. Including Mexicans, Indians and foreigners, it has a population, of about five hundred, which consists, chiefly, of Mexicans and Indians. There are fewer foreigners at this town, than at any other in the country, in proportion to the population, unless, perhaps, there may be fewer at Poabalo below. The buildings of this town, like those of Monterey and Poabalo below, are small, and cheaply constructed, the walls of which, are of "adobies," and the roofs of tiles. In all, there are about seventy buildings, among which, there are a few framed dwelling-houses, which are chiefly situated in the suburbs, and are principally owned by foreigners.

The only towns remaining to be noticed, are Yerba Buena and Sonoma, the former of which, is the fourth town in reference to its population, but it is the second, if not the first, in point of local position. Yerba Buena is the Spanish name, given this place, which signifies, in the English language, good herb, and which was given it, because of a certain herb's growing, in great abundance, in its vicinity. This place, however, among the foreigners, has always borne the name of St. Francisco, which name, it will be most likely, to retain. It is located on the north side, of the bay of St. Francisco, about two miles from the entrance of that bay, near latitude 38 deg. north, containing a population of about two hundred, which consists of Mexicans and Indians, but there are more foreigners at this place, than at any other town in the country, in proportion to the population. It contains about fifty buildings, which, unlike those of the other towns enumerated, are, chiefly, wooden buildings, which is owing to the fact of their having been built, by the foreigners. This is a very delightful site for a town, but it is rather limited in extent, it being but about eighty rods, from the bay, to the base of the range of hills, which lie between it and the ocean. That portion of the site which lies between the bay and the hills, is a beautiful, gradually undulating plain, immediately in front of which, is an extensive and safe harbor, in which hundreds of ships, of the largest class, may ride in perfect safety. This situation, although limited, may very easily be extended, to a sufficient extent, with the trivial expense, of a few excavations and other improvements. The extensive and secure anchorage, in the vicinity of this situation, as well as its proximity to the entrance, and to the coast, has thus far, given it the preference, to the numerous other sites, which are found at various points, upon this great bay. The most extensive and secure anchorage, is to be found, in almost every portion of this bay, in connection with which, are numerous situations for towns and cities, which are of large extent, and extraordinary beauty. In view of these considerations, I am inclined to the belief, that some other point, which is more advantageously situated, and more extensive, will, eventually, be selected as the situation, of that great commercial emporium, which is, beyond a doubt, destined, at no distant period, to be reared up, at some point upon that great inland sea. The importance of the site upon which Yerba Buena is situated, must readily be seen, for although, it is not the most eligible site, which may be found upon that bay, yet, as it is the first town commenced in that vicinity, it may, for that reason alone, acquire a lasting preference, over all other, even more favorable situations. The Hudsons' Bay Company having seen, the superior importance, of this section of country, located at that place, at an early day, where it now has an extensive trading establishment, at which, a very extensive trade, is now carried on, both with the Mexicans and the foreigners. The gentleman in charge of that establishment, is Mr. Raye, who is not only a very intelligent business man, but also an honorable, kind and hospitable gentleman. He receives and entertains foreigners with the utmost kindness and attention and without regard to their national origin, his unremitting attentions are bestowed upon them, while they remain at Yerba Buena, and even when they take their departure, this gentleman is seen waving his hat, in tokens of kind remembrance, and lasting friendship. Sonoma is the only town, which remains unnoticed, and which is situated on the north side of the bay of St. Francisco, near latitude 38 deg. and 20 min. north. It contains about twenty wooden and "adobie" buildings, with a population of about one hundred, consisting of Mexicans and Indians. The site occupied by this place, is a most beautiful and fertile, though small valley, in some part of which, there will, most likely, eventually, be a town of some considerable importance.

The principal settlements, which are disconnected with the forts, missions and towns, are chiefly within ten or twelve leagues of the coast, with the exception of those upon, and in the immediate vicinity, of the Sacramento, which are from ten to fifty leagues from the coast, and which are the most extensive of all the interior settlements of California. These settlements are made up, almost entirely, of foreigners, and chiefly, of Americans, consisting of about two hundred persons, thirty-three of whom, arrived with me, in that country, in the autumn of 1843, but the greater portion of them, had resided there for several years previous. They all have fine herds of cattle and horses, with farms, under a good state of cultivation, upon which, they grow a great abundance of wheat, corn, oats and flax, as well as a great variety and superabundance of vegetables, and that too, with very little labor or expense. Many of these settlers are in very prosperous circumstances, and they are all doing extremely well, considering the very short period, of their residence in that country. They usually sow annually, several hundred acres of wheat, from which they are not only able to supply themselves, but also to supply all the emigrants who are annually arriving, as well as to furnish much for exportation. All the farmers, throughout the different portions of the country, are succeeding extremely well; they all grow considerable grain, and especially wheat, but they devote their chief attention to the rearing of cattle, horses, and sheep. As has been before stated, many of them have, as many as fifteen or twenty thousand head of cattle, and as many horses, and from five to fifteen hundred sheep. The foreigners here, conduct their agricultural labors, very much as they do in the states, but, their improvements are materially different; they very seldom construct rail fences, as they find it is less expensive, to inclose their lands by ditches, or to employ a few Indians to guard their crops, until they are matured and harvested. Crops are thus very easily protected, as the country is but sparsely settled, and as the plains and valleys, everywhere abound, with oats and clover, so that there is very little inducement, for the various herds to intrude upon the cultivated lands. In the present thinly settled state of the country, an Indian will effectually guard, a hundred acres; hence crops are protected, in this manner, with much less expense, than they could be by fencing. Fencing, by ditching, is attended with much less expense, than fencing in the ordinary manner, not because timber cannot be obtained, but because the Indians perform all labor of that kind, with much expertness, and because they are entirely unacquainted with the business of making rails. The buildings, upon the various farms, here and throughout all the interior, like those in the towns, are, chiefly, of "adobies," which are found, by experience, to make much the best buildings. These buildings are preferred for various reasons; they are much less expensive, and they are much cooler, and more pleasant in the summer, and warmer in winter, than either those made of stone, the ordinary brick, or of wood. But the chief circumstance, which gives them the preference, is that the Indians are able to perform all the labor, in their construction. The roofs are either of tiles or shingles, and the first floors are, generally, of "adobies" of the same size and kind, as those of which the walls are constructed. The farmers find all the materials, for this kind of buildings, wherever they wish to build, and by calling a few Indians to their aid, they are able, at any time, to complete a very comfortable building, of this kind, in a very few days. This species, of building, is thought to be equally permanent and durable, as either those constructed of brick or stone, especially in a climate of so very little rain, and of such extraordinary dryness and aridity. The same kinds of buildings, I find, are used, in all the southern portion of Mexico, where they are much preferred, and for the same reason, that they are here preferred.

All of these settlements, as well as those connected with the forts, missions and towns, are supplied with all the means of subsistence within themselves, they not only rear their own herds, grow their own grain and vegetables, but they also make their own cloth; and they are all supplied with flouring-mills, which answer all the purposes of each settlement. These mills are either horse-mills or wind-mills, yet they are found to answer all useful purposes, of all the different settlements, forts, missions and towns. These are the only kinds of flouring-mills, in the country, as yet, but a steam flouring-mill was in contemplation, and in truth, it was commenced, and in a forward state of progression when I left that country. Lumber is generally sawed by hand, as there are but few saw-mills, as yet, in the country. There were but two saw-mills in operation in the autumn of 1843, one of which was owned by a Mr. Graham, and the other by a Mr. Yunt, both of which gentlemen, are countrymen of ours. Besides these, there was also a steam saw-mill, which was then, recently commenced, by a Capt. Smith, who is the proprietor of the steam flouring-mill, before alluded to, and who is also a countryman of ours. Both of these mills were in a state of completion, when I left that country, the frames and other wooden work, were very nearly finished; the engine, and other machinery had been received, and were being erected. It was thought that both of these mills, would be fully completed, by the first of January

1843, at farthest. These mills are being erected at Bodaga, which has been before described, and which is a very favorable position, for machinery of that kind, especially, for a saw-mill, as the whole surrounding country, abounds with the most admirable timber, for lumber and ship-building. Here I will take occasion to remark, that the reason of machineries not being established, in this country, to a greater extent, is not that there is not a sufficient number of sites, favorable for that purpose, for there are very few portions of the country, but that abound with the most eligible sites, for extensive machinery of any kind. Many of those portions of the country, in the vicinity of the different bays, and of the coast generally, as well as those portions far in the interior, afford numerous favorable situations, for extensive machinery. The only cause of machineries' having been introduced to so limited an extent, are, that the very sparce settlement, and the general inattention to the industrial pursuits, would not, heretofore, have warranted such expensive enterprises, and that, foreigners of that sterling enterprise, requsite to develop the resources of that delightful country, have not, until quite recently, turned their attention to that remote region. But now, a different state of things exists; a new era in the improvements of California has commenced; here as in Oregon, foreigners from all countries, of the most enterprising and energetic character, are annually arriving, selecting and improving the most favorable sites for towns, and selecting and securing extensive grants of land, in the most desirable portions of the country.

Chapter 12

THE POPULATION OF CALIFORNIA

The entire population of Upper California, including foreigners, Mexicans and Indians, may be estimated at about thirty-one thousand human souls, of whom, about one thousand are foreigners, ten thousand are Mexicans, and the residue are Indians. By the term foreigners, I include all those who are not native citizens of Mexico, whether they have become citizens by naturalization, or whether they remain in a state of alienage. They consist, chiefly, of Americans, Englishmen, Frenchmen, Germans and Spaniards, but there is a very large majority of the former. The foreigners are principally settled at the various towns, and upon the Sacramento; those of whom who, are located at the latter place, consist almost entirely of our own citizens. The foreigners of this country are, generally, very intelligent; many of them have received all the advantages of an education; and they all possess an unusual degree of industry and enterprise. Those who are emigrating to that remote and almost unknown region, like those who are emigrating to Oregon, are, in all respects, a different class of persons, from those who usually emigrate to our frontier. They generally possess more then an ordinary degree of intelligence, and that they possess an eminent degree of industry, enterprise and bravery, is most clearly evinced, from the very fact, of their entering upon this most arduous and perilous undertaking. Very few cowards ever venture voluntarily, to meet all those imaginary and real dangers, to which they are necessarily exposed, in crossing the Rocky mountains or doubling Cape Horn; and no indolent man, even if he possess the bravery of Caesar, can ever summon the requisite energy; and if he possess the bravery of Caesar, and the strength and energy of Hercules, and lack the enterprise, he will have no disposition to attempt a feat, so arduous and irksome. Hence, if he possess an unusual degree of cowardice, he dare not, if nature has supplied him with a great competency of indolence, he cannot; and if he be not blessed with more then an ordinary share of energy and enterprise, he will not emigrate, either to Oregon or California. The above gives some of the leading traits of character, of the foreigners of California, but extraordinary kindness, courtesy and hospitality, are additional traits, which they possess to an unusual degree. A more kind and hospitable people are nowhere found; they seem to vie with each other, in their kindness and hospitality to strangers; and at the same time, they treat each other as brothers. Here, you see the citizens and subjects, of almost every nation in the civilized world, united by the silken chains of friendship, exerting every energy, and doing every thing in their power, to promote the individual and general welfare. Upon the arrival of a stranger among them, the question is not, is he an Englishman, an American or Frenchman, but is he a foreigner? which latter, if he is found to be, he receives all that kindness and hospitable attention, peculiar to the foreigners of California. These are truly a happy people; among whom, no distinction of clime is recognized, national preferences and prejudices do not exist, religious rancor is hushed; and all is order, harmony and peace. The sages of by-gone days, sighed for such scenes as here exist, but they realized them not; the children of fancy, dreamed their dreams of union and harmony, but the foreigners of California, enjoy their desired realities.

The Mexicans differ, in every particular, from the foreigners; ignorance and its concomitant, superstition, together with suspicion and superciliousness, constitute the chief ingredients, of the Mexican character. More indomitable ignorance does not prevail, among any people who make the least pretentions to civilization; in truth, they are scarcely a visible grade, in the scale of intelligence, above the barbarous tribes by whom they are surrounded; but this is not surprising, especially when we consider the relation, which these people occupy to their barbarous neighbors, in other particulars. Many of the lower order of them, have intermarried with the various tribes, and have resided with them so long, and lived in a manner so entirely similar, that it has become almost impossible, to trace the least distinctions between them, either in reference to intelligence, or complexion. There is another class, which is, if possible, of a lower order still, then those just alluded to, and which consists of the aborigines themselves, who have been slightly civilized, or rather *domesticated.* These two classes constitute almost the entire Mexican population, of California, and among them almost every variety and shade of complexion may be found, from the African black, to the tawny brown of our southern Indians. Although there is a great variety, and dissimilarity among them, in reference to their complexions, yet in their beastly habits and an entire want of all moral principle, as well as a perfect destitution of all intelligence, there appears to be a perfect similarity. A more full description of these classes, will be found, in what is said, in reference to the Indians, for as most of the lower order of Mexicans, are Indians in fact, whatever is said in reference to the one, will also be applicable to the other. The higher order of the Mexicans, in point of intelligence, are perhaps about equal, to the lower order of our citizens, throughout our western states; but among these even, are very few, who are, to any extent, learned or even intelligent.

Learning and intelligence appear to be confined, almost entirely, to the priests, who are, generally, both learned and intelligent. The priests are not only the sole proprietors, of the learning and intelligence, but also, of the liberty and happiness of the people, all of which they parcel out to their blind votaries, with a very sparing hand; and thus it is, that all the Mexican people are kept, in this state of degrading ignorance, and humiliating vassalage. The priests here, not only have the possession of the keys of the understanding, and the door of liberty: but they also, have both the present and ultimate happiness of these ignorant people, entirely at their disposal. Such at least, is the belief of the people, and such are the doctrines there taught by the priests. At times, I sympathize with these unfortunate beings, but again, I frequently think, that, perhaps, it is fortunate for the residue of mankind, that these semi-barbarians, are thus *ridden* and restrained, and if they are to be thus priest ridden, it is, no doubt, preferable, that they should retain their present *riders.*

Notwithstanding the general learning of the priests, they are the most dissolute and abandoned characters of the whole community. They indulge, without restraint, in all the vices common to those people, and, especially, in those of drunkenness and gambling. To such an extent do they indulge in the former of these vices, that it is not unusual, to see them so much intoxicated, as to prevent the discharge of their ordinary religious duties. It may not be inappropriate here, to give one or two instances, which were related to me by respectable gentlemen, in California, and which may show, to what extent those priests, indulge in these vices. One Sabbath morning, as my informant was passing along the street, in one of those towns, he observed a priest standing at the counter of a grocery, and in the act of satiating his artificial appetite, not with the delicious wine of California, but the inebriating brandy of the states, of which, he seemed already, to have received a surcharge, for his deranged system, appeared to be almost entirely, beyond his control. By a fast hold upon the counter, however, he was enabled to hold his position, but not to change it, though the latter appeared to be an object, which he had a very great anxiety to accomplish. Finally, a lad, who was evidently in search of the priest was seen passing from grocery to grocery, until he fell in with the object of his search, our hero, when he informed him, that the people were in attendance, at the church, waiting his arrival, to which the priest replied, that it was very well, he would go, so saying, he took another glass of brandy, when, with the aid of the boy he staggered on church-ward, with more then ordinary rapidity, as he had, by this time, ample propelling power. But his movements were very irregular, which was very much owing to the inadequacy of the power, at the helm, which was the small lad, despite of all whose powers, he frequently made the most tremendous leaps and plunges, which appeared to threaten an immediate wreck. By the aid of the helmsman, however, and the gradual diminution of the propelling power, that awful calamity was averted, and this great craft, was safely moored in the desired haven, amid the shouts of the multitude, and to the infinite joy and gratification of the whole crew. Whether this was the last voyage, my informant was not advised, but that it was not the first, he was fully advised, for he had witnessed several similar arrivals and departures, in person.

When I shall have related one other instance of this kind, I will have done with this class of the Californians. The instance to which I allude, was related to me, in substance, by a respectable foreigner, of that country, who witnessed the whole occurrence, as here related. As my informant was passing in the street, of one of those towns, his attention was attracted to a gambling house, upon entering which, he saw four or five gentlemen engaged at a game of cards, among whom, were several officers of the government, and other gentlemen of standing, as well as a very devoted and learned priest, who appeared to be much interested in the game, and very much excited, not only from the effects of large betting, but also from the effects of large drinking. While my informant remained in the room, which was about thirty minutes, he saw this religious personage, bet and stake, not less than one hundred dollars, and drink not less than three glasses of brandy. My informant now left these high dignitaries, about "half seas over," excepting the priest, who appeared not to deal in halves; he did not appear willing to bet half of a hundred, to drink half of a glass of brandy, nor did he appear willing to be half drunk, for he was more than two thirds drunk. Very early the next morning, my informant passed the door of the same establishment, when, upon hearing unusual confusion, he again stepped in, and to his utter astonishment, he found the same gentlemen in the same condition as that in which he left them the evening previous, with the exception of an increase of their numbers and their excitement, the latter of which, was strongly indicated, by their boisterous and angry declamations, as well as the thunderings of their repeated stamping upon the floor, and their successive furious blows upon the table. A further difference, however, was, that the floor was strewed with the victims both of Morpheus and Bacchus, amongst whom, were two priests. But our hero, who seemed to take every thing by the entirety, had taken the whole night, and appeared inclined to take the whole day; he was now in high glee, and was evidently triumphing over the fallen victims with whom he was surrounded. He had out-drunk, out-gambled, out-generaled and out-juggled them all. As any new or interesting circumstance occurred, he was frequently heard to exclaim, in a jocular way, "qod est in corde sobrii, est in ore ebrii," what soberness conceals, drunkenness reveals. In the midst of this high glee, and this learned display, a servant appeared, who informed the learned divine, that his attendance was now required at the church, where the people had already convened. The learned, polite and drunken divine, now arose, and thus addressed his fellow bacchanalians; "gentlemen, you will excuse me, for a few minutes, as I have a religious duty to perform, when I shall have done which, I will immediately return, but in the mean time, go on with the game; good morning gentlemen." Of course, the learned prelate was excused, who having performed his religious services, soon returned and renewed his bacchanalian revelings with renewed vigor. How different are the priests of California from those of the same denomination, of christians in our own country? There, as above seen, we find among them, the most cruel oppressors, the most absolute tyrants, and the most devoted and dissolute debauchees, of the whole land, while here, we find among the clergy of the same denomination, not only the most humane, just and honorable citizens, but also the most meek and sincerely devoted christians.

The Indian population, as before stated, amounts to about twenty thousand, most of whom, are found in the interior and mountainous regions, yet they are found, in greater or less numbers, in all the different valleys. They are usually found, congregated in villages, in many of which, there are, frequently, many hundreds, and even thousands, who occupy small huts, of most singular construction. These huts consist of mere conic elevations of earth, about eight or ten feet in height, and about twenty feet in diameter, with a small aperture at the top of each, of about two feet in diameter, which affords an entrance into each; besides which, there is also, an entrance at the side of each, near the surface of the earth. In each of these villages, there are, usually, from ten to fifty of this kind of primitive buildings, which are capable of accommodating, from ten to twenty persons. They have the external appearance, of being constructed entirely of earth, but upon entering them, they are found to be constructed, internally of timbers, which sustain the earthen covering. The Indians of this country, are not migratory, but it is seen, that they have, in numerous instances, abandoned their old haunts, and re-established in other portions of the country, but for what cause, it is difficult to ascertain, with any degree of certainty, for the sites which have been thus abandoned, appear in many instances, to possess advantages much superior, to those which have been subsequently selected. As far as can be ascertained, the desolating ravages of war, have been the chief causes of these repeated removals, for villages of fifty, or even a hundred of these huts, are frequently seen, which have the appearance, of having been their ancient haunts, but which, are now abandoned, the ground at, and around which, is covered with human skulls. Upon examining several of these huts, of these abandoned villages, I very readily found, that whatever the cause of this mortality, might have been, it was, evidently, inflicted upon them, when within their huts, for the earth of the external covering of the huts, having fallen in, was extensively intermixed with skulls, and other human bones. At the villages which they occupy, there are no apparent evidences, of that extensive mortality, which formerly prevailed, to such an alarming extent among them, at their abandoned villages. All of the various tribes, of this country, are found in their aboriginal state of barbarism, as perfectly wild and timid, as the herds of beasts, with which they are surrounded. Upon approaching one of their villages, without their previous knowledge, a scene of most extraordinary confusion, and noisy clamor is presented; all scudding at once, into their earthen house, not a human soul is to be seen, excepting those who present their heads through the aperture at the apex, of each of the huts, and who are, in a most clamorous and confused manner, drawing upon your humanity and mercy, and begging you to spare them, collectively and individually. The nearer you approach their village, the more boisterous and clamorous they become, in their loud and confused appeals, to all the better feelings of your nature, to spare their tribe, from the dire calamity, of extermination, or, at all events, to save their village, from which the earth may be repeopled. After having remained a few minutes, amid their loud lamentations, furious cries, frantic yells, and wild gesticulations, your pity and sympathy, are excited, and sure enough you conclude to spare their village, at least, and leave them, making the very heavens resound, with their loud, clamorous shouts, of exultation and joy. These Indians are much more advanced, in civilization, then any others found in this country, with the exception of those who have been connected with the missions, or those who have become Mexicans, which, by the by, is a very slight transition.

In many other portions of the country, they do not even build huts, nor do they wear any kind of clothing; being mere children of nature. Nothing whatever is attached to their persons, excepting, perhaps, a few feathers, which are attached to the heads of the chiefs, by means of the hair, and which are designed, to designate their rank; but when they are about to engage in some extraordinary chace, they also tie either a bark or grape-vine around their waists, drawing it so tight, as to almost sever their bodies. When going to war, they also tie a vine or bark around the waist, in addition to which, they besmear their faces, and their bodies generally, with the white clay before alluded to, which having done, and having provided themselves, either with a kind of rude bow, or equally as rude war-club, they are prepared for any warlike emergency. Many of these tribes, which are found far in the interior, and in the mountainous regions, subsist almost entirely upon edible root, grass seeds, oats, acorns, and insects, such as crickets and grasshoppers, the former furnishing them a substitute for bread, and the latter for meat. In those portions of the interior, where they subsist mostly upon insects, such insects us crickets and grass hoppers are extremely numerous; so numerous, in fact, that it is not unusual to see fifty or sixty bushels, at one of these villages, which are dried and prepared for food. In order to take these insects, fire is set to the dried vegetation, which, in many places, is literally covered with them, and which, as it burns, leaves them upon the ground partially burned, when, without waiting for the command, arise, slay and eat, they all, old and young, male and female, with their rude baskets, and whatever else they happen to possess, now go forth, to the in gathering, of the rich harvest. In this manner, many bushels are soon gathered, which are exposed to the rays of the sun, until they are perfectly dried, when they are laid up in store, for their future necessities. The wildness and timidity of these tribes, are such, that upon the appearance of white persons, at their villages, all of the males, both old and young, immediately flee in the utmost confusion, to the surrounding hills and mountains, while the females remain; and as you advance, they commence a most doleful moaning and crying, and, at the same time, persist in offering you such food as they have collected. It would excite both your curiosity and compassion, in passing their villages, which have been thus abandoned, by the males, to hear the mournful lamentation, and the piteous crying of the timid women, and the deafening screaming, and wild clamor, of the frightened children, and to see the females cautiously approaching, upon the right and left, with rude dishes, containing insects, which they are now offering you, with a view of appeasing your wrath, and thereby, averting the awful calamity which evidently awaits them, and all their insectile neighbors. In passing through the extreme interior of this country, I have often come suddenly upon several hundred, of these wild, naked creatures, when, like the wild beasts of the forests, they would leap and scud away, plunging into the river, and swimming across, they would soon be lost to our sight, in the vast plains, upon the opposite shore. Those of the tribes, which build huts, are, usually, found upon, and in the vicinity of the streams; they subsist, chiefly upon fish, which they are able to take at any season of the year, and as many of them have bows, of a very superior kind, they are also able to kill much game. Many of these tribes take the salmon, and other fish, not only in quantities sufficient for their own purposes, but they also, supply all the different settlements with an ample abundance, for the most trivial compensation. Most of these tribes are entirely friendly, and they are of the greatest service to the various settlers, who are able to perform all their labors, upon their farms, by the aid of the Indians, with very little expense, and with very little trouble, or inconvenience to themselves.

The government of California, being the government of one military chieftain, whose will is the law of the land, may be defined to be, a *military despotism*. The present executive, is Manuel Micheltorena, who is also the commander in chief, of the militia, of both Californias. He resides at Monterey, where he arrived in the autumn of 1843, when he was very favorably received, although there had been much opposition to his appointment. He was appointed by the government of Mexico, to fill a vacancy, occasioned by the removal of one Juan Baptiste Alvarado, who was elevated to that station, by the people in 1836, in opposition to the government of Mexico, the previous governor, Echuandra, having been forcibly deposed, by the Mexicans and foreigners combined. This was the result of the revolution of 1836, in which the Mexicans and foreigners succeeded, in a very few days, not only in acquiring complete possession of the country, and establishing an independent government, but they also succeeded, in shipping the whole crew, of Mexican officers, "in good order," for Matzatlan, on their way to city of Mexico, and thus the country was rid, of a horde of governmental robbers. When the government of Mexico, became advised of the course pursued by the Californians, and that the Mexicans and foreigners had combined, to accomplish their purposes, it proceeded, immediately, though very reluctantly, to ratify the revolutionary act of the Californians, by issuing a commission to the "rebel" governor, by which, he was authorized to hold the office, which he had thus acquired, by his treasonable intrigue. The chief cause, of the government's so readily, recalling its rejected governor, and confirming the act of the "rebels," was, that it was now fully advised, that the foreigners had determined to adhere to the revolutionists. This course, they had been persuaded to pursue, by the "rebel" governor, and several other influential Californians, who pledged themselves to the foreigners, that upon their succeeding, the government should be declared independent of Mexico, and that they should be entitled to all the privileges, and immunities of citizens. These with numerous other inducements, were held out to the foreigners, in order to induce them to aid, in the pending revolution, which they did, and which resulted as before stated, in the elevation of this Alvarado to the governorship, and as they thought, in the acquisition of their independence of Mexico. But this Alvarado, a libel upon the human race, accepted the appointment from the Mexican government, and commenced a series of indiscriminate insult, and oppression upon all foreigners, within his inhuman grasp; but the foreigners, not being inclined to submit, tamely, to this repeated wrong and outrage, were now in feeling, at least, in formidable and hostile opposition, to his supreme highness, the rebel governor. His insignificant excellency, continued his insult, cruelty and oppression, from day to day, and from month to month, but finally, after the lapse of about three years, perceiving that he was receiving his just

deserts, the disapprobation and supreme contempt, of all foreigners, as well as that of all the better class of the Mexicans,
now determined to make one last, desperate effort, to redeem
his lost character.

After consulting his own black heart, and those of some of
his villainous comrades, in disgraceful, cowardly oppression;
he determined to adopt some means, which might terminate,
either in the extermination, or expulsion of all the foreigners
from California, and in order to accomplish his fiendish purpose, he now commenced his unheard of cruelties, and barbarous oppressions, with renewed vigor and malignancy. His
extreme and justly deserved unpopularity, had a great tendency, to prevent his desired success, in infamy and crime,
until the autumn of 1840, when, by the aid of others, more
skilled in low treachery, and black villainy, he finally, fell
upon a scheme, which to some extent, effected his sinful and
criminal purpose. The course fixed upon, was to report,
among all the Mexicans, that the foreigners had combined,
for the purpose of revolutionizing the government, and establishing a republic, and that all the preliminary measures, preparatory to the accomplishment of that object, were already
adopted. All this, he well knew, to be absolutely false, yet he
also knew, that the credulous and suspicious Mexicans
would, very readily, credit it, especially, as it came from so
credible a source, but notwithstanding the *high source* from
which it was derived, he took particular care, to have it well
confirmed, by three or four other malicious villains. Lest the
falsity, of this base and murderous intrigue, might be seen,
even by the benighted rabble, his criminal excellency, was
extremely cautious, to enjoin upon every Mexican, to whom
he reported this base falsehood, that he keep the whole matter, a profound secret, and above all things, that he should not
divulge to any foreigner, although he might be his most inti-
mate friend, or even closely allied, by the ties of affinity or

consanguinity. This injunction of secrecy, he well knew, to be highly essential to his cowardly purpose, for he was not ignorant of the fact, that there were many of the foreigners, whom he had implicated, in the treasonable schemes alluded to, whose words simply, would be entitled to greater weight, than the solemn oath of himself, and his whole fraternity; nor was he ignorant of the fact, that if the foreigners should acquire, the least knowledge, of his infamous designs, his excellency would soon, cease to exist as *governor*, or in any other *manner*. The whole matter was, therefore, kept a profound secret, as far as the foreigners were concerned, for there was not one of them, in the entire country, who had the least intimation, that any thing unusual, was in contemplation.

His ungrateful and black-hearted excellency, having accomplished his unholy preliminaries, now dispatched a few of his niggardly hirelings, in the dead of the night, to the residences of most of the foreigners through out the country, with orders to bring them, in irons, before his supremely contemptible excellency. Nothing could have been more congenial, to the feelings of this pusillanimous crew, than the base and cowardly enterprise, in which they were about to engage; that of attacking innocent, unoffending men, under cover of night; without giving them the least intimation of their despicable designs, and that too, after having treated them, but the day before, with all the apparent kindness, and affected politeness, at the command of their hypocritical natures. Contemptible hypocritical cowards; base midnight assassins! In most instances, the first notice which the foreigners had of their approach, was a volley of musket balls, poured in upon them, through their windows and doors, as they were reposing upon their couches, with their families, in deep, midnight slumber. Many of them, most manfully resisted, this unceremonious attack, but being finally overcome by numbers, forty of them were taken, put in irons, taken to Monterey, and delivered to that demon in human form, his more then criminal excellency Alvarado. Here these brave *Anglosaxons* were dragged about, from place to place, during all the following day, many of them suffering most intensely, from the wounds which they received, the night before, and others, from the sore gallings of their ponderous shackles. Among them, was one Graham, who suffered extremely; for having fought bravely, and desperately, upon the night previous, he had received several very severe wounds, from musket balls, the breeches of muskets, and from swords; but he endured it all, with the fortitude of an American, which he is by birth; a brave determined American! These unfortunate men, still loaded with irons, were now thrown into dungeons, where they were confined for several days, suffering the most exquisite torture, from the continual gallings, of their massive fetters, parching thirst, and gnawing hunger. But to heighten their sufferings, they were all thrown together, into a little, narrow, filthy dungeon, the floor of which, was the wet muddy ground, and into which the air was admitted only at a small aperture, at which, scarcely sufficient could be received, to sustain life. Under this cruel, oppressive treatment, many of them were rapidly sinking; and had become so far exhausted, that they were no longer able to stand at the little aperture, to avail themselves of the oxygen, essential to the support of life, but were actually fast declining, under the influence of the carbonic acid gas, which occupied the bottom of the deep, dark and wet cell. Their companions, now seeing their exhausted condition, immediately, took them to the aperture spoken of, where after inhaling the atmospheric air for a few minutes, they were partially revived, and thus, for several days, those who were able, going frequently to this aperture, and those who were not able to stand, being carried to it, they were able to aid respiration, and to sustain life, though with the greatest possible difficulty, and most intense suffering.

Having thus satiated, his more then barbarous revenge, this heartless, soulless wretch, alias governor, now ordered his helpless, and almost lifeless victims, to be loaded with additional irons, and to be shipped for Matzatlan, and to be taken thence, to the city of Mexico, there to be dealt with, as the supreme authorities might direct. Arrangements were accordingly made, when these now pale, emaciated and dejected men were dragged from their dungeons, torn from their families and friends, loaded with massive fetters and chains, and thrown on board the vessel, by which they were to be conveyed to Matzatlan, or the grave, they knew not which, nor had they much solicitude as to the result. So violent was the suffering, of these unfortunate men, that one or two of them sunk under it, and died before reaching Mexico, while many others, suffered under severe illness, not only during their confinement, but also for months after their release, and all were reduced to an extreme state, of feebleness and emaciation. Upon arriving at the city of Mexico, an investigation was instituted, not only by the Mexican authorities, but also by the foreign ministers, the result of which was, that they were all, at once, released, with a tender of a small amount of money, as a remuneration for the insults and injuries, which they had thus wrongfully sustained. Some of them received the trivial remuneration, which was offered them, while others refused, absolutely, to receive so trivial a remuneration, and hence, have not, to this day, received a farthing. And is not this a gross neglect of our government, thus to permit her citizens to be chained, and dragged in irons, under the most cruel and barbarous treatment, suffering every thing but death, and even death itself, and that too, without the slightest cause, without a shadow of provocation? The result of all this affair, as far as the base tyrant, the governor is concerned, is all very well, but by no means as he had anticipated. As before remarked, he acquired his ascendancy forcibly, and against the will of Mexico, and the only reason of Mexico's suffering such an outrage upon her rights, was her dread of the foreigners, who adhered to him, in his treasonable elevation. But now, finding that the foreigners had abandoned him, and were most bitterly opposed to him, the government availed itself of this opposition of the foreigners, and unceremoniously removed this ungrateful, cowardly oppressor, and, as before stated, appointed the present governor in his stead. And now, being thus supplanted, as the fates will have it, and "plane uti factum oportuit," just as it ought to be, he is everywhere looked upon, with the most indignant contempt, not only by the foreigners, but also by the Mexicans, for he has proved equally treacherous to both, and has shown himself unworthy of the confidence of either; the consequence of which is, that he is now to be seen wandering about, like a "discontented ghost," having neither talent, worth, nor power, sufficient to attract the attention of any human soul, he drags droanishly about, from place to place, unobserving and unobserved.

Notwithstanding the complete prostration, in public opinion, of the treacherous monster of whom I have just spoken, the present governor, had many misgivings, as to the propriety and safety, of his attempting to enter upon this discharge, of his gubernatorial duties, in California, without a competent military force, to ensure his protection. Having advised the proper authorities of Mexico, of his fears and doubts, and some of the grounds upon which they were predicated, one thousand criminals were extracted, from the various prisons, and committed to his charge. With this formidable band of cut-throats, as their brands and cropped ears showed them to be, he set out upon his march to the Californias, where he arrived in the fall of 1842, remaining in the extreme southern part, of Upper California, until the fall of 1843, when he collected sufficient courage, to enable him to advance to the seat of government. The timorous movements of the governor, and, especially, the fact of his being unwilling to venture among the Californias, without an armed force, for his protection, created much dissatisfaction among them, which became so general, at one time, that they determined to interpose their omnipotence, to prevent his excellency from marching his omnifarious troops, to the seat of government. But before I left that country, his generalship was permitted to march northward, and was in full possession of the chief town, there to be seen marching and parading his cropped and branded troops, about the streets, with all imaginable pomposity. Disease and dissertion had reduced these troops, to two hundred, before they arrived in California, but there were quite enough of them left, to afford some of the rarest specimens of humanity, that I have ever beheld. They were indeed a motley crew; some were cropped, and others were branded; some were without shoes, and others were without shirts; some had guns, others had spears, others lances, and others nothing; and the latter were equally as well armed as the former, for those who had guns, had no ammunition. Thus armed and equipped, this omnifarious soldiery, is prepared to meet, in mortal combat, even a Caesar, a Hannibal, a Bonaparte or a Washington, but they cannot be induced to meet a Jones. These soldiers, like all others of Mexico, are mere Indians, many of whom, are as perfectly wild and untutored, as the most barbarous savages of the forest; yet it is with these wild, shirtless, earless and heartless creatures, headed by a few timid, soulless, brainless officers, that these semi-barbarians, intend to hold this delightful region, as against the civilized world.

The Judiciary of this government, is extremely simple; it is divested of all that complexity, peculiar to our judiciary system. The judicial officers consist simply of a few alcaldes, or justices of the peace, who are appointed for each town, and settlement, throughout the country, and who have unlimited jurisdiction, in the precinct for which they are appointed. The chief duties of these alcaldes, are merely to adjudge all trivial difficulties, which arise among the people, and to issue passports for those who wish to pass from one precinct to another, and prohibit their passing without them. A passport, issued by the alcalde, is a mere written authority, given you, to pass to and from, such places as are designated, without limiting you to any particular time, though they always contain the words, valid for the time necessary, or words of similar import, and a request, of the alcalde, to the civil and military authorities, to permit you to pass unmolested. The officers are latterly, very inattentive to that branch of their duty, for it is very seldom now, that a foreigner is interrogated in reference to his passport; perhaps it is never the case, unless the foreigner is an entire stranger, and the officers have some good reason, to apprehend some improper conduct. In passing from place to place, no Mexican even spoke of my passport, unless it was, when I applied for its renewal, which I sometimes did, as I passed from one precinct to another, although it was not strictly necessary. Upon one occasion, when I applied for a passport, I remember to have spoken to the "commandants," in reference to the propriety of being thus required, like slaves, to obtain a permission, to pass from place to place, when he remarked, that the authorities were not as strict, with foreigners, in that respect, as they had formerly been, for instance, he remarked, that if I should pass throughout the entire country, the question would never be asked, whether I had obtained a passport. The reason of this great difference, in respect, he said, was that from the long residence of foreigners among them, they were satisfied, that they were not as evilly disposed, as they had formerly been supposed to be; but the true reason is, that they have not the balance of power, in their favor, as they formerly had, which if they had, all their former hostility and barbarity, would be renewed, with infinite pleasure. The foreigners are annually increasing in numbers and power, the inevitable tendency of which, is clearly seen and understood, even by the Mexicans, hence it is, that foreigners are now treated with the utmost respect, kindness and hospitality. The bombardment of Vera Cruz, the triumph of Texas, and the impromptu conquest of California, by Com. Jones, have long since, taught them the propriety, of respecting the rights of foreigners.

Now, instead of that inhuman oppression, which was formerly inflicted upon foreigners, without measure and without mercy, they are trusted with all the deceptive kindness imaginable, and instead of that hostile opposition, which formerly existed to the emigration of foreigners to that country, every inducement is held out, to encourage foreign immigration. Large grants of land are given to each emigrant, averaging from one to eleven square leagues, the quantity depending upon the number of members, composing the applicant's family, and his means of improving, by building, fencing or otherwise. In order to obtain a grant of land, it becomes necessary for a foreigner, first to make an application for naturalization, then to present a petition addressed to the governor, praying for a grant of the land which he may have selected, and of which, he, at the same time, presents a general map, representing its extent and surface. This being done, he is entitled to the possession of his land, and when the process of his naturalization is accomplished, he is entitled to his deed, which is made by the government, of California, under the hand and seal of the governor. Although the quantity of land usually granted is from one to eleven square leagues, yet it is seldom that either extreme is taken, perhaps there are no instances of any individuals having obtained but one league, though there are some instances, of their having obtained eleven square leagues. There are also several grants of twenty or thirty square leagues; among these extensive grants, is Captain Sutter's, which contains thirty square leagues, or two hundred and seventy square miles. Grants of this extent, are given only upon the condition that the grantee settle a certain number of families upon it, within a certain number of years, according to the provisions of the colonization law, which law, however, it is said, has recently been repealed. Any person arriving in that country, is at liberty to take any lands which, are not taken, or which have not been applied for, even without making any application for that purpose, but in such case, he is liable to be dispossessed at any time, by the lands being regularly applied for, by another. All those who emigrated to that country, with me, settled in that manner, and made some extensive improvements, without having made an application for a title, yet they all designed to make their applications, in due time. The reason of their not making their application, immediately, upon their arrival, was, that it was, at that time, rumored, that foreigners would be enabled to obtain their titles, without becoming citizens, which they all very much preferred, if it could be accomplished. I am aware that a certain high functionary, at Washington city, who represents the government of Mexico, insists that foreigners can not obtain lands, in California, merely by becoming citizens, but that their obtaining lands, depends entirely, upon the option of the governor of California. Now how this may be, I do not pretend to say, but I do say, that the only prerequisites, required, are those just stated, and in reference to this matter, I speak from my own personal knowledge, as I called upon the governor, with a view of applying for the grant of a certain tract of land, when he informed me, as above stated. But as I did not think proper to become a Mexican citizen, I did not obtain my title, and as I am fully determined *never* to become a Mexican citizen, the presumption is, that I shall never obtain a title to the lands for which I applied, especially if it is the destiny of Mexico forever to retain possession of the Californias. In reference to the option of the governor to grant lands or not, as contended by the Mexican functionary alluded to, it is not at all material, more specially, as it happens to be his *preference*, or at least his *practice*, to grant lands to all foreigners, who make application in conformity with the requisitions before stated. And should his preference suggest a different course, I am inclined to the opinion, that his excellency would still find it much more conducive, both to public policy and peace, to grant lands upon the same terms, to all who make application for that purpose; and thus, avoid creasing distinctions and prejudices, between native and naturalized citizens.

Chapter 13

Manners and Customs of California

The Mexicans here, are a peculiar people, not only in reference to their intelligence, government, and all other particulars before mentioned, but also in reference to their manners and customs. The lower order of them live in mere huts, the walls of which are constructed of poles, which are set upright, side by side, one end being permanently fixed in the ground; the other ends are attached with raw hide ropes to a pole, which is placed horizontally on each side of the walls thus constructed, and about six or seven feet from the ground. The four walls being thus erected, poles are then placed transversely from one wall to the other, which are covered either with hay, flags, or cornstalks, constituting the roof, when the hut is completed, having neither floor nor chimney. – The second and higher orders, occupy such buildings as those which have been described upon a former page, most of which are also without either chimneys or floors. No furniture is generally found in or about the houses of the lower orders, excepting here and there a raw bullock's hide spread upon the ground, which, together with a blanket or two, constitutes their beds and bedding. Their clothing generally consists of nothing more then a shirt and a pair of pantaloons, yet some of them also have a kind of rude, primitive hat, and sandals. The chase and servitude to the higher orders, furnish them a livelihood; they subsist almost entirely upon meat, fish, oats and edible roots. Those of the second and higher orders, who reside in the interior, although they have "adobie" houses, yet they generally have neither beds, chairs, tables, nor any other furniture, excepting such beds as those before described, and a raw hide spread upon the ground, which constitutes a table, with a few stools or bullock's heads, which answer as chairs. Their apparel consists of a shirt, a pair of pantaloons, some kind of a hat and shoes, or sandals, in addition to which, some have a pair of breeches and a blanket, with a perforation in the middle, through which they put their heads, and thus form, as they think, a very convenient coat or cloak. Meat, fish, beans, bread and fruit, constitute their food. But they subsist chiefly upon the former, as a matter of preference. Should you call at the residence of one of these Mexicans, even of the highest class residing in the interior, you would not only be received very kindly, but you would also be annoyed with continued proffers, of all the luxuries which they possess. And should you remain until noon, a large quantity of beef will be roasted before the fire, which, when done, will be attached to a few sticks, which are driven into the ground for that purpose, in the middle of the room, when you are invited to sit down with them, and partake of the rich repast; at the same time, you are offered a stool or beef's head as a substitute for a chair, if there happens to be one convenient, if not, you are expected to sit upon the ground. Being thus located, you now commence the dissection and mastication of the half, or quarter of a beef, as the case may be, with which you are now confronted; but in this operation, you labor under the disadvantage, of having none of the ordinary instruments, used upon such occasions; hence you are under the necessity of using your pocket knife, or such other knife as you may chance to have in your possession. Among some of these people, in addition to the roasted beef, you would also be furnished with a little bean soup, and, perhaps, some bread; but they all view

plates, knives and forks, and the like, as mere useless append-
ages. Should you call upon those of the lower order, with the
view of obtaining a dinner, the presumption is, that the whole
affair would result in a disgusting failure, if not on their part,
in an attempt to procure something for you to eat, at least,
upon your part, in your attempt to eat what they have succeeded in procuring; but whatever they have, they will readily
offer you, with much apparent anxiety to accommodate. The
higher order of those who reside in the different towns, and at
the missions, generally live very well, much, in fact, as the
foreigners do, who are equally as abundantly supplied with all
the necessaries and luxuries of life, as citizens of our own
country, or those of any other. All classes of the Mexicans are
unusually kind and hospitable to foreigners, as far as it relates
to their reception and treatment as guests. Whatever attention
and kindness you may receive at their hands, while guests,
and however long you may remain with them, they will
receive no compensation, but to your proposition to remuner-
ate them, they invariably reply, "God will pay."

Labor of all kinds is performed by the Indians and the
lower order or the Mexicans, but those who are not bound in
servitude to others, labor very little, as a competency of food
and raiment, is readily acquired, with very little exertion.
Among all classes, oxen are principally used for the draught,
drawing by their horns, instead of their necks, as in the ordinary manner; a strong piece of timber about as large as an
ordinary yoke, is placed, upon the necks of the oxen, just back
of the horns, to which it in permanently attached, by means of
a raw-hide rope. To the middle of this new-fashioned yoke, a
strong raw-hide rope is affixed, to which the cart, plough, or
whatever else is to be drawn, is attached, when all is in readiness for actual service. Those oxen, yoked in this, manner,
draw most extremely large draughts, but by no means as large
draughts as they could draw, if yoked in the ordinary manner.

The plough, which is in use among the Mexicans, is certainly among the most simply constructed, and cheapest of farming utensils, being, generally, a mere forked stick, one prong of which, being pointed, answers, as the share, and the other having a notch cut at the end, to which a rope maybe attached, constitutes the beam, while the main stalk, extending back a few feet from the union of the two prongs, constitutes the handle. This is the California plough, which is in general use, throughout the entire country; but as an improvement upon this plough, some of the Mexicans construct one in a different manner, though with the same regard to cheapness, being two sticks of timber, so attached as to form a plough, very much like that just described; and designed only as a substitute for that, when a natural fork cannot be conveniently found. Horses are seldom used otherwise then as saddle-horses, but we frequently see large draughts, drawn by them, which, instead of being harnessed in the ordinary manner, are put under the saddle, the girth of which is drawn extremely tight, when one end of a strong raw-hide rope, is attached to the stone, wood, or whatever else is to be drawn, while the other end is firmly attached to the pommel of the saddle. Every thing being thus arranged, the Mexican, with his heels loaded down with ponderous, gingling spurs, now mounts his steed, to whose sides he plies his heels with such pointed exactness, such force and confused gingling, that, as the only alternative, he leaps and darts away with his immense load, notwithstanding its very great ponderosity. With horses harnessed in this manner, it is quite common to see Mexicans on their way to market, their vehicles being a dry bullock's hide, to which one end of a long raw-hide rope is attached, the other end of which, is attached to the pommel of the saddle, of their riding horses. Upon this hide, thus dragging upon the ground, are heaped vegetables, fowls, and whatever else they may have in readiness for the market, as well as two or three women and children, which, from all appearances, are not designed for the market, or, at all events, it would seem that they would not sell to a very good advantage, without the preparatory expense of a thorough scouring. Upon arriving in market, I have frequently seen these inventive geniuses, with their strange omnibuses, and omnifarious loading, passing about from place to place, until they disposed of all their load, excepting that part of it which partook somewhat of humanity, when they also disposed of their extraordinary vehicles, and returned to their homes as they best could, some on horse back, some on foot, and others, I knew not how, unless by "steam," to raise which, they appeared to be making some efforts, which I thought, would most likely succeed. These are the vehicles in common use, among the Mexicans, but many of the foreigners, as well as some of the higher order of the Mexicans, have carts, wagons, and even carriages, but these are very seldom seen, and especially the latter; as traveling is, as yet, almost entirely on horseback and by water, the former of which methods, is, however, much the most generally adopted, both by the Mexicans and foreigners.

As we are passing, perhaps the reader would be pleased to notice the proceedings of a Mexican alcalde's court. An individual, wishing to institute proceedings in one of their courts, for the recovery of a demand, applies to the alcalde for that purpose, who, instead of issuing a summons, despatches a servant post haste, to the residence of the defendant, informing him, that his attendance at the alcaldes' office, will be required on a certain day, to answer the complaint of the plaintiff; and that, if he do not appear at the time and place designated, the alcalde will proceed to the determination of the matter exparte. The day thus fixed upon arrives, and the parties appearing, his honor, now interrogates the defendant in reference to his delinquency, when he proceeds to offer such excuses as may occur to him, setting forth his reasons for not having made payment previously, or he commences to curse his antagonist most vociferously; and insulting and abusing him to every extent, declaring absolutely, that he will not pay him, which is the "general issue" in California. According to the rules of practice in the alcalde's court, the plaintiff is now entitled to the floor, which he takes with the greatest eagerness, when he commences to answer all the excuses and arguments of the defendant, or to repel his insults, by more direct, and more numerous insults, as well as by more vehement, and more profane cursing. If the proceedings have taken the latter course, his honor has nothing to do, but to weigh the insult and profanity, and give his judgment according to the preponderance, as it may be found in favor of the plaintiff or the defendant; but if they have taken the former course, his honor proceeds to determine, as to the weight and validity of the defendant's excuses, which are thrown into the Mexican's scales of justice, with the plaintiffs demand; and, as before, the decision is according to the preponderance. In weighing and determining causes as above, much less depends upon the quantum of insult, profane cursing, the validity of the excuse, or the justness of the demand, than upon the weights which are employed, which are usually of gold, sometimes, however, they are of silver, but when those of the latter metal are used, they are made much heavier, the proportion between those of the latter and former metal, being nearly as sixteen to one. These weights are always employed upon such occasions, and they are furnished, for that purpose, either by the party himself, or by a friend; in English they are called bribes, and it is now reduced, by experience, to an absolute certainty, that he that will not bribe, can not succeed at *law*, in a Mexican alcalde's court. At *law*, I say, I mean the game above alluded to, which, perhaps, partakes as little of *law* as it does of divinity. A foreigner of respectability, informed me, that he found it necessary in one instance, to resort to the *law* for the recovery of a demand, which he held against a farmer, who was amply able to pay him at any time, if he was so disposed. In order, therefore, to regulate his disposition, this gentleman applied to an alcalde, who immediately issued his warrant, (an athletic servant,) and soon the delinquent was ushered into the alcalde's august presence, where he commenced to offer his numerous excuses, the principal of which was, that his cattle were not sufficiently fattened for the slaughter-house, and, consequently, to kill them then, would subject him to a very great loss. The kind hearted, lenient judge, now appeared to symphathize greatly with the defendant, which, however, was the effect of the golden weights, which had already been thrown into the scales, which were now, evidently, preponderating in the defendant's favor. The magnanimous judge, pausing a few moments, but finding no disposition on the part of the foreign gentleman, to apply either the golden or silver weights, now asks the defendant, when his cattle will be so fattened as to enable him to kill them and discharge the plaintiffs demand, to which the defendant replies, that he thinks they will be amply fattened in about twelve months; "very good" replies the alcalde, "let the cause stand continued until next autumn." The parties now, severally, returned to their homes, the defendant much elated with his triumphant success at *law*, and the plaintiff, laboring under the sting of his unexpected defeat, is perfectly disgusted with every thing that bears the name of law, alcalde, or defendant. But the year soon rolls around, and the parties again appear before his honor, the dignified and bribed alcalde, who, immediately, proceeds to propound the same questions to the defendant, as before, in reference to the fitness of his cattle for the slaughter-house. Although the defendant did not give the same answer as before, yet he gave one, which more clearly exhibited the baseness, and contemptible meanness of both himself and the perjured alcalde, which was, that his cattle were sufficiently fattened, but that he was unable to procure sufficient laborers. The parties now again returned to their respective homes, the defendant rejoicing in "the glorious uncertainties of the law," and the plaintiff, more fully then ever, convinced of its tendency to obstruct justice, and to promote villainy and crime; and, hence more fully then ever, determined to have no more to do with either law, alcaldes, or defendants.

The chief amusements of the Mexicans, are their fandangos or balls, cock-fights, and bull and bear-fights. The fandangos, or balls, are conducted among these people, much in the same manner, that they are elsewhere, or so nearly so, at least, that there is nothing connected with them, which I shall particularly notice, although there are many very extraordinary and interesting scenes, that occur upon these occasions, which might be so described, as to afford some amusement, yet, as their description would afford no important information, I pass them unnoticed. The cock-fights are always attended by large core courses of people, especially upon the Sabbath, when not only the common people, but also the officers of the government, as well as the priests, all of whom march in solemn procession, directly from the church, after divine service, to the cockpit, where they anticipate much from the approaching exhibition of inhuman cruelty. Various opinions are now entertained and expressed, as to the probable success of the various game cocks; and all is high joy, noisy merriment, among the priests and all others, the latter of whom, are frequently heard to utter the most vehement, exulting, and triumphant shouts of acclamation and joy, with repeated and vehement outcries of "huzza, for the priest's cock!" The bull-fights are much the most common amusements, and it is almost incredible, with what ardor and zeal, the citizens of all classes, and of both sexes, crowd together, at these inhuman scenes of cruelty and blood. In the vicinity of every town of any importance, there is a vast arena in the form of an amphitheatre, designed for sports of this kind, which is circumscribed by a strong post and rail, or board fence, around the exterior of which, are successive circular seats, rising above one another to the height of fifteen or twenty feet, and of sufficient extent, to accommodate several thousand persons. Timely notice is always given of these bull-fights, and a general attendance, universally follows; savoring so strongly of barbarity, cruelty and indolence, it could not fail to attract the attention of the admiring thousands, of those semi-barbarians. The governor with all the principal officers, together with the priests, always occupies the highest seats upon such occasions; and their smiling approbation, especially of the priests, whether drunk or sober, is always considered a much higher encomium, then the thundering plaudits of all the surrounding multitude. And the priests are quite certain to laugh, whether there is any thing to laugh at or not, especially, if their merriment has been sufficiently excited by the enlivening and inebriating draughts, to which they are accustomed. Upon these occasions, you will frequently see, one fourth of all the Mexican population present, occupying the various seats before described, which, when thus occupied, are covered with an extensive awning. Being thus arranged and accompanied by a band of music, or, rather, of *noise*, and the bull-fighters, having marched into the arena, the signal is given, and the bull is loused, when the fight commences. Some of the bull-fighters are on foot, others are on horseback, the latter being generally well trained in equestrian exercises, and all being armed with swords, spears, or lances, they now commence action, either on the offensive or defensive, but generally, on the defensive; for usually, the moment the bull is turned loose he makes a most furious charge, either upon the footmen or horsemen, when he receives repeated lacerations, from both spears and lances. If he attacks a horseman, his repeated assaults are resisted by the horseman, until a footman comes to his aid, who thrusts a spear or lance into him, from behind, and, at the same time, exhibits a red flag, and thus his attention is diverted from the horseman, who would otherwise have been an easy prey. His attention is now turned to the footman, who is in a similar manner, relieved either by a horseman or by another footman. This scene is repeated from time to time, and, until the fatigued and wounded bull moves slowly away to one side of the arena, as if desirous of avoiding further conflict, when a most tremendous burst of applause resounds through the air, amid which the priests are heard, loudly exclaiming, "non potest fieri melius! non potest fieri melius!" as well as heart could wish! as well as heart could wish!

These repeated and continued plaudits, excite the pride and renew the energies of the tormentors, who proceed to the renewal of the bloody scene, but the indisposition of the bull to renew the contest, appears to afford a serious obstacle, yet the ingenuity of these cruel tormentors, readily invents the means of arousing his last and dying energies. Hundreds of squibs and crackers, are now brought, which are attached to one end of wires, the other ends of which are pointed and bearded, which are then thrust into the neck, shoulders, and back of the sinking animal; but he is so far exhausted, that he entirely disregards them, until fire is applied to them, when the incessant cracking, hissing, smoking and blazing, arouse all his declining vigor. He now shakes his head most furiously, amid the firing, smoking confusion, then bellowing aloud, and distending his tongue, as if calling into requisition all his powers, he plunges and leaps at his antagonist, and striking the horse, prostrates him, rider and all, upon the ground, amid the deafening shouts of the multitude, and the vociferous exultations of the priests, who are heard above all others, loudly exclaiming; "prospere procedit opus! prospere

procedit opus!" the business goes on well! the business goes
on well! But, in the mean time, the bull is goring and lacerat-
ing his fallen victim, with the greatest fury; and soon it is
found that the horse is dead, and that the rider, from the fall of
the horse upon one of his legs, and the successive blows of
the bull's head and horns upon the other, is unable to maintain
an upright position; but by the aid of a few of his brave comrades, he makes good his retreat, when the very heavens
resound with thundering shouts, and vociferous peals of
laughter from the exerted multitude, who appear to be entirely
indifferent, which of the animals succeeds, whether those in
quadruped or human form. This scene is also enjoyed to every
extent by the priests, who are now heard exclaiming most
vociferously, "exitus acta probat," all is well that ends well,
which they repeat time after time, not only with the view of
evincing their extreme delight, but also with a view of exhibiting some proofs of their more then ordinary learning. The
attention of all, is, again, turned to the offending bull, upon
which repeated assaults are made, both in front and rear, and
he is soon dispatched, when one end of several strong ropes,
is attached to his hinder legs, and the other, to the pommels of
the saddles, and he is soon dragged out of the arena. But soon
another bullock is brought in, and the same inhuman scene is
again performed, which is followed by similar circumstances,
and so on continuously, until five or six bulls have been thus
inhumanly tortured and slain, when the whole multitude disperse, amid the most indescribable confusion, and return to
their respective places of abode, with ample topics of conversation for many months to come. The "bear-fights," as they
are called, are conducted, in a manner, quite similar to that
just described, the only difference being, that those human or,
rather, inhuman combatants, the Mexicans, are not called into
requisition. The combatants, in these conflicts of death, are a
bear and a bull, which are turned into the arena together, the

bear being, generally, turned in first, where he is permitted to remain alone, until all things are in readiness for the fatal combat, when the bull is also brought in, upon which, the bear rises slowly upon his hinder legs, and sits upright, until he is assailed. The bull, casting wildly about the arena, soon perceives his powerful antagonist, when he curbs his neck, and moves slowly towards him, turning first one side towards him, then the other, until he approaches near him, when, at once, he darts forward, and thus engages in mortal combat. The result of these conflicts is, invariably, either that the bull strikes his adversary with such irresistible force that he is thrown upon his back, and the horns of the bull are thrust into him with such force, and in such quick succession, as to leave him lifeless in a very few minutes, or, that the bear, acquiring some advantage in the outset, gives him such tremendous blows with his paws, as to dash him to the ground, when, continuing the assault, his horned adversary is soon, and easily, rendered a lifeless prey.

The market, trade, and commerce will now be briefly noticed, when I shall have done with California. There is, at this time, an ample market, in all the various portions of this country, for all the surplus products of whatever kind; and this market is certain and uniform, being subject to none of those fluctuations, to which our market, in all portions of the States, is subject. Wheat has uniformly sold, in all portions of this country, for about one dollar per bushel, which it is now worth; corn is worth fifty cents per bushel; beans one dollar per bushel; and potatoes fifty cents per bushel; cattle are worth from one, to five dollars per head; horses from three, to ten dollars; sheep, from one to two dollars; and hogs from one to three dollars; hides are worth from one to two dollars each; tallow from two to five cents per pound; beef from one to three cents per pound; butter from five to twenty cents per pound; and flour from five to eight dollars per barrel; which prices, with very few exceptions, have remained the same for successive years. The Hudsons' Bay Company, and the Russians, at present, afford an ample market for all the wheat, which is, as yet, grown in this country; and they, as well as the American merchants, afford an extensive market for the furs, hides, and tallow, as well as much of the beef, butter and vegetables, yet for the latter, especially the beef, butter and vegetables, the ships of war and the whale ships, afford the most extensive and valuable market. The increasing emigration, however, will afford an extensive market for most of the surplus grain, as well as for many cattle and horses, sheep and hogs, for many years to come; yet the market, for all the products of the country, will be, ultimately, found in the South American States, the various islands of the Pacific, the Russian settlements, China and England. The very great variety of the productions, will require a variety of markets, producing the tropical productions, it requires a northern market; and as it produces the northern productions, it requires a southern market. The staples will eventually be, beef, pork, fish, various kinds of grain, flour, wool, hides, tallow, furs, lumber, cotton, tobacco, rice, sugar, and coffee, as well as coal, iron, and various other minerals. This very great variety of productions will afford the people of this region, all the means of subsistence within their own country, will vastly enhance its wealth, and add, in an eminent degree, to the prosperity and happiness of the people.

The trade of this country is chiefly carried on at the different towns, where, considering the extreme newness and unsettled state of the country, it is already very extensive. At each of the towns before enumerated, there are several stores, at which an extensive business, is daily transacted, which is found to be very lucrative. All kinds of dry goods, groceries, hardware, and cutlery, are much dearer here, then they are either in Oregon or the States, being sold here, at prices, about five hundred per cent higher, than they are in either of those countries, which is owning to the imposition of excessive, and unparalleled duties upon imports. The enormous amount of duties, that is annually received by the government, or, rather, the prodigal officers of the government, notwithstanding the innumerable leaks, is estimated at two hundred thousand dollars. Wages of labor, both for mechanics and ordinary hands, are very high; those of the former being from two to five dollars per day, and those of the latter, from one to three dollars per day. The cause of wages' being so very high, is attributable to the fact, of there being so very few mechanics in the country, and the great aversion to industrial pursuits, which has, heretofore existed, in that country. This aversion to industry, evidently arose, from the fact of their being no apparent necessity to labor, or, in other words, from the unparalleled facilities, which here exist for acquiring a competency, and even a superfluity, by the easy process of doing nothing. Indians are readily employed, and, in any numbers, at the trifling expense of merely furnishing them such clothing, as a coarse tow shirt, and a pair of pantaloons of similar cloth, and with such food as meat alone, or whatever else you may feel disposed to furnish them; for any thing, which you might feel disposed to provide for them, would be preferable to the crickets and grasshoppers, upon which they have formerly subsisted. There are several foreigners, who have from one, to four hundred of them employed upon these terms; and when thus employed, should they leave their employer, without just cause, he is authorized to retake them, wherever he may find them, in whosoever service they may be engaged. It is usually understood, that slavery does not exist, in any form, in any portion of the Mexican dominions, yet the natives, both in California, and several other portion of that country, and in truth, in all portions of it, are in a state of absolute vassalage, even more degrading, and more oppressive then that of our slaves in the south. Whether slavery will, eventually, he tolerated in this country, in any form, I do not pretend to say, but it is quite certain, that the labor of Indians will, for many years, be as little expensive to the farmers of that country, as slave labor, being procured for a mere nominal consideration.

Considering the very short space of time, which has elapsed, since the different governments have turned their attentions to this country, and the very little which is, as yet, known in reference to it, its present commerce is scarcely paralleled; some conception of which, may be drawn from what has been said upon a former page, in reference to its extensive imports and duties. Fifteen or twenty vessels are, not unfrequently, seen in many of the various ports at the same time, displaying the national flags of all the principal powers of the world. Merchant vessels of the United States, England, France, Russia, and Mexico, as well as the ships of war, and the whale ships of the four former governments, are to be seen, at almost any time, in the different ports of this country, and of all of which, there are frequent arrivals and departures. The ships of war, which cruise in the Pacific, touch very frequently at the various ports of this country, for the purpose of obtaining fresh supplies of water, and provisions, and maintaining the rights of their respective governments, as wall as for the purpose of capturing, now and then, a small town, or seizing, here and there, upon an island of the Pacific. The merchant vessels are much the most numerous, and are, chiefly, those of the United States, which arrive in that country each spring, and depart for the States every autumn or winter. Arriving in the spring, they are engaged in the coasting trade, until the latter part of the fall, or the early part of the winter when they depart for the States, with cargoes of hides, tallow, or furs, which have been collected during the previous year. About one half of the merchant vessels, engaged in this trade, always remain in the country, engaged in the coasting trade, while the residue return to the States, England, or France, for the purpose of renewing their stock of goods. Several of these vessels usually belong to the same houses, either of Boston or New York, which always keep a number in the country, while they employ others, constantly, in exporting the products of California, and importing goods for that trade, which they dispose of at most extraordinary prices. The whale ships touch at the various ports, for the purpose of obtaining supplies of provisions and water, and also for the purpose of trade with the inhabitants. Besides the ships and vessels above enumerated, there are numerous others, as well as various barques and brigs, which annually touch at the various ports of this country, not only from the States, England, France, and Russia, but also from the Sandwich Islands, the Russian settlements, and China.

The foregoing will enable us to form very correct conclusions, in reference to the present and future commerce of this infant country, the former of which, considering the newness of the country, and the sparseness of the population, is scarcely equalled, and, if the present may be considered as a prelude to the future, the latter is destined, in a very few years, to exceed, by far, that of any other country of the same extent and population, in any portion of the known world. We are necessarily driven to this conclusion, when we consider the vast extent of its plains and valleys, of unequalled fertility and exuberance; the extraordinary variety and abundance, of its productions, its unheard of uniformity, and salubrity of climate; in fine, its unexhausted and inexhaustible resources, as well as its increasing emigration, which is annually swelling its population, from hundreds to thousands, and which is destined, at no distant day, to revolutionize the whole commercial, political, and moral aspect of all that highly important and delightful country. In a word, I will remark that in my opinion, there is no country, in the known world, possessing a soil so fertile and productive, with such varied and inexhaustible resources, and a climate of such mildness, uniformity and salubrity; nor is there a country, in my opinion, now known, which is so eminently calculated, by nature herself, in all respects, to promote the unbounded happiness and prosperity, of civilized and enlightened man.

Chapter 14

A DESCRIPTION OF THE DIFFERENT ROUTES

Having perused the foregoing pages, the reader may have determined to emigrate to the one or the other of these countries, if so, his next inquiry is, in reference to the routes, the equipment, supplies, and the method of traveling, all of which will now be noticed, in their proper order. In all there are eight distinct routes to those countries, six of which lie through the different passes, mentioned upon a former page; one of the remaining two is that by the way of New Orleans, Vera Cruz, the City of Mexico, and Matzatlan; and the other is the route by sea, by the way of Cape Horn. There are but five of the above routes, which are worthy of a particular notice; all of which, I will now proceed briefly, to describe. The most northern of them, is that lying through the great gap, between Brown's and Hooker's Peakes, through which the Canadian emigrants, and the fur traders of the Hudsons' Bay Company, annually pass, in their journeying from Canada, to the lower settlements in Oregon. As this route is very seldom, if ever, traveled by citizens of the United States, it is not deemed important, to enlarge in its description. I shall, therefore, proceed to the description of that lying through the great southern pass, near latitude 42 degrees north. Upon this route, the emigrant sets out from Independence, Mo., and travels thence, five or six days in a direction, about west by north, to the Kansas or Caw river, crossing which, he proceeds thence northwest, about five days, to the Platte river; thence continuing up the Platte, upon the south side, to the junction of its north and south forks, thence up the south fork, on the south side, one day, to the usual ford; where crossing the river, and continuing thence, in a direction about northwest by north, three days, to the norm fork; thence up the north fork about four days, to Fort Larimie, and Fort John. Leaving these forts, the emigrant pursues a course, about west by north, over the Black hills, seven days, to Sweetwater, near Independence rock; thence up Sweetwater, nine days, to Little Sandy; thence west by north four days, to Green river, or the Colorado of the west. Crossing Green river, and continuing thence, down it three days; thence west, one day, to Ham's fork, which is a branch of Green river; thence up Ham's fork, three days; thence west by north, one day, to Muddy river, which is a branch of Bear river; thence down Muddy and Bear rivers, three days, to the soda springs; thence north northwest up the valley, two days; and thence west over the high lands one day, to Fort Hall. From this fort, those who go to Oregon, continue down Lewis' river, fifteen days, to Fort Wallawalla; and thence down the Columbia, ten days, to the lower settlement in Oregon. Those who go to California, travel from Fort Hall, west southwest about fifteen days, to the northern pass, in the California mountains; thence, three days, to the Sacramento; and thence, seven days, down the Sacramento, to the bay of St. Francisco, in California. The former part of this route, is but one vast concatenation of plains and prairies, of almost unbounded extent. The entire country, from Independence to Fort Larimie, is a vast plain, entirely destitute of timber, with the exception of the small portions occasionally found upon, and in the immediate vicinity of the streams. The principal timber, found upon all this portion of the route, is found upon the Kansas or Caw river, and its tributaries; besides which, there is very little found even upon the streams. No scarcity of timber for fuel, is experienced, until you arrive upon the Platte; when, for the first time, you are reduced to the necessity, of substituting the excrement of the buffalo for fuel, which you are under the necessity of doing, the greater part of the distance, this side of the mountains, and, for considerable distance, after crossing the mountains. From Independence, to Fort Larimie, no serious obstructions are found; as upon all this part of the route, you cross neither mountains, nor unfordable streams. The Kansas, and the south fork of the Platte, are the only streams of any importance, which are crossed upon this portion of the route; and they are, always, very readily forded, at the season of the year at which emigrants pass through, that region. The buffalo are usually seen upon this portion of the rout, about fifteen days drive from the States; but they are also found, some seasons, within ten days drive from the States; while, at other seasons, they are not found, within twenty days drive. This, however, depends much upon the forwardness, or backwardness of the season, and the fact, of their having been hunted by the Indians, who inhabit that region. If the season is backward, they will not have migrated from the south, as early as the season, at which emigrants pass through that country; and if they have come out upon their northern migratory tour, in time for the emigrants, it frequently happens, that the Indians of that section hunt them to such an extent, that they are completely dispersed from all that region. The buffalo are also, generally found upon all portions of this route, from the Platte to the Rocky mountains, and even, for several hundred miles west of the Rocky mountains, both in Oregon and California; and wherever they are found, they are always seen in the greatest abundance, and are killed with the greatest facility. The only hostile Indians, that are seen between the States and Fort Larimie, are the Pawnees, who are a powerful and warlike tribe, and who are, generally, very troublesome to the emigrants; yet they are, generally south of this route, at the season, at which emigrants pass through that portion of the country. The Cumanches, and the Sioux sometimes visit this region, but they are, very seldom here met by emigrants; yet there are several other tribes, inhabiting and visiting this portion of the country which, although much less powerful and warlike, are, at times, very troublesome to emigrants and others. Fort Larimie is situated on Larimie's fork of the Platte, about seven hundred miles from Independence About one mile south from this fort, there is, also, another fort, which is called, Fort John, and which is situated near the same river. These forts are constructed, in a manner, quite similar to Fort Hall, which has been before described; and they are occupied by traders and trappers, for similar purposes. The trade, at these forts, is entirely with the Indians, which consists in the exchange of dry goods, provisions, guns, ammunition, blankets, and whiskey, for furs, buffalo robes, buffalo beef, and horses; in which, both of these establishments appear to be doing a very extensive and lucrative business. The gentlemen of these forts, are the first white persons, with whom the emigrants meet, after leaving the States, unless they chance to meet with companies of traders and trappers, on their way to the States.

From these forts, to Fort Hall, a distance of about six hundred miles, the country through which the route lies, is, generally, very hilly and mountainous. The former part of this portion, includes that section of country, denominated the Black hills, which present a very extraordinary appearance. When viewed from an elevated position, they present one interminous succession of treeless, shrubless, rolling swells and hills, which much resemble the rolling billows of a tempestuous ocean. Traveling over these hills, is attended with much inconvenience and fatigue; as it is but one continued scene of alternate ascension and decension, from morning until night, for several days in succession, and until we arrive at Independence rock, which, from its peculiarity and notoriety, requires a passing notice. It is situated near Sweetwater: about one hundred rods from the ordinary encampment, upon that stream. It is composed of solid granite, covering an area of about five acres, and rising in conical form, about four hundred feet, above the level of the surrounding country; it is seen at a great distance, and, hence, serves as a land mark, both for the mountaineer and the emigrant. Many portions of this extraordinary rock, present an extensive, perpendicular, smooth surface, upon which the various trappers and others, who have passed through that region, have inscribed their names, the numbers of their parties, and the date of their passing. The first party, which noticed this singular rock, in this manner, was a party of American trappers, who chanced to pass that way, upon the fourth day of July, when, wishing to be Americans, even in that secluded region of aboriginal barbarism, they proceeded to celebrate that great day, which gave birth to human liberty. This they did, by a succession of mountain revelings, festivities and hilarities which having been concluded, they all inscribed their names, together with the word "Independence," upon the most prominent, and conspicuous portions of the rock; hence its name and notoriety, which are as firmly established by that act, as that rock of ages itself. Independence rock, thus consecrated, is destined, in all coming time, to stand forth as an enduring monument to civil liberty, and American Independence! A greater part of the distance, from Independence rock to Green river, is comparatively level, and affords a very eligible wagon way; but from that river to Fort Hall is the most broken and mountainous portion, of the entire route.

All this portion of the route, from Fort Laramie to Fort Hall, like that east of Fort Laramie, is, usually, entirely destitute of timber, but as a general thing, sufficient is found for fuel. On this portion of the route, buffalo are very seldom found west of Green river, but they are very abundant, between that river, and Fort Laramie: especially upon Sweetwater, and in the vicinity of Independence rock; and they are, also, very numerous off the route, west of Green river, and even west of Fort Hall, both in Oregon and California. The only hostile Indians, with whom emigrants meet upon this portion of the route, are the Sioux, the Shyanes, and Eutaws, yet these are not called hostile, by mountaineers; of this, however, the reader, will be enabled to judge, for himself, from what has been said upon a former page. The Sioux particularly, can, scarcely, be thought to be friendly, if we judge them by their acts; the taking of myself and Mr. Lovejoy, prisoners of war, and the robbing of our hunters, whenever an opportunity presented, to say the least, were not very strong indications of friendship.

From Fort Hall to the Pacific, by the Oregon route, a distance of about eight hundred miles, there is but one continued succession of high mountains, stupendous cliffs, and deep, frightful caverns, with an occasional limited valley. There is much less difficulty, in obtaining wood for fuel, upon this portion of the route; yet there are many places below Fort Boisia, where wood, for fuel, can not be obtained, only as it is purchased of the Indians, who always take immediate possession of every stick which they find, either upon the shores, or floating down the streams. Although the Indians appear inclined to monopolize the entire wood trade, yet the course, which they pursue, is highly serviceable to the emigrants; for, if they were here left to their own resources entirely, they would be unable to procure, either wood, or the excrement of the buffalo. From the dalles to the Pacific; there is ample timber, as much of the country is covered with dense forests. This portion of the Oregon route, from Fort Hall to the Pacific, has always been considered, wholly impassable for wagons, or any other vehicles; yet it is said, that the emigrants of 1813, succeeded in getting their wagons entirely down to the Wallammette settlement. This they may have done, but I am confident, from my own experience, that each wagon must have cost the owner of it, more time and labor, then five wagons are worth, even in Oregon. By recent explorations, however, a very good, and much more direct wagon way, has been found, about one hundred miles, southward from the great southern pass, which, it will be observed, lies principally through the northern part of California. The California route, from Fort Hall to the Sacramento river, lies through alternate plains, prairies and valleys, and over hills, amid lofty mountains; thence down the great valley of the Sacramento, to the bay of St. Francisco, a distance from Fort Hall, of nine hundred miles. The Indians are, in many places, very numerous; yet they are extremely timid, and entirely inoffensive. Wagons can be as readily taken from Fort Hall to the bay of St. Francisco, as they can, from the States to Fort Hall; and, in fact, the latter part of the route, is found much more eligible for a wagon way, than the former. The most direct route, for the California emigrants, would be to leave the Oregon route, about two hundred miles east from Fort Hall; thence bearing west southwest, to the Salt lake; and thence continuing down to the bay of St. Francisco, by the route just described. The emigrants, up to this time, however, have traveled together, as far as Fort Hall, because of this being the only settlement, in that vicinity, at which they are enabled to procure horses, and provisions. The soda springs, however, will, undoubtedly, be found to be the point, at which the routes will most advantageously diverge, both in reference to directness, and to the obtaining of supplies; for there is no doubt, but that a town, of very considerable importance, will spring up, at that point, in a very few years. The entire distance by this route, from Independence, either to Oregon or

California, is about twenty-one hundred miles; and the usual time required in performing the journey, to either of those countries, will be found to be about one hundred and twenty days, exclusive of delays; yet the great disadvantages, under which parties have, heretofore, labored, have caused them to occupy much more time, than that above stated, in performing the journey. It a surprising fact, that upon this entire route, from the States, either to Oregon or California, there is not a stream that emigrants cross, but that is fordable, at the season of the year, at which they pass through those regions. A much better way, is generally found, the entire extent of this route, than can be found, in any portion of our western States, the same distance, especially from the States to California, by the route just described.

The route, which I propose next briefly to notice, is that lying through the pass before described, which is situated, at latitude 34 deg. north. This route is that usually traveled, by the Santa Fe traders and Mexican emigrants, as well as emigrants from our southern States. Because of the very little importance of this route to our people, *at present,* it is not deemed proper to detain the reader, with a detailed description. Although this route is now deemed, rather unimportant to citizens of the United States, yet, if the time ever comes, when the intermediate country, shall belong to a civilized people, this route will become of the greatest importance, especially to the southern emigrants and travelers, who, traveling almost directly west, would save all the distance to Independence, the present place of rendezvous. Until that happy event, no further description need be given of this route; as, because of the inveterate suspicion and animosity, which the inhabitants of that region, now entertain, of all foreigners, it is almost impossible for them to pass through that country, with any degree of safety. Foreigners, in traveling by this route, are not only subject to the serious effects, arising from the suspicion and animosity of the Mexicans, but they are also, subject, to the serious and dangerous consequences arising from their innate thievish and murderous propensities. The route, by way of Vera Cruz, is among the most important routes to those countries, and hence, will require a more particular notice. The emigrant, who travels by this route, ships, at New Orleans, for Vera Cruz, where, if he sails from New Orleans, he arrives in seven or eight days; thence by stage, three days, to the city of Mexico; thence by stage, six days, to Guadalaxara; thence on horseback, five days, to Tepic; thence on horseback, two days, to St. Blas; thence, by water, twelve days, to California, or twenty days to Oregon. By adding about the same time, as that above stated, for delays, we will have, very nearly, the time required, in performing the journey to Oregon or California, by this route, which will be found to be, about one month and a half to the former place, and about one month and six days, to the latter place.

This is the route, by which I returned to the United States; but I was more than three months, in reaching the States, even from California; yet many of the usual delays, may be avoided. It is very expensive, traveling by this route, the entire expense being, about five hundred dollars. From Guadalaxara, the traveler is not only under the necessity of employing servants, and purchasing horses; but he is also under the necessity, of purchasing and taking with him, such provisions as he requires, as well as a traveling bed; for, without preliminary arrangements of this kind, he would, generally, find himself without food, and always without a bed. The principal dangers, to which travelers are exposed, in passing through that country, are those of being robbed, and insulted or murdered, because of their non-conformity to the prevailing religious ceremonies, in which, all things else, appear to be wholly absorbed. Robberies are, most frequently, committed between the city of Mexico and Vera Cruz, which is owing to the opinion, which prevails among the people, that upon the arrival of foreigners into their country, they necessarily have money in their possession; and so upon their departure, the impression is, that they have collected their money, and other property; and hence, that is the most lucrative field for robbers, which, it undoubtedly would be, were it not for the extensive competition. About two thirds of all the robberies, committed upon this route, are committed between those two places. There is no method of guarding against these robbers; for you are not permitted to carry arms, or what is tantamount to the same thing, you are told by the Mexicans, that they will not travel in the stage, if arms are carried; the consequence of which is, that you are under the necessity, either of taking all of the seats in the stage yourself, or disposing of your arms, the latter of which courses, you would be most likely to pursue. Having disposed of his arms, the traveler proceeds upon his dangerous journey, throwing himself upon the mercy, of a merciless bandit, of wreckless robbers, he perfectly reconciles himself to his fate, expects nothing else than to be robbed, and he is very seldom disappointed. The stage is seldom robbed, less frequently, then twice or thrice a week; and passengers are, very frequently, shot from the box, as they are riding with the driver, especially if they are foreigners. Several graves are seen, by the road side, in one day's travel, of foreigners, who have been thus shot from the box, or otherwise killed, in their attempt, to resist the attack of the robbers, which, by the by, is a very dangerous undertaking, unless there are several foreigners together. These robbers, thus rob and kill, without regard to persons, or to *personages*, it seems, for our ministers do not escape their avaricious grasp. The only security, which travelers have against the ravages and outrages, of this community of thieves, is, to travel in numbers sufficient to insure their own protection; for which purpose, four or five foreigners, well armed, are amply sufficient.

An armed escort of about fifteen soldiers, is furnished by the government, ostensibly for the purpose of protecting travelers; yet this escort is, always, composed of the most wreckless, and efficient robbers of the whole land. These soldiers always travel with the stage, on horseback, for which service they are not only paid by the government, but also by the passengers; yet their innate ungratefulness, treachery and cowardice, are fully displayed, upon the approach of the robbers, when they, at once, flee for their own security, and leave the passengers, to the mercy of a horde of inhuman banditti. Several instances of this kind, were related to me, by the drivers, who are generally Americans, and who, by the by, are very kind, jovial fellows. One of these drivers informed me, as an extraordinary instance of this kind, that in driving the stage from the city of Mexico to Vera Cruz, he was attacked by a band of robbers, who ordered him to dismount, and hold his horses, and at the same time, ordered the escort to secure a retreat, while it was practicable; both of which commands, were readily obeyed, when the robbers advanced, with drawn guns, and swords, and ordered the passengers to prostrate themselves, one by one, upon the ground, with their faces downward, which, as they were unarmed, they, of course, readily did; when the robbers immediately proceeded, to break open their trunks, and valises, and to search their persons. Having done which, and having secured all the money, and other valuable property, of those who were fortunate enough to have either, and most cruelly, and inhumanly beating those, who had neither, they then ordered, their impoverished victims, to prepare for their departure, which they did, with very little delay. The *brave* escorts, observing this, now galloped up, and demanded a portion of the spoils, a part of which, *they* said, they were entitled to, as they had given way, in order to enable the robbers, to accomplish their criminal purposes. But the robbers having the organs of acquisitiveness, and destructiveness, equally as fully developed as the *brave* escort, and having the possession, had greatly the advantage, in this contest for the spoils; being aware of which, they now ordered the *government robbers,* to desist in their contest for the spoils, and to avail themselves of a speedy flight; and thereby save their lives, which they were assured, any further contest would greatly jeopardize. Knowing that there was much more "truth than poetry" in the above, the *government robbers,* now, immediately made good their retreat; and thus, the *illegal* succeeded, and triumphed over the *legal robbers.* There really appears to be a connivance, at these repeated, and wanton robberies, by a great majority of all the Mexican people; of which, I was finally convinced, by numerous instances, which were related to me, by several gentlemen, both foreigners and Mexicans, of *Mexican gentlemen's,* being stationed at the various public houses, whose duty it is, to keep the operatives in villainy and crime, duly advised of all favorable opportunities, which may present, for the accomplishment of their sinful purposes.

The greatest dangers, to which foreigners are exposed, in traveling by this route, are those of being insulted or murdered, for a non-observance of the interminable, and extremely annoying religious ceremonies, with which they are everywhere surrounded. At the ringing of a certain bell, or rather a volley of ringing, from scores of bells, which occurs about eleven o'clock, of each day, all things human, everywhere in view, as well as many *things* that do not appear to be *exactly* human, fall upon their knees, where they remain for a few minutes, uncovered, when they are permitted again to engage in their ordinary avocations. Upon the passing of a certain "black coach," which is called by the foreigners, in derision, the "gocart," which is said to contain the "Holy

Ghost," all persons, whether male or female, black or white, brown or yellow, prostrate themselves in a proper attitude of man worship, and thus remain upon their knees, whether in the mud, or on the pavement, until the sacerdotal corps, shall have passed away; when they retire to their respective places of abode, business, amusement or lounging, amid the most confused and tremendous thunderings, of hundreds of bells, which are now tossed and thrown with unusual energy. The black vehicle, above alluded to, instead of containing the "Holy Ghost," as said, contains nothing more nor less, than one of those superhuman dignitaries in black, who is said to be on his way, to the residence of some person, who is very ill, with the view of administering to him, the last propitiatory, clerical aid. Because of the non-conformity of the foreigners, to these unmeaning, superstitious ceremonies, of this priest ridden people, they are very frequently publicly and grossly insulted, knocked down in the streets, and even killed. Numerous instances of foreigners having been slain, for the above reason have, frequently, occurred in all the different portions of that country, and, even, in the city of Mexico. A short time since, a countryman of ours, was inhumanly butchered in the city of Mexico, although he was kneeling, in conformity to the above superstitious practice. Being a shoemaker, he was in his shop, engaged at his business, when he was informed by a Mexican, that the "Holy Ghost" was passing, and understanding, that he was desired to do reverence to the "man in black," he arose, and knelt upon his seat; but he was informed, by the Mexican, that he must come entirely out of his room, and kneel in the street. As he did not, immediately, comply with this request, but remained kneeling in his room, the Mexican rushed upon him, stabbed him to the heart, and laid him at his feet, a lifeless corpse, an unoffending victim of barbarous superstition, and tyrannical priestcraft. The foreigners, being much exasperated, at this atrocious act of barbarous inhumanity, held a public meeting in reference to it, but being interrupted by the rabble, they were soon compelled to disperse, not, however, until they had made arrangements for the interment of the body, which they, immediately, proceeded to do; but as they were moving in solemn procession to the grave, they were assailed by a mob, with clubs, brick bats, and all manner of deadly missels. So furious was the assault upon them, that they were under the necessity, of leaving the corpse in the street, and applying to the civil authorities for protection. A few soldiers were now sent to their aid, when they again moved on to the grave, where, as they were in the act of performing the ordinary religions rites, they were again assailed, and driven from their purpose; but finally, the mob was partially dispersed, when, availing themselves of the favorableness of the moment, they, in great haste and confusion, consummated the interment, and immediately retired, in order to secure their own personal safety. These are a few among the many dangers, to which foreigners are exposed, in traveling by this route, as well as a few, among the numerous instances, that might be given, of the enormous evils and oppressions, which necessarily arise, from unrestrained priestcraft and religious intolerance.

The route by sea, is the well known route around Cape Horn, by which there is, latterly, very extensive travel to those countries, bordering upon the Pacific ocean. Opportunities are, annually, presented of obtaining passage, by this route, either from Boston or New York, to Oregon, California, or the Sandwich Islands; and passage is readily obtained, from either of the latter places, to the other, twice or thrice, annually. Those wishing to return, from either Oregon or California, to the States, find very frequent opportunities, as vessels sail, frequently, each season from both those countries, to the Sandwich Islands, from which place, passage can be obtained, at almost any time, to Boston or New York, and as vessels sail regularly, every autumn, from Oregon to California, and from California to the States. The latter opportunity, can be the more certainly relied upon, as the arrangements of the merchant vessels are such, that several of them arrive and depart annually. Leaving Boston or New York, in the month of August or September, they arrive in California, in the month of December or January; and on their return to the States, they leave California, in the month of November or December, and arrive at Boston or New York, in February or March. The usual time required, by this route, is about one hundred and twenty days; and the expense is about three hundred dollars, exclusive of all expenses, previous to departure. The doubling of Cape Horn, was, formerly considered a very hazardous undertaking; latterly, however, it is not so considered, by experienced navigators. The greatest objections, which can be urged against traveling by this route, are the unpleasant, cheerless monotony, and the irksome confinement, incident to this method of traveling. Now, having taken this cursory view of the different routes, perhaps it would not be uninteresting to the reader, to briefly examine, the comparative advantages, and disadvantages, of each, in reference to safety, time and expense. Upon a full review of this subject, we shall find that the route, lying through the southern pass, near latitude 42° north has a decided preference, in all the above particulars. It will be observed, that traveling by this route, is much less hazardous, that but about the same time is required as in traveling by the route by sea, and very little more than is required, in traveling by the route, by the way of Vera Cruz and the city of Mexico; and that the expense is much less, by this route, than by either of the others, must be very evident. As nothing is required upon this route, but such teams and provisions, as the farmer must necessarily have at home, it may be truly said, that it costs him nothing but his time; for he can expend no money, as he travels entirely among tribes of barbarous Indians, who know nothing of money or its value.

Chapter 15

THE EQUIPMENT, SUPPLIES, AND THE METHOD OF TRAVELING

In treating of the equipment, supplies, and the method of traveling, I shall confine my remarks, entirely, to the over land route, which lies through the great southern pass; as the chief emigration, to those countries, is, at this time, by that route, which from present indications, is destined to become the great thoroughfare, between the States, and both Oregon and California. All persons, designing to travel by this route, should, invariably, equip themselves with a good gun; at least, five pounds of powder, and twenty pounds of lead; in addition to which, it might be advisable, also, for each to provide himself with a holster of good pistols, which would, always, be found of very great service, yet they are not indispensable. If pistols are taken, an additional supply of ammunition should, also, be taken; for, it almost necessarily follows, that the more firearms you have, the more ammunition you will require, whether assailed by the Indians, or assailing the buffalo. If you come in contact with the latter, you will find the pistols of the greatest importance; for you may gallop your horse, side by side, with them, and having pistols, you may shoot them down at your pleasure; but should you come in mortal conflict with the former, the rifle will be found to be much more effective, and terrific; the very presence of which, always, affords ample security. Being provided with arms and ammunition, as above suggested, the emigrant may consider himself, as far as his equipment is concerned, prepared, for any warlike emergency, especially, if nature has, also, equipped him with the requisite energy and courage.

In procuring supplies for this journey, the emigrant should provide himself with, at least, two hundred pounds of flour, or meal; one hundred and fifty pounds of bacon; ten pounds of coffee; twenty pounds of sugar; and ten pounds of salt, with such other provisions as he may prefer, and can conveniently take; yet the provisions, above enumerated, are considered ample, both as to quantity, and variety. It would, perhaps, be advisable for emigrants, not to encumber themselves with any other, than those just enumerated; as it is impracticable for them, to take all the luxuries, to which they have been accustomed; and as it is found, by experience, that, when upon this kind of expedition, they are not desired, even by the most devoted epicurean. The above remarks, in reference to the quantity of provisions, are designed to apply only to adults; but taking the above as the data, parents will find no difficulty, in determining as to the necessary quantum for children; in doing which, however, it should always be observed, that children as well as adults, require about twice the quantity of provisions, which they would require at home, for the same length of time. This is attributable to the fact, of their being deprived of vegetables, and other sauce, and their being confined to meat and bread alone; as well as the fact, of their being subjected to continued and regular exercise, in the open air, which gives additional vigor and strength, which greatly improves the health, and, therefore, gives an additional demand for food. I am aware, that an opinion prevails among many, that when arriving in that region in which the buffalo abound, meat can be very readily obtained, and hence, much less meat need be taken; but this is an error, which, unless cautiously guarded against, will be very apt to prove fatal: for to be found in that wild and remote region, depending upon the buffalo for meat, would, in nine cases out of ten, result in immediate or ultimate starvation, especially, if there should be a large body of persons together. It is true, that immense herds of buffalo, are found in that region; but it would be impossible to kill them in sufficient numbers, to sustain a large party, unless many persons should devote their entire attention to the business of hunting; and, even then, it could not be done, unless the company should delay for that purpose, which would, in all probability, produce consequences, equally as fatal as starvation; for, unless you pass over the mountains early in the fall, you are very liable to be detained, by impassable mountains of snow until the next spring, or, perhaps, forever. Then it would seem, that, although the buffalo are vastly numerous, they cannot be relied upon yet to avoid encumbering himself with the very large quantities of meat which his family would require, the emigrant can drive cattle, which will afford him a very good substitute, not only for the beef of the buffalo, but, also, for bacon; and what is more important, is, that they can be relied upon under all circumstances.

Very few cooking utensils, should be taken, as they very much increase the load, to avoid which, is always a consideration of paramount importance. A baking-kettle, frying-pan, tea-kettle, tea-pot, and coffeepot, are all the furniture of this kind, that is essential, which, together with tin plates, tin cups, ordinary knives, forks, spoons, and a coffee-mill, should constitute the entire kitchen apparatus. Bedding should consist of nothing more then blankets, sheets, coverlets and pillows, which, being spread upon a buffalo robe, an oiled cloth, or some other impervious substance, should constitute the beds, which are found much preferable, because of their being much less bulky, and weighty. Feather-beds are sometimes taken by the families, but in many instances, they find them, not only burthensome and inconvenient, but entirely useless, consequently, they leave them by the way, and pursue the course above suggested. Our common horses, are preferable for the saddle, but it becomes necessary to take such numbers of them, that they may be occasionally changed; for it is found by experience, that no American horse can be taken entirely through, being daily used, either under the saddle, or in the harness. Many prefer mules for the saddle, but they are objectionable, because of their extreme intractability, and their inflexible inertness, in which they appear to indulge, to a much greater extent then usual, upon this kind of expedition. For the harness, mules are preferable to horses; for, notwithstanding their extreme inertness and slowness, they are found to endure the fatigue, and to subsist upon vegetation alone, much better than horses; but oxen are considered preferable to either. If mules are taken, it is advisable to take more of them, than are required for ordinary teams, in order that they may be changed as occasion may require; for they, even, frequently become so fatigued: and exhausted, that they, like the horses, are left by the way, to be taken or killed, by the Indians. Oxen endure the fatigue and heat, much better than either horses or mules; and they also, subsist much better, upon vegetation alone, as all herds are, of course, required to do, upon all portions of the route. There is no instance, within my knowledge, of any emigrant's being required to leave his oxen by the way, because of excessive fatigue, or extreme poverty; for, as a general thing, they continue to thrive, during the entire journey. But there are other considerations, which give them a decided preference, among which is the fact, that they are not liable to be stolen by the Indians, who are aware, that they travel so extremely slowly, that it would be impossible for them, to drive them so far, during the night that they could not be retaken, during the next day; hence, they will not hazard the attempt, especially as they would be serviceable to them, only as food; and as the country abounds with buffalo, and other game, the meat of which they very much prefer Another consideration, which gives cattle the preference, is, that they do not ramble far from the encampment, as do horses and mules; nor are they necessarily tied, or otherwise confined, but are permitted to range about uncontrolled, both by day and night; and, yet, they are always to be found, within sight or hearing of the encampment. In selecting horses, mules and oxen, for this expedition, none should be taken, which are under five, or over ten years of age; nor should calves or colts, under one year of age, be taken; for, from the tenderness of their hoofs, and their inability otherwise to endure fatigue, they are invariably left by the way. The hoofs of older cattle, even, are frequently worn to such an extent, that, at times, it appears almost impossible, for them to continue the journey, but being driven on, from day to day, their hoofs soon become again so indurated, as to obviate all further inconvenience. Some urge the propriety of working cows, instead of oxen, both the advantage and propriety of which, are very questionable; for, it will be admitted, that they are much inferior to oxen, in point of physical strength, and, hence, cannot be as serviceable for the draught; but it is urged, that, although they are more feeble, and, hence, less serviceable for the yoke, yet they are preferable, because they answer the double purpose of drought animals, and milk-cows; but the force of this reason is lost, when we take into consideration, the unwholesomeness of the milk of animals, whose systems are, thus, enfevered by exposure to excessive heat, and extreme physical exertion. Good and substantial wagons should always be selected, and however firm and staunch they may appear, they should, invariably, be particularly examined, and repaired, before leaving the States; for, otherwise, the emigrant may set out, with a very good wagon to all appearances, the defects of which, when he shall have traveled a few hundred miles, will have become very obvious; the consequence of which, is, that he is left without a wagon, and thrown upon the kindness of his friends, for the conveyance of his family and provisions. Whether wagons are new or old, it is, perhaps, preferable, always, to have the tires reset, previous to leaving Independence; otherwise, before traveling one thousand miles, into that vastly elevated region, from the intense heat of those extensive, sandy plains, and the extreme aridity of the atmosphere, the tires become so expanded, and the wooden portions of the wheels, so contracted, that it will be found very difficult to keep them together, in which, however, by the constant and regular application of water, you may possibly succeed. Those who go to Oregon, if they design to perform the journey in the ordinary time, of 120 days, should take their wagons, with a view of leaving them at Fort Hall, and performing the residue of the journey, on horseback; otherwise, the repeated interruptions, below that point, will, most likely, present an insuperable barrier, to the accomplishment of their object. Horses, which have been accustomed to wearing shoes, should also be shod for this journey, but others should not, as to shoe the latter, only imposes an unnecessary expense, and spoils the hoof, by cutting away that horny substance, which, hardened by the intensely heated sand, would answer all the purposes of shoes. Mules, like horses, if they have not been previously shod, ought not to be, for the same reason, as that above stated; and oxen and cows, ought never to be shod; yet many pursue a different course, and thereby, incur much useless expense, and inconvenience. Those horses and mules, which it becomes necessary to shoe, should be shod, previous to leaving the States; and one or two pairs of extra shoes, should be taken for each, which may be set by the blacksmiths on the way; as there are, always, several mechanics of that kind, belonging to each company. Besides the foregoing supplies, emigrants should, also, provide themselves with good wagon covers and tents, tent poles, axes, spades, and hoes, as well as strong ropes, of about sixty feet in length, for each horse or mule, with a supply of stakes, to which they are to be tied; in addition to which, every wagon should be supplied with extra axletrees, chains, hammers, and the like; and the different mechanics should also take a small portion of their tools, as they are, always, needed by the way. Should there be physicians and surgeons, attached to the company, as there most usually are, they should supply themselves with a small assortment of medicine, and a few surgical instruments. In addition to all the foregoing, perhaps, it would also be advisable for each emigrant, to provide himself with some such goods, as are adapted to the Indian trade, such, for instance, as beads, tobacco, handkerchiefs, blankets, ready made clothing, such as cheap summer coats, pantaloons, vests and coarse, cheap shirts, butcher knives, fishhooks, and powder and lead. Being equipped and supplied, as here suggested, the emigrant may set out upon this wild, yet interesting excursion, with high prospects of enjoying many extraordinary and pleasing scenes; and of safely arriving at his desired place of destination, without suffering any of that extraordinary toil, unheard of hardship, or eminent danger, which his own fruitful imagination, or the kind regard of his numerous friends, may have devised.

Nothing now remains to be done, but to notice the method of traveling, which I shall proceed to do, with as much brevity, as is consistent with the importance of the subject. Emigrants should, invariably, arrive at Independence, Mo., on, or before, the fifteenth day of April, so as to be in readiness, to enter upon their journey, on, or before, the first day of May; after which time, they should never start, if it can, possibly, be avoided. The advantages to be derived, from setting out, at as early a day as that above suggested, are those of having an abundance of good pasturage, in passing over those desolate and thirsty plains; and being enabled to cross the mountains, before the falling of mountains of snow, or floods of rain, which usually occurs, in that region, early in October. Before leaving the rendezvous, emigrants should, always, organize, by dividing into such companies, and electing such officers, as shall be deemed necessary. Having organized, they commence their onward, westward march, under the direction of their officers, and moving merrily on, they soon arrive at their mid-day encampment, when the wagons are driven up, so as to form a large elliptical inclosure, into which the horses may be driven, in case of an incursion, or an attack by the Indians. This inclosure is called a "caral," and is formed, by dividing the whole number of wagons, into equal divisions, each of which, is under the control of an officer, who is designated for that purpose, and who moves on, in advance of his particular division, to the place pointed out, by the principal officer, as the encampment, where one of the wagons of each division, is placed at the head of the encampment, side by side, about ten feet distant from each other. By the side of each of these, and about half the length of the wagon, to the rear of each, is another wagon driven; at the side, and half to the rear, of the latter wagons, are two others driven, and so on continually, until the rear of the inclosure, is as nearly closed as the front. The cattle and horses, are now turned loose, upon the plains, where they are guarded and herded, by a guard, consisting of several persons, who are designated for that purpose; and who remain upon the plains, beyond the herds, until all have dined, and until the command is given to prepare to march, when they immediately commence to drive the herds from all directions, toward the camp. Each now proceeds to catch, harness and saddle his horses, and yoke his oxen; and soon the caravan is again in motion; and moving onward, with increased speed, it arrives, in a few hours, at the nocturnal encampment. At this encampment, as at the former, the wagons are again divided, into two equal divisions, which now move, side by side, following their respective officers, until they arrive at the place designated, as the encampment. Here one of the officers, followed by his division, falls off to the right, and the other, to the left, forming right angles; and moving in opposite directions, to designated points, when the former division wheels to the left, and the latter, to the right, forming right angles, as before; when moving on, to another designated point, the former division again wheels to the left, and the latter to the right, forming right angles, and continuing in the same direction, until the two divisions meet, and thus form a large square "caral" or inclosure. Horses are now unharnessed; cattle are unyoked, and all are turned together, upon the unbounded plains, where they are permitted to graze, under the watchful care of a vigilant guard, until nightfall; when after all have supped, and the cloths are removed, the command is given, and the vast herds are crowded together, into the inclosure, before described; which is, now, everywhere surrounded, with erected tents and blazing fires. Within this "caral" or inclosure, stakes are thickly driven, to which the horses and mules, are firmly tied; when sufficient guards are sent out and stationed, at designated posts, where they remain for about two hours; when they are relieved by others, who, after the lapse of two hours, are also relieved, in a similar manner, and so on, during the night. In the morning, upon the signal's being given, other guards are sent into the plains, in the vicinity of the camp, in order to receive and guard the horses and mules, as they are turned out of the "caral," and until the command is given to march, when the tumultuous caravan is again in motion, amid the deafening confusion of the loquacious, noisy thousands.

Nothing different from the foregoing, worthy of remark, occurs, from day to day, in reference to the method of traveling, until the company arrives, in the territory of the hostile Indians, which commences at the Kansas river, and extends throughout the residue of the journey. Throughout all portions of the country, beyond the Kansas, emigrants are required to proceed with much more caution, especially, in the country of the Pawnees, Sioux, Shyanes, Eutaws, and Blackfeet. Wherever there are evidences of hostile Indians being in the vicinity of the company, it is advisable, always, to enjoin upon all, to avoid a separation from the main body of the company, and, at the same time, to keep an advance and rear-guard out, as the company is on the march. Should the guards discover an approaching enemy, the safest course is, to throw the caravan, at once, into a defensive attitude, which is very readily done, by forming a "caral," in a manner, quite similar to that first described; the only difference being, that the teams of both cattle and horses, occupy the interior, instead of the exterior, of the "caral," without being detached from the wagons. Being thus formed, the entire caravan assumes an impregnable attitude; the wagons affording complete protection to the women and children, as well as the teams, and at the same time, affording a secure breast-work for the men, should they be driven to the necessity of using them for that purpose. Upon the approach of the Indians, and their friendly designs, timidity or cowardice being discovered, the company is soon enabled to continue its march, as though no interruption had occurred. Upon many portions of the route, it becomes necessary thus to form the wagons, several times each day, in order to dispose of various marauding and war parties, with whom emigrants, frequently come in contact. In many portions of this country, it is found to be unsafe, to turn the horses or mules loose, upon the plains, either at night, or during the day; instead of which course, they should be tied with long ropes to stakes, which are driven for that purpose, being well guarded, and moved from time to time, as circumstances may require. Whether this course should be pursued, is, of course, determined by the officers, in view of all the surrounding circumstances, which if adopted, is found to answer every purpose, of turning the horses and mules loose upon the plains; and it is much more convenient, as they are much more readily taken, when the company is in readiness to march. A sufficient and vigilant guard, should, always, be kept out, whenever the company is encamped, whether during the day or night. These guards may be distinguished, as day, and night guards, the former of which, should always be sent out, whether in the morning or at noon, before the horses and mules are turned out, in order to receive them, and the more effectually, to prevent their rambling far from the encampment, as well as the more readily to drive them in to the "caral," in case of an incursion by the Indians. The night guard should, always, be sent out previous to nightfall; when the fires should, invariably, be extinguished, in order to prevent being discovered by the Indians, from the surrounding hills and mountains. The day guards should not, generally, be permitted to discharge a gun, only in case of an attack, as the discharge of firearms by the guard, is considered, as an indication of the hostile movements of the enemy; nor are the night guards ever permitted to discharge their firearms, unless human beings are descried, endeavoring to effect either a clandestine, or forcible approach.

The Indians, being aware of this arrangement among mountaineers, have, in many instances availed themselves of the preference, which the above arrangements, give animals, in quadruped form, to those in human form. Being aware that, in human form, it would be very dangerous to approach the encampment of white men, in the night, they change their forms, and approach in the form of an elk, or some other familiar animal; but they usually prefer the form of the elk, as it is the most common animal in those regions. In order to effect the requisite metamorphosis, to enable them to enter the camp of the whites, they prepare the hide of an elk, entire, retaining his ponderous horns, which being thus prepared, is placed upon one of the most daring "braves," who proceeds to the encampment; and, upon all fours, moves about the camp, apparently feeding as he goes, until he observes the greatest space between the sentinels, when he passes on, elk like, among the horses. He now goes on, from horse to horse, cutting the ropes with which they are tied, until he has loosed a greater part of them, when he throws off his disguise, mounts a horse, and, with most hideous whoops and yells, unlike an elk, he soon puts the horses to flight, and the guard to a nonplus; and leaving all in the utmost confusion, he gallops swiftly away, closely pursuing his numerous, frightened prey, when, soon, he is joined by hundreds of his villainous comrades. With the precaution, however, of securing the horses properly, within the "caral" as before suggested, no danger whatever is to be apprehended from the elk, in human form. Another method, by which the Indians effect an entrance into the encampment by deceptive means, is, by drawing near to the camp, in various directions, and commencing a most tremendous howling, in precise imitation of wolves; and so perfect is the mimicry, that it is almost impossible to distinguish their howl from that of the real wolf. By this deceptive course, the sentinels are thrown off their guard; for as they hear what they suppose to be wolves, in almost every direction from the encampment, and that too, very near, they are naturally led to the conclusion, that there are no Indians in their vicinity, as wolves and Indians seldom occupy the same country together in harmony. In order to avoid the misfortunes which so frequently befall emigrants from the accidental discharge of firearms, guns should never be carried capped or primed; yet they should, always, be carried loaded, and otherwise in order for action, upon a moment's warning. More danger is to be apprehended, from your own guns, without the observance of the above precaution, than from those of the enemy; for we, very frequently, hear of emigrants being killed from the accidental discharge of firearms; but we very seldom hear of their being killed by Indians. The importance of observing the above regulation, cannot be too strongly urged; for as the entire company, of hundreds or thousands, as the case may be, is frequently thrown together, and confined within a very small compass, the accidental discharge of a gun, is likely to be attended with serious and fatal consequences. A practice prevails among the emigrants, of disbanding, and disposing of their arms, to the Indians and others, upon arriving at Green river, or Fort Hall, and pursuing the residue of the journey, in detached and unarmed companies. This practice should, by all means, be invariably avoided, as it is beyond those points that the Blackfeet, the most hostile tribe in all that region, are met, if they are at all seen; and as all the Indians, who inhabit that portion of the country, although they are said to be friendly, as before remarked, avail themselves of every opportunity, of insulting, and even robbing, every small party, with whom, they may chance to meet. Both numbers and arms, sufficient for self-protection, are as indispensably necessary, upon this, as upon any other portion of the route; although an adverse opinion, is prevalent, among all the mountaineers, of that region, yet experience, amply sustains the opinion, just advanced.

In hunting the buffalo, the greatest precaution should be observed, as the hunters are not, unfrequently, attacked and robbed, of both their meat and horses; hence, it is advisable, that they should, always go out, in sufficient numbers, to insure their protection. The method of taking the buffalo, is either by approaching them unobserved, or by giving them chase, on horseback, and shooting them down as you pass them; the latter of which methods is, perhaps, preferable; and, hence, it is most generally adopted. In hunting the buffalo, emigrants are very liable to lose the fleet horses, which, after having been used a few times in the chase, with whatever timidity, they may have, at first, approached the buffalo, will, the moment buffalo are seen, evince the greatest anxiety to commence the chase; and, if restrained, in the least, they prance to and fro, under the steady restraint of the rider, or standing, they gnash the bit, and stamp and paw the ground, with all the wild ferocity, of those trained for the race course, or the battle field; and, unless perfectly secured, by being permanently tied or held, they dart away, and commence the chase without a rider. There have been numerous instances, upon the appearance of the buffalo, of their having broken loose in this manner, although saddled and permanently tied; and having commenced the chase at the top of their speed, until they arrived in the midst of the buffalo, when horses and buffalo together, leaped away over the vast plains, and were never seen or heard of afterwards. Companies should never consist of more then five hundred persons; for, as they are enlarged, the inconvenience, difficulties and dangers, are increased. The inconvenience of encamping a large company upon the very small encampments, to which emigrants are frequently necessarily confined, the difficulty of obtaining a sufficiency of pasturage, for such extensive herds; and the increased danger, arising from accidents, where large bodies of armed men, are thrown together, without the aid of military discipline; as well as the inconvenience and difficulty, arising from the protracted marches of large caravans, and the danger arising from the extreme tardiness, with which large companies, are thrown into a defensive attitude, in case of an attack, must be obvious to all, even the most inexperienced, in this method of traveling. By the careful observance, of the foregoing directions and suggestions, as well as a close adherence to their own experience, emigrants will avoid all those hardships and dangers, which they would, otherwise, necessarily experience. It is true, that emigrants in traveling, through these wild regions, are cut off in a measure, from society, deprived of many of the luxuries of civilized life; and it is also true, that their way is not studded, with magnificent churches, and spacious houses of public entertainment; but they have enough of the enjoyments of society, for their present purposes, and as many of the luxuries of life, as are conducive to health and happiness: and, although they have not the benefits of churches, yet every camp of the emigrants is truly, a camp-meeting, and presents many of the exciting and interesting scenes, exhibited upon those important occasions; and, although they have not all the conveniences, of commodious public-houses, yet nature's great inn, is always in readiness for their reception; and they experience the continual manifestations of the peculiar care and protection, of its great Proprietor, whether high, upon the eternal mountains above, or deep, in the untrodden vales below.

The task assigned me at the outset, I have now, faithfully, though briefly, and imperfectly, performed; yet, notwithstanding its brevity and imperfection, it is hoped that it will afford some valuable and practical information, in reference to both those highly important countries. Nothing, however, has been attempted, but an extremely brief, though practical description of those countries, which was designed, to enable the reader, to draw tolerably correct conclusions, in reference to their extent, mountains, rivers, lakes, islands, harbors, soil, climate, health, productions, governments, society, trade and commerce; and to give the emigrant, such practical information, relative to the routes, the equipment, supplies, and the method of traveling, as is thought to be essential, to his success and safety: all of which, I have now done, as far as consistent with the extent of this little work, and my original design. In leaving this subject it is natural for us, not only to review what we have just seen, in reference to those countries, and to contemplate their present, prosperous condition, but also, to anticipate their condition, in reference to the progressive future. In view of their increasing population, accumulating wealth, and growing prosperity, I can not but believe, that the time is not distant, when those wild forests, trackless plains, untrodden valleys, and the unbounded ocean, will present one grand scene, of continuous improvements, universal enterprise, and unparalleled commerce: when those vast forests, shall have disappeared, before the hardy pioneer; those extensive plains, shall abound with innumerable herds, of domestic animals; those fertile valleys, shall groan under the immense weight of their abundant products, when those numerous rivers, shall teem with countless steamboats, steam-ships, ships, barques and brigs; when the entire country, will be everywhere intersected, with turnpike roads, railroads and canals; and when, all the vastly numerous, and rich resources, of that now, almost unknown region, will be fully and advantageously developed. To complete this picture, we may fancy to ourselves, a Boston, a New York, a Philadelphia and a Baltimore, growing up in a day, as it were, both in Oregon and California; crowded with a vast population, and affording all the enjoyments and luxuries, of civilized life. And to this we may add, numerous churches, magnificent edifices, spacious colleges, and stupendous monuments and observatories, all of Grecian architecture, rearing their majestic heads, high in the aerial region, amid those towering pyramids of perpetual snow, looking down upon all the busy, bustling scenes, of tumultuous civilization, amid the eternal verdure of perennial spring. And in fine, we are also led to contemplate the time, as fast approaching, when the supreme darkness of ignorance, superstition, and despotism, which now, so entirely pervade many portions of those remote regions, will have fled forever, before the march of civilization, and the blazing light, of civil and religious liberty; when genuine *republicanism*, and unsophisticated *democracy,* shall be reared up, and tower aloft, even upon the now wild shores, of the great Pacific; where they shall forever stand forth, as enduring monuments, to the increasing wisdom of *man,* and the infinite kindness and protection, of an all-wise, and over-ruling *Providence.*

Printed in the United States
2755